INSIDE TRACK

ALSO BY ROBIN OAKLEY

Valley of the Racehorse: A Year in the Life of Lambourn

INSIDE TRACK

ROBIN OAKLEY

Murry — Nutyper

BANTAM PRESS

LONDON · NEW YORK · TORONTO · SYDNEY · AUCKLAND

TRANSWORLD PUBLISHERS
61–63 Uxbridge Road, London W5 5SA
a division of The Random House Group Ltd

RANDOM HOUSE AUSTRALIA (PTY) LTD
20 Alfred Street, Milsons Point, Sydney,
New South Wales 2061, Australia

RANDOM HOUSE NEW ZEALAND LTD
18 Poland Road, Glenfield, Auckland 10, New Zealand

RANDOM HOUSE SOUTH AFRICA (PTY) LTD
Endulini, 5a Jubilee Road, Parktown 2193, South Africa

Published 2001 by Bantam Press
a division of Transworld Publishers

Acknowledgements Page 6: RO in the *New Statesman*, May 2000 © Robin
Oakley, by kind permission of the *New Statseman*. Page 12: Michael Gove
on RO in *The Times*, 5 March 1997 © Times Newspapers Ltd. Pages 39–40:
RO's BBC Grand National script, April 1996 © BBC by kind permission of
the BBC. Pages 76–77: RO on Thatcher in the *Sunday Express*, 4 June 1974
© Express Newspapers, reproduced by kind permission of Express Newspapers.
Page 104: Frank Johnson on the SDP from *SDP: The Birth, Life and Death
of the Social Democratic Party* (1995) © Ivor Crewe and Anthony King,
reproduced by permission of Oxford University Press. Page 108: RO on the
SDP in the *Daily Mail*, 13 September 1981 © *Daily Mail*, reproduced by
kind permission of the *Daily Mail*. Pages 109–10: RO on Peckham in the
Daily Mail, October 1982 © *Daily Mail*, reproduced by kind permission of
the *Daily Mail*. Pages 112–14: RO on Tony Benn in the *Daily Mail*, 26 May
and 3 October 1981 © *Daily Mail*, reproduced by kind permission of the
Daily Mail. Page 240: RO on Neil Kinnock in *The Times*, 2 December 1986
© *The Times*, reproduced by kind permission of *The Times*.

A catalogue record for this book is available from the British Library.
ISBN 0593 047699

Typeset in 11¼/16pt Times by Falcon Oast Graphic Art Ltd

Printed in Great Britain by
Clays Ltd, St Ives plc, Bungay, Suffolk

1 3 5 7 9 10 8 6 4 2

To Carolyn, Annabel and Alexander
who are all the world to me

CONTENTS

PREFACE

I DIDN'T HAVE THE VOICE TO BECOME A ROCK STAR, AS THOSE WHO attended the karaoke celebrations at the end of the BBC's party conference coverage will testify. I was always going to be too heavy to be a jockey. And so I became a journalist, an ambition I first formed when editing a school magazine at age thirteen. I have never, ever regretted that decision. I have been lucky enough to be close to the heart of great events. For newspapers, radio and television I have travelled to more than fifty countries. I have met a fascinating range of people. And I have never for a single day of my working life been bored.

But why should a journalist, especially a journalist with distaste for the self-importance of some in the trade and with growing worries about the power of today's media, have written what my friends keep referring to as my 'memoirs'? In the first place, I do not regard these as memoirs, a term which implies imminent disappearance into some south coast sunset home, equipped with the addresses of the letters pages of the national papers, a plentiful supply of green ink and a bottle or two of good malt. I remain with CNN very much a working journalist. I have written this book because I wanted to share with others the fun and fascination of the political journalist's life.

To some we are sad, anorakish figures, far too involved with the minutiae of Westminster life. But the joy of it is that political journalism is the last refuge of the generalist in an ever more compartmented world. We can be dealing with education on Monday, defence on Tuesday, genetically modified foods on Wednesday, who's up or down the promotional ladder on Thursday and the British effort to host the World Cup on Friday. It is an ever-changing canvas. The constant challenge of taking complicated subjects and learning enough about them rapidly to be able to explain to others what is going on is exhilarating. So is seeking out the motives behind political actions. So is watching the force of personality in politics and marking the birth, growth and decline of political ideas amid the sheer pace of daily journalism.

Even then, one journalist's life is not worth a book. So this is not just a book about me, but also one about the many leading political figures whose fortunes and foibles I have chronicled over more than thirty years, and about the world in which we cohabit. It is a book which draws upon many conversations with leading political figures over the years, some conducted on restricted terms. I have not included confidences involving those still deeply embroiled in the political world where they might be embarrassed by them, but I have used other privileged material which gives the flavour of their lives or helps to make a point without doing them real harm, and I have written freely about politicians who are no longer involved in the daily round – especially those who have already published their own memoirs.

This is a book, too, about the relationships between journalists and politicians and about the way we ply our respective trades, because I believe political journalism and the modern generation of politicians are between them beginning to destroy rather than to sustain democratic politics.

This spring, on an assignment for CNN, I interviewed the new foreign minister of Bosnia, who told me that when his country was controlled by communists they made use of criminals, whose power began to grow. Under the nationalists who succeeded the communists, the criminals achieved an even greater status, first becoming the equals of the politicians and then beginning to dominate them. The task for his government, he said, was to reassert democratic political power and to reduce the criminals to their natural level in society. Substitute 'media' for 'criminals' in that statement and you have a fair description of the condition which we have reached. The media have achieved too much power. Whom did the Prime Minister tell first about the postponement of the election from May 2001? Not his senior colleagues but the *Sun*, which had to be kept sweet. Just compare the obituaries these days for journalists like John Diamond and Auberon Waugh with the obituaries for former Cabinet ministers; there is no doubt who are the real celebrities now.

We have some wonderfully sharp editors and columnists, and some very entertaining newspapers, journals and TV interviewers. Long may they flourish. But there is one essential difference between the politicians whom we are all so ready to criticize and those of us who hold 'important' jobs in journalism. They were elected, we were not; and we should perhaps remember that a little more often. So should they. Instead of setting up focus groups and reading newspaper editorials, and then regurgitating what they are told dressed up as party policy, the politicians should rediscover the art of leadership, telling us what they believe and seeking to win our support for genuine conviction.

In thinking about the fun which the life of journalism has given me I am conscious of the many deep debts which I owe. First I must thank my parents, Joe and Barbara Oakley, for giving me the experience and education that made my career possible. Deepest of all is the debt I owe to my wonderful wife Carolyn, a ray of sunshine to all who meet her, and to my children Annabel and Alexander. The penalty of a political journalist's life is that it involves long hours, much travelling and endlessly cancelled social arrangements. I have always wanted to be a family man; often I have not been, and somehow they have loved me in spite of that. How Carolyn has put up with my late nights and early mornings writing this book along with the day job none of our friends can understand.

I owe a debt, too, to the working colleagues from whom I have learned so much and whose company I have so relished; especially Phil Webster and the political team on *The Times* through my six years there, the late, much-lamented Gordon Greig on the *Daily Mail*, and the first-class producers with whom I worked at the BBC, like Kevin Bakhurst, Simon Smith, Colin Tregear, Adrian Wells, Lorna Donlon, Marcus Herbert, Robert Rea, Audrey Green and Julian Joyce. Mine was the face that went out on the screen associated with our efforts; they and our wonderful picture editors, unseen, had often put more into the finished product than I had. My only regret there is that many more of them would have become closer friends if I had found the time to go off to the pub now and then instead of staying for one more story.

Finally, at Transworld I would like to thank Selina Walker and Simon Thorogood for their encouragement through the frantic dash of producing this book between November and June, for their reassuring calm in the face of the computer glitches which twice lost me five thousand words as I rolled the boulder up the hill, and for their meticulous and sympathetic editing. The mistakes are all mine.

Robin Oakley
June 2001

PROLOGUE:

KINDLY LEAVE THE STAGE

ON THE NIGHT OF THURSDAY 11 MAY, 2000 I THOUGHT MY WORLD had come to an end. At around 9.30 that evening I was having a meal at home with my wife, daughter and son-in-law when I received a call from the office of Tony Hall, the BBC's head of news. Would I please go and meet Tony at the Dolphin Square Hotel at 10.00 p.m.? I assumed that some huge news story was about to break and that this must be for a conference on how we would handle it.

I arrived at the hotel to be told mysteriously, 'Mr Bailey is already upstairs,' and was directed to a gloomy end-of-corridor room, no. 613, where the lights were turned down. It contained neither Tony Hall nor Ric Bailey, the BBC Millbank news editor. Instead a shifty-looking Mark Damazer, the head of political programmes, was sitting under a standard lamp, a typed statement in his hand. What little light there was glinted off his bald head.

The purpose of this melodramatic cloak-and-dagger meeting was rapidly made plain. With the hangdog expression in which he specializes, Mark told me that the BBC wished me to take early retirement, beginning almost immediately. He realized that I would be disappointed by this decision (understatement of the year) and agreed that I had every right to feel bitter. But the BBC had to look to the future. They had decided that Andrew Marr, a former editor of the *Independent*, was to be my successor (when I got the job, eight years earlier, I had won it in open competition under a full board process) and, for reasons which he was not at liberty to reveal, Andrew was available to them only within a narrow time-frame.

I was shocked by the decision and bitterly angry at the way in which the BBC was treating somebody who had given them eight years of total commitment as political editor. So my language, and my reflections on Mark's and Tony Hall's family history, were not of the kind viewers were accustomed to hear on the *Nine O'Clock News*. What, I demanded to know, had I done wrong that I should be treated like this?

Nothing, he replied. They were deeply grateful to me. I had done a great job and Mark would be happy to say so publicly. To be fair, he later did, giving me the most fulsome praise at my Westminster leaving party for the nation's politicians.

His explanation was that when I had approached him a few months earlier, pointing out that the next general election might slip beyond my official retirement date (I would be sixty in August 2001) and saying that I wanted to stay on to cover that, it had started them thinking about the succession. They had made their choice, and Andrew Marr was willing to come only if he were appointed immediately. (He had been about to commit himself, I learned later, to a big internet venture.)

I had a file bulging with management tributes to my work at the BBC, especially through the 1997 election. I had never been criticized by a single BBC executive, and while I was aware that I was not the most natural of TV broadcasters, lacking the easy body language in front of the camera that I envied in friends like news presenter Huw Edwards, I knew too that the *Nine O'Clock News* editor who greeted news of my impending departure by telling me, 'You never called a story wrong,' was not far off the mark. But there were no two ways about it. I was out.

Why did it have to be done quite so brutally? Why all this ridiculous late-night drama? Why could we not have discussed the matter in the light of day in Mark's office? The answer was soon clear. The story of what they had been doing behind my back had begun, as most things do in the BBC, to leak. They wanted to agree terms fast before the *Observer* broke the story on Sunday. We could either go our own ways in conflict or seek to co-operate in the presentation of my departure. Since at only fifty-eight I was likely to need future work from the biggest broadcasting organization in Britain, I had little option but to co-operate.

Totally shell-shocked, I had to spend all the next day in another Dolphin Square room, no. 215, negotiating my leaving terms with the BBC, who wanted them kept secret. One thing I insisted on was that I should not leave until the natural hiatus of the summer recess. I knew it would not be easy going on broadcasting for two months under public sentence of death, but had I agreed to leave within days it would have looked as though I was being hustled out for committing some heinous offence.

It was a gritty, painful process. But there was one moment I enjoyed. After the BBC team of three made their first offer I said it would not do: I was obviously going to need a good employment lawyer and the whole process would have to be delayed, because the best one I knew was just about to have a baby in Downing Street. I did enjoy the expression on their faces at the thought of those headlines: 'Cherie Blair versus the BBC'. They knew I had the contact and could not be sure I would not follow it through. And, as Alastair Campbell later reminded me, Cherie does quite like high-profile cases.

Eventually the BBC negotiators and I made progress. We agreed an outline deal by 7.00 p.m. I then had to listen to a series of phone calls between Mark and Tony Hall debating whether they should release the news that Friday night or on the Saturday in time for the Sunday papers, whose media correspondents they did not favour. In their panic they seemed totally unaware that by seven o'clock on a Friday night most of Fleet Street had already put the first editions of the bulky Saturday morning papers to bed.

Next day the agreed statements went out. The BBC one, in Tony Hall's name, said:

Robin, who will be 60 next year, has decided to retire a year early. He has done a tremendous job for the BBC since he became political editor in 1992, chronicling with immense skill and wisdom the political drama of the 1990s. He leaves the job as political editor with our very best wishes, but he will be back on Radio Four this autumn presenting *The Week In Westminster* throughout the conference season. We will explore other ways of using his considerable talents.

Mine said:

Because I was due to retire next August I had been talking to the BBC for a while about my time of leaving, particularly because of the growing uncertainty about the date of the next general election. Although I would have liked to have covered that election before going the BBC have decided that they would like the whole period – through the election and the next parliament – to be covered by my successor Andrew Marr. I can see the logic of that and so I have decided to pursue other interests from this autumn.

Before the statements went out, executives phoned round the political staff – not as a courtesy to let them know what was happening before it became public, but merely to tell them not to talk to the press. Despite such efforts the newspapers had a field day reporting my sacking. (I could not quibble at that description. I have reported enough political resignations over the years in the same terms!)

Fleet Street loves to have a go at the BBC and its journalists, and although 'Oakley replaced by Marr' was not much of a story except to me, Mrs Oakley and my bank manager, many decided to spice it up as a political plot. Andrew Marr was presented as Downing Street's choice for the job and labelled as a friend of the Prime Minister and a New Labour crony of director-general Greg Dyke. I did not buy the conspiracy theories, and what particularly irritated me was that in order to make them work some reporters branded me as some kind of Tory creature, when I had always been careful not to be in anybody's camp. Partly, I think, they worked on a process of 'guilt by association'. It so happened that I had worked for most of my pre-BBC career on Tory-sympathizing newspapers: the *Sunday Express*, the *Daily Mail* and *The Times*. I write my racing column for the elegantly Tory *Spectator*; but then, the *New Statesman* never asked.

To define myself, because the BBC was primarily interested in protecting its own back and could not easily praise in public the man it had just sacked, I wrote an article for the *New Statesman* which the magazine ran under the heading 'There's no Toryism in my closet'. In this I said that what had amazed me about the stories was how few journalists had bothered to contact me to check anything before writing them. In fact, the only one who did track me down at Lingfield races on the Saturday, Nicholas Hellen of the *Sunday Times*, rang me at an inopportune moment. Taking his call, I missed placing what would have been my only winning bet of the afternoon. But then, it clearly wasn't my week!

In the *New Statesman* piece I went on:

I happen to belong to an old-fashioned school of journalism which believes in political reporters being as far as possible without opinions and subjugating any they have in the interest of that very old-fashioned word fairness. That is why as political editor of the Conservative-leaning *Times* I made Neil Kinnock my Politician of the Year one Christmas. That is why when most wishful-thinking newspapers were predicting John Major's imminent downfall in his leadership election I talked to many middle of the road Tories who were rarely seen before a camera or quoted in a newspaper. I concluded, and told BBC viewers, that he would survive, as he did.

That is also why, in some recent years, I have been the only political editor at Liberal Democrat Spring conferences, to ensure that their proceedings made it on air, and to compensate for other occasions when time constraints meant that the Lib Dems dropped off the end of political packages. Politicians of all parties have known that I report without fear or favour. In my 14 years as political editor, first on the *Times* and then on the BBC, the complaint has never been one of bias.

I do not want to sound too much of a goody-two-shoes. Like

most journalists, I have exaggerated and I have been selective on occasion. But I do believe fervently in unbiased, independent and objective political reporting. Despite what happened at the end of my time with the BBC, I remain a passionate admirer of BBC journalism. Ironically, in view of what happened, I was probably the most enthusiastic subscriber to the BBC ethos in the whole corporation. I had never before worked with people so keen to get it right and so unhappy when they reckoned with hindsight that they had got it wrong. And I found that a blessing in days when there were as many spin doctors outside the government as within it.

Many Fleet Street papers nowadays are dominated by small groups of politically active figures who see themselves as players on the field rather than reporters in the stands. The careers of many political journalists these days depend less on building contacts, ferreting out new information, writing well and displaying good judgement than on their ability to select facts or fancies to fit the pre-ordained theories of such small groups. The concept of a straight-down-the-middle reporter or commentator dong the job without engagement on either side of the argument is alien to them. No wonder, then, that our politicians sometimes moan about the treatment they get.

The big hole in the conspiracy theories peddled when the BBC gave me the push was that I got on well with Alastair Campbell and with New Labour. They did not like everything I said, but they never accused me of prejudice. When I left the BBC, Tony Blair wrote to me.

'As a government we haven't necessarily agreed with everything you've done all the time. Nor, I suspect, did our predecessors,' he declared. 'That's the nature of politics and of journalism. But I believe that at all times you made enormous efforts to report and assess issues fairly and accurately and in a way which held the interest of viewers and listeners. You have been a credit to the BBC, to journalism and to political life.'

Although I am a long way yet from giving up, and am relishing my latest role reporting politics all over Europe for CNN, in due course I'll happily settle for that as my professional epitaph.

As for my departure from the BBC, they were within their rights to push me out early. But the clumsy way in which they did so, panicking in the face of a leak, did untold harm to them, to me and to my successor Andrew Marr, a respected commentator who I am sure will earn himself a fine reputation as political editor. By acting in the way they did – telling him, for example, that they were simultaneously negotiating with me – they ensured maximum resentment among the many BBC colleagues who resented my ousting, so making life harder for Andrew when he arrived. By failing to mount a selection board for the job, they alienated all those excellent correspondents and presenters within the BBC who felt they had the right to be considered as candidates to succeed me. Newsreader Huw Edwards and correspondents John Pienaar, Nick Robinson, Jon Sopel and Mark Mardell should all have been in the hunt. And, by provoking the drama, they directed the brightest possible spotlight on Andrew which, initially at least, made life very uncomfortable for him.

Helped by the hundreds of kind strangers who have come up to me since my departure and told me how they have missed me on the BBC news, I have learned to live with the hurt and with the slur cast on my reputation by the manner of my ejection. Thanks to CNN, I have a happy and stimulating alternative career outside the BBC. I am enjoying the TV life now more than I have ever done. But I do not deny that for me the BBC was something special. Having the only job within the corporation that I wanted, I never bothered with empire-building, ego-stroking or internal politics. I turned down too many dinner invitations with senior BBC figures because they clashed with the *Nine O'Clock News*, which I saw as more important. I simply had not imagined that the corporation's executives could behave in the way they did. But if I had my time again, even in the knowledge that it was to end thus, I would still take the eight years with the BBC.

Let those who follow after me, however, remember the words sent on to me by one senior figure who had himself suffered in an equally brutal putsch. 'Your problem is that you love the BBC too much,' the letter said. 'Just remember that underneath all the sentiment the BBC is no more than a bureaucracy. Like any bureaucracy it has a cold heart. You will find it is quite incapable of returning the love you feel for it.'

Some weeks after my sacking, having heard not a word from either Tony Hall or Greg Dyke, I wrote to them both requesting ten minutes of their time before I left the BBC. After three postponements I saw Tony and told him what I felt. Greg Dyke could not spare the ten minutes.

1

LEAD ME NOT INTO TEMPTATION:
THE TV GAME

SO WHAT HAD GONE WRONG, AND SHOULD I HAVE SEEN MY enforced early departure coming? Like many coup victims in business or politics, for months afterwards I would wake at 3.00 a.m. in a stomach-twisting mixture of pain, fury and frustration, asking myself such questions, alternating between wanting to punch somebody on the nose and wanting to crawl into a hole. But really, I knew the explanation.

Journalism, like so much else, is subject to fashion. Executives in any organization survive and prosper by creating and managing change. In an organization like the BBC, those who are not directly involved in programme-making – and there are an astonishing number who are not – make their names by changing programmes, changing schedules or changing people. Some of them take a particular delight in doing so, I am convinced, because they would really rather like to be doing the front-line jobs themselves but lack the bottle to do so. They resent our obvious enjoyment of our roles and our lack of desire to be performing theirs.

For them, my style of straight-up journalism – no cherries, no ice cubes, no parasols on the edge of the glass – had reached the end of its shelf life.

'Why do you always have to look quite so serious?' my wife Carolyn used to complain to me.

'The stuff I have to deal with mostly is pretty serious,' I used to counter. 'I can't really pop up at the end with an inane grin.'

But she had a point, and as the craggier-faced correspondents began to be weeded out and confined to radio duties soon after I left, referring to themselves sardonically as the 'Tufties' – too ugly for television – it soon became clear that we were in for the era of News With A Smile. As the media correspondents have been pointing out, the fashion is now for chumminess at the expense of gravitas, for what media correspondent Jane Robins in the *Independent* called 'cuddly news'. Perhaps I wasn't qualified for that.

Maybe I should have taken an early warning from a full-page article in my old paper *The Times* before the 1997 election, which said that the real battle being fought out on the screens at the election was over who was to succeed me. Michael Gove, who had clearly been talking to some of my potential rivals, wrote that, like John Cole, I was a painstaking reporter with Fleet Street battle honours, but that my 'calm, detached, rational style' was not to the taste of some in the BBC hierarchy who wanted something bouncier in the excitable mode effectively employed by Michael Brunson on ITN.

I did not pay much heed at the time, largely because practically the only guidance I was given on arrival at the BBC was, 'The one thing we don't want you to be is another breathless Brunson.' Gove's verdict was that I enjoyed 'the respect of colleagues in the Parliamentary lobby for the range of his knowledge, quality of his prose, scrupulous professionalism and quiet authority'. But, he added,

> Ever since Oakley arrived at the Beeb he has been like Juninho at Middlesbrough, a classy player under-appreciated by those around him. There was resentment among the corporation's older sweats that the post of political editor had gone to someone whose background was in print, not broadcasting ... Oakley has proved an authoritative broadcaster, but that has not quelled the critics. There are rumours that after the election, elements in the BBC will try to ease Oakley out.

There were other straws in the wind. A year or so before I went, editors like me and senior correspondents who were frequently on screen were offered sessions with grooming and colour consultants. Having been campaigning for years to smarten me up, my wife was delighted. She was less delighted by a front-page *Independent* piece from Jane Robins, under the headline 'BBC reporters told to get smart', which quoted a newsroom source as saying, 'Have you seen our reporters? Scruffy doesn't even begin to describe them.' Her article revealed that BBC correspondents were being offered expert advice on how to improve their looks, and she reported that the BBC denied this was in response to viewer complaints. 'All this raises fears that such "chain-store types" as the political editor Robin Oakley and the Northern Ireland correspondent Denis Murray are facing makeovers,' she continued.

A day or so later Denis rang me and advised me to read the *Independent* letters page. There was an item under the heading 'Sartorial Snub' which read

Sir: With reference to your article 'BBC reporters told to get smart'
I object strongly to your implication that my colleague Robin Oakley
and I are 'scruffy' and to your assertion that such 'chain-store types'
as ourselves fear a makeover. Firstly, if you think that on BBC wages
we can afford to shop for clothes in chainstores then your correspondent hasn't done enough research. Secondly, we do not fear
makeovers as, clearly, in the case of both Robin and myself, it would
be impossible to improve on nature.
Denis Murray, Ireland Correspondent, BBC Belfast

I e-mailed him back that I thought his anorak very fetching.

Good correspondents, I am sure, are not judged by their
clothes; but I have no objection to any professional advice which
helps to make our reports easier on the eye. For a start, it helps
if the cameraman tells you when your tie isn't straight. You don't
want viewers worrying about this when they should be concentrating on your words. But my concerns about modern
political journalism go rather deeper than the state of a reporter's
haircut or the colour of his or her coat. And on most of these I
think the BBC comes out well on the credit side of the ledger.

Much in journalism has improved over the years, especially in
its investigative arm. Governments have grudgingly been nudged
into raising the curtain here and there. Corporations have begun
to appreciate that their obligations are not to shareholders alone.
The public have a right to know who gave us tower blocks as the
answer to urban problems and who let careless companies turn
our rivers into sewers. They should have been able to see before
belated official inquiries reported what advice the government
was getting on BSE or what drugs cocktails were given
to our troops in the Gulf War. And why should the evidence to
disaster inquiries be kept secret for years?

I welcome the steady decline in deference, perhaps helped along by the collusion between the royals and the tabloids in turning the Windsors into a soap opera. And I am pleased that a sharper eye is now kept on the revolving-door syndrome, whereby politicians and senior civil servants decamp from Westminster and Whitehall to well-paid positions with companies operating in the spheres they recently policed.

But while the investigative media can hold up their heads, I worry about the trends in modern political journalism. Too much political reporting is now served up with a slant. We are allowing policy and politics to become separated, and by making little differentiation between the way in which we report politics and heavyweight boxing we risk turning people off the democratic process.

I believe that journalists should enlighten, not impose. But too many editors now see themselves and their teams as participants in, not commentators on, political life. My friend Trevor Kavanagh, the political editor of the *Sun*, is a top-class journalist. But when serious columnists start writing that he is one of the most powerful figures in the political world, and when he is invited on political programmes to be asked how the *Sun*, not the political parties, will respond to the latest government initiative, that stirs anxiety. Neither Trevor nor I nor Rupert Murdoch has been elected to any public office.

When the Conservative minister Michael Mates, famous for his gift of a watch to Asil Nadir with its 'Don't let the bastards grind you down' inscription, followed David Mellor and Norman Lamont into resignation and made his statement in the Commons, I remember the political editor of one of the tabloids – a cheery fellow with whom I would happily enjoy a drink any day – emerging from our press gallery above the Speaker's chair, grinning widely, jabbing his thumb into the air ahead of him and exulting, 'Played three, won three!'

The Labour party, out on the political field of play, were entitled to do that. As journalists on the terraces, we were not. We did not play. We watched, we commented and we reported, and there is a difference in the roles.

Within television, I believe that too much attention is being focused on the style of the news-giver and too little on the quality of the news itself. I do not believe in too much 'personality' being inserted between the news and the audience, though I guess my critics might argue that is because I don't have enough personality to insert. Certainly, in a world in which the media are playing an ever more powerful role, the obsession with personality is reflected in politics too. When people are assessing a politician's ability these days they do not dwell on his or her capacity for original thought; they do not rate his or her ability to drive legislation through the Commons; they do not pay much attention to his or her ability to motivate a team or run a department. The prime concern is whether he or she is 'good on TV'. The former Home Secretary and later European commissioner Leon Brittan, for example, has one of the most outstanding minds I have met in politics. His clarity of thought and expression in outlining policy proposals was second to none. But on TV it seemed he had all the appeal of yesterday's catfood; and I have no doubt this limited his political career.

I am happy, to a degree, to defend the soundbite culture. We live in a rushed age, and politicians have to learn to express themselves pithily. If they do not, then they (and our reports containing their efforts) risk becoming victims of channel-flippers with a multiplicity of outlets to turn to. But when Walter Cronkite points out that in 1968 the average soundbite on

American TV channels was 42.3 seconds and that it is now down to 7 or 8 seconds, we have to hear the warning. I agree with his concern that while TV may be raising the floor of knowledge for non-readers, it is also, through its limited exploration of difficult issues, lowering the ceiling of knowledge for others. The BBC and other broadcasters do, it is true, make strenuous efforts to avoid 'dumbing down'; but it is one thing having executives nodding gravely at seminars about the mission to explain, quite another trying to persuade a programme editor on the day of a motor-way pile-up to find space for a complicated piece about the euro.

Running properly resourced news services is expensive; but the ghettoization of news programmes on specially reserved channels must in my view be resisted at all costs if television is to continue to play its role in democracy. We must especially fight the tendency for politics and policy to be separated. One argument I pursued ceaselessly with BBC executives was over their growing eagerness during recent years to hand over most of the policy stories to specialist correspondents rather than to political reporters. There is no cry in society I resist more vigorously than that glib invitation, 'Let's take it out of politics,' when people are talking, say, about the health service, or transport, or education. Politics is meaningless unless it is about all those things which affect people's lives: the quality of the local country bus service, the availability of a bed for a sick relative at the local hospital, the shortage of books in the nearest primary school. Since 1997, under a New Labour government with a huge majority, the political story has largely been about the steady development of policy. But as green papers, white papers and bills were published, BBC execu-tives in their morning meetings decided too often that they should be reported not by the political team but by the transport or med-ical or social security specialists.

I opposed this not out of any jealous impulse to protect my territory. Nor did I have any objection to the individual specialists. Far from it. You could not find a more knowledgeable or capable reporter or commentator than the BBC's social affairs editor Niall Dickson or the then legal affairs correspondent Joshua Rozenberg (who has since opted for life on the *Daily Telegraph*). But when all the stories affecting people's lives went that way, the political staff were left with nothing but constitutional questions, parliamentary rows and sleazy tales of hands in the till or trousers down. In consequence, more and more people decided that 'politics' was nothing to do with them. Polls and focus groups (yes, the BBC is prey to them too) measured that alienation and programme editors said: 'Ah, there you are. People want less politics.'

The sixteenth-century philosopher Richard Hooker once wrote: 'He that goeth about to persuade the multitude that they are not so well governed as they might be shall never want for attentive and favourable hearers,' and for that reason the relationship between politicians and journalists will always be an awkward one. Sir Bernard Ingham, Margaret Thatcher's long-time press secretary, likened it to the tension between cat and mouse, or fox and goose. The American writer H. L. Mencken once suggested it was more like the relationship between dog and lamp-post; I think I know which side Bernard, a gruff Yorkshireman, would have had in mind as the lamp-post. But whether either side likes it or not, the roles are inevitably intertwined. In my opinion Enoch Powell was right when he said that politicians who complain about the media are like ship's captains who complain about the sea; and this is becoming ever more true in a world of strong media and weak politicians. But if the politicians have from time to time abused their role, then we have to be careful not to prostitute ours too.

It is so easy for the media to get above themselves. MPs used to confess to me quite candidly during my time at the BBC that they would rather do a couple of questions with me in front of a camera than make a twenty-minute speech in the Commons; for the TV appearance had a hundred times better chance of catching their constituents' attention. There is, for instance, a far bigger audience for the BBC's *Question Time* than there is for the live afternoon broadcasts of Prime Minister's Questions. Ministers deliberately trail their policy announcements on the *Today* programme, even at the risk of a trouser-fraying worrying from John Humphrys.

As for election times, here the whole process of politics has changed. Today there are fewer public meetings; street canvassing is declining, with a crime-conscious electorate less ready to answer the door at night, and many people locked away behind entryphone systems; and the town hall meeting is dying. Leading politicians make far fewer set-piece speeches than in the days when Clement Attlee toured the country to woo the electorate in a family saloon driven by his wife, Violet. Harold Wilson made seventeen major speeches in his last general election campaign; Tony Blair and William Hague made only a handful this year. But party leaders now subject themselves to almost daily grilling at televised press conferences. They do innumerable interviews for all branches of the media, and with academics calculating that some 7 million out of 39 million electors change their minds (not all, of course, in the same direction) in the course of a three-month run-up to the polls, there remains a huge amount to play for. For their part, the media gratefully accept their role, putting out extended news bulletins and extra election pages, election night specials and a wide range of audience participation programmes. So far has this process gone, indeed, that we have reached the point of absurdity. Róbin Cook went down one garden path at the 1997 election and knocked on a glass-panelled front door. After some time, a cross-looking woman edged the door open a few inches and peered suspiciously around it. He declared: 'I'm here for the Labour Party, seeking your support on May 1.'

'I haven't got time to talk to you,' his constituent responded crossly, 'I'm watching the election on television.'

The role of the media, especially the electronic media, in elections has increased with the detribalization of politics. People move and change their jobs more often, class and family structures have weakened, and opinion polls fluctuate wildly, as for example during the petrol protests in September 2000. Old loyalties have gone out of the window and governments now have to justify themselves to a fickle electorate on an almost weekly basis. And so the bulk of the hefty resources which parties have convinced themselves they need to conduct an effective campaign are spent on attempts to manipulate the media.

Yet today's focus-group-driven politics is not an entirely new phenomenon. Harold Macmillan once asked Rab Butler to 'find out what the middle classes want, put it down on one side of A4 and let us see if we can give it to them'. But the power of a press and television corps elected by no-one has been increased by a generation of politicians who are too ready to kowtow to the media. I sometimes feel that today's politicians give the electorate more followership than leadership, and if they complain of the media throwing their weight about they have only themselves to blame.

On occasion in my BBC days Tony Blair, a Prime Minister with a majority of 179 behind him, would say to me rather nervously after an off-the-record chat, 'I hope that's in line with what Alastair's told you.' So eager were he and his government not to fall foul of the media that his press secretary Alastair Campbell, at that time Downing Street's point of daily contact with political correspondents, had become the most powerful adviser in the land.

When Tony Blair went to St Petersburg in March 2000 to chum up with Vladimir Putin, not yet then elected President, I interviewed him on the plane on the way back. Had he felt comfortable, I enquired, doing business with a man whose background was not in democratic politics but as the head of the dreaded KGB?

'Well,' the Prime Minister conceded, 'there are some advantages to such a background. This is the first time one of my overseas trips hasn't leaked in advance.'

The St Petersburg trip marked the end of the so-called 'ethical dimension' to New Labour's foreign policy. When I went on to ask Blair about the brutality in Chechnya, he said that the Russians had a serious problem with terrorism.

'Yes,' I conceded. 'But was the right response to raze a city like Chechnya to a pile of rubble?'

He could not quite bring himself to say 'No.' Foreign affairs is truly governed by the law of the jungle. When countries are too big to push around, repression and mass murder become 'internal affairs'.

Then I threw in a new line. Having learned that the Sunday newspaper journalists on the plane had been briefed about a new government initiative on drugs, I knew it would help the BBC to have a clip of the Prime Minister talking about what might be the main Sunday story. So, at the end of the interview, I asked Mr Blair what plans he had to tackle the drugs menace. Looking somewhat bemused, he gave me a standard reply about the evils of the drug trade and departed for his quarters.

'That was a crap reply on drugs,' Alastair Campbell said as we chatted afterwards. 'He obviously wasn't listening when I told him about that. Do you want me to get him to do that answer again?'

'It would certainly help,' I replied, hardly imagining that the Prime Minister would interrupt his supper or his Putin debrief with his foreign affairs advisers to do so. But within five minutes he was back, fully briefed. We set up the camera again and went through the question and answer on the drugs initiative once more. This time Blair's response was sharper and far more specific. Would a Prime Minister fifteen or twenty years ago have done that?

It is fashionable to castigate Labour as a party which will do anything in its attempts to manipulate the media. Certainly, it was more than a coincidence that the one time in Blair's first term when the corps of political correspondents was invited, with wives, to a Downing Street drinks party was when Michael Cockerell was making a documentary about Number Ten's relationship with the press. Suspicious of a set-up, I went to Yorkshire instead that day to do a piece about the local elections.

But while Tony Blair may be an extreme case among party leaders in his media consciousness and his willingness (sometimes) to charm those whom Denis Thatcher used to condemn as 'the reptiles', he is not alone. If you were on a plane with John Major and you said something which interested him, you might get a call from Chequers when he was working on his next speech to discuss the point. William Hague's team would invite correspondents to dinners for an off-the-record chat to discuss where the Tories might be going wrong. The Liberal Democrats had me along, in a non-aligned capacity, to talk to their MPs at a strategy conference before the last election about how they were perceived, warts and all. Even Paddy Ashdown, a generally robust politician who was prepared to plough a lonely furrow or two, would occasionally weigh the media's view. One day during Paddy's time as leader of the Liberal Democrats, an aide of his called me one day with a bizarre enquiry. 'The boss wants to know if he can get away with using the word "bollocks" in this weekend's speech. What do you think? Would you report that passage?' My advice was to go ahead. It was, after all, a colloquialism to be heard in any pub exchange. But in the end he, or they, chickened out.

We in the media are, of course, highly susceptible to flattery. You don't spend your working life in pursuit of a big byline without wanting somebody to take you seriously from time to time. But these were more than ego-stroking exercises, and you would sometimes see the results in Prime Minister's Questions.

'Party loyalties apart, because I have none, I'm pleased to see the return of a government with a decent majority. At least it means you can take the tough decisions the country needs without being in thrall to the tabloids,' I said to Tony Blair the week after he had been elected in 1997. But I had overlooked his desperate desire to be the first Labour leader to win not just one but two full terms of office: in the event, he was to prove just as concerned to please the *Sun* and *Daily Mail* leader writers as was John Major with his pitifully thin and ever-crumbling majority of twenty-one. Through the past couple of decades, the cynic who first wrote that politicians are the people who tell lies to journalists and then believe what they read has seen his point proved for him time and time again by parliamentarians apparently unwilling to wrest back control of the agenda from the unelected. One little incident summed up for me the shoulder-shrugging attitude that has taken over.

When Steve Norris, as robust and courageous a politician as I know on many issues, was London transport minister in John Major's government he made some impromptu remarks in front of a Commons select committee inquiry into vehicle exhaust pollution. The first most journalists heard of them was a report from a news agency headlined 'Transport minister pulled up over commuter gibe'.

'Transport minister Steve Norris is at the centre of a row after he dismissed public transport commuters as "dreadful human beings",' said the striking opening sentence. 'Mr Norris sparked an angry response when he praised the benefits of private car travel by saying "You have your own company, your own temperature control and don't have to put up with dreadful human beings sitting alongside you." ' This looked like arrant and politically damaging snobbery. The Press Association included in its story a quote from shadow minister Michael Meacher, who declared, 'This is a gross insult to public transport users and shows the deeply held Tory belief in a two-tier society, whether in health, education or transport services.'

Before we ran the story on the BBC, I asked a correspondent to check the exact words used and their context. As even Labour members of the committee confirmed to us, what Norris had said, in the course of pressing the need for a better class of public transport, was that people in general were deterred from leaving their cars at home and using the Tube by the difference they were likely to experience in terms of comfort and the company in which they might find themselves. One of my colleagues put out on the internal BBC copy system a report which said that the Transport Department was insisting that Mr Norris's remarks had been taken seriously out of context. What he had actually said was: 'It is difficult to get people on to public transport because the attitude they have [to the car] is . . . you have your own company, your own temperature control, your own music and don't have to put up with dreadful human beings sitting alongside you.'

'The Labour chairman of the Environment Select Committee, which questioned Mr Norris this morning, has confirmed that this was indeed the context in which the remarks were made,' the report continued. Another Labour member, John Denham, confirmed that Mr Norris had not been giving his own views but was describing the typical reasons people gave for not using public transport.

I pointed out that item and the actual words used to programme editors, advising them to make the context clear if they used the story. The BBC's main bulletins then decided it was not much of a story after all and ignored it. But ITN ran it, and the tabloid newspapers the next morning duly savaged Mr Norris with headlines like 'Transport minister's gaffe' and stories calling for his resignation.

I felt we had played fair and acted responsibly. But our bit of straight reporting, or non-reporting if you must, was completely undermined by Norris himself. Yes, he agreed that he had been quoted out of context; but then, instead of complaining about the widespread misrepresentation of what he had said, he shrugged his shoulders, held up his hand and said, 'Sorry, I got it wrong,' telling a press conference that he had been a 'pompous prat'. He had decided that against the full weight of the tabloids the quickest way to kill the fuss was to accept the blame and get on with life. If politicians will not fight for straight reporting themselves, how can we do it for them?

*

So what is the role of political journalists? While I agree that we must be fair to politicians, we are not there to make life easy for them. At the risk of sounding a bit of a pompous prat myself, let me go back to the words first used by John Delane, a nineteenth-century editor of *The Times*, which have always seemed to me the best summary of what our trade is about. Delane had been chided by Lord Derby for an attack on Palmerston, and Derby had urged that newspapers should share responsibilities with statesmen. Not so, said Delane. The roles were entirely separate:

> The first duty of the Press is to obtain the earliest and most correct intelligence of the events of the time and instantly, by disclosing them, to make them the common property of the nation. The Statesman collects his information secretly . . . he keeps back even the current intelligence of the day with ludicrous precautions. The Press lives by disclosures: whatever passes into its keeping becomes a part of the knowledge and the history of our times.

News has best been defined as something which somebody has an interest in not having published, and it is the natural instinct of governments to control and conceal. Even Churchill, that great beacon of democracy, wanted to take control of the BBC during the General Strike of 1926 and turn it into a vehicle of public propaganda. So disclosure is our first task. It is also our job to probe behind the propaganda to beliefs, to seek out the hidden agendas, to test whether policies are properly thought-out remedies or mere headline catchers for politicians who feel the need to be seen doing something. We have to pick up the whispers of concern at Westminster and amplify them so that all can join in the debate. But this – crucially – does *not* mean we have to pre-empt the result of that debate. Nobody seems content to report the facts any more: everybody wants to trumpet their opinions.

Early on in Czechoslovakia's Velvet Revolution I was invited to Prague to speak on the role of the media in a democracy. It was as if the country had been handed over to the National Union of Students. Over nearly two hours an astonishing range of questions came thick and fast: Should you frame your policies on the basis that humanity is good or evil? How much should you pay your judges? How do you run a parliamentary whipping system? But it was President Vaclav Havel's words which stuck with me: 'Politicians must always remember to look out of the windows of their aeroplanes,' he declared. What he meant was that those who spend their lives in ministerial conference rooms, cosseted by appointments secretaries and flattered by visiting dignitaries, must not lose touch with the lives of ordinary people. I see this as part of my role too. It is my job to ask ministers not the clever-dick questions which might score me points with the chattering classes, but the ones which matter to people who do not spend their daily lives around Westminster.

In an age, therefore, when so many people have become disillusioned with politics, I believe the media too – and I am not talking here just of the BBC, so often sloppily taken as a coconut shy when people are talking about broadcasters as a whole – have to question how much they might be to blame for that disillusion and what they can do to help redress the situation. We do, after all, boast proudly that we are part of the democratic process.

Of course, the problem of disillusion is a complex one. After hopes of a New World Order with the fall of the Berlin Wall, the collapse of apartheid and the early breakthroughs towards peace in the Middle East, many people now feel let down by leaders who have been incapable of preventing the bloody conflicts in the Balkans, the collapse of much of the former Soviet empire into gangsterdom, the scourge of AIDS across Africa and the genocide in Rwanda. Governments have appeared increasingly impotent in a globalized world where some companies have budgets larger than many countries. Less robust than their pre-decessors in much more volatile times, political leaders have grown more frightened of admitting to the need for taxation to run the services the people demand. Fearful of media reactions and anxious to avoid all the blame they can, they have become readier to refer key decisions to the mass electorate in referendums. We've had them in Britain on the Scottish Parliament and Welsh Assembly. We are promised them on the single currency and on proportional representation for Westminster. William Hague's Tory opposition, in pursuit of populist bandwagons, took to demanding them on almost any-thing decided in Europe.

What this has meant in Britain is that MPs, conscious of how little attention is paid to them by an over-strong executive, have felt increasingly impotent as Brussels has grown more powerful, judges have become increasingly ready to challenge Parliament's actions and the media has steadily run more of the agenda. But they have done nothing to reassert themselves.

There is little the media can do about this directly. Politicians have to recover their nerve and start to reclaim ground them-selves. But we can do something about the most damaging trend, the tendency to present all of politics as nothing more than a struggle for personal power among unprincipled and self-serving cynics. This leads to politics finding space on the news bulletins only when there is a row, a personality struggle or a battle. The politics of the single currency, for example, was widely reported even on serious programmes only when it became evident that there were marked conflicts within the government between Robin Cook, Stephen Byers and Peter Mandelson at one end and Gordon Brown at the other over tactics on the euro. The 'personality factor' simplified things: this was a story that could be sold.

James Fallows, the Washington editor of *Atlantic Monthly*, drew attention to the problem in the 1990s in his book *Breaking the News: How the Media Undermine American Democracy*. Modern journalists, he argued, believe that being independent boils down to acting in a hostile fashion. Thus important subjects like crime and health become merely arenas for the political power struggle. 'For the American media in the 1990s public life is sports: no clash, no story.' The increasing cynicism of the mainstream media in presenting politics made public life a depressing spectacle which people were prepared to follow only if it were turned into a form of 'infotainment'.

'Lead us not into temptation, O Lord,' I used to say to myself, not always quite loudly enough. Like most TV journalists, I have sometimes given an exaggerated importance to rebels. I have often taken the most extreme quotes from interviews with the leading players to present the arguments at their starkest and thus make a better 'story'. When St Peter is calling the evidence and the chaps in red capes with pitchforks and swishy tails are stoking the fires in anticipation, my defence will be that sometimes, given the time constraints of TV journalism, it has been my only hope of getting the main points of my story across. But I and other journalists should remember every time we justify such stratagems that those of us who have actually sat through the entire speech or seen the whole story are in a tiny minority. Most of our audience have not shared that experience. They have to rely on our judgement and our selection. We try to deliver that judgement as fairly and objectively as we can. But I can see why politicians complain that there is more and more interpretation and less and less reporting, particularly with the modern fashion of having the reporting delivered not in a 'package' containing excerpts of the politicians' words but in an interpretative 'two-way' exchange between correspondent and programme presenter.

There is still much to be said, I believe, for the old-fashioned package. If you take a fair selection of the politicians' views and craft every linking phrase with care, you can often impart more telling information in a package than you can in a two-way exchange, where a presenter's mild obsession with one aspect of the story or a late studio decision to trim the discussion may leave the whole piece unbalanced. Certain kinds of stories are undoubtedly best handled through the two-way interview. On complicated theoretical questions, for instance, and on late-breaking stories, it is the only sensible approach. But there is an equally strong case for presenting as much as possible of the political narrative in politicians' rather than journalists' words. They, after all, are the ones who have been elected; it is their articulation of their own arguments that the voters should be able to hear. But in recent times that has not been a popular view. My belief in the value of carefully compiled packages increasingly ran against the received wisdom in BBC executive circles. It probably did not enhance my appeal there. But fashion moves in cycles, and in a few years' time, I have no doubt, a TV executive will be making his reputation by reviving the art of the package report.

Methods, morals, mistakes I might have made and the meaning of it all – these were what used to flood through my mind on those mornings when I lay awake through the early hours regretting the finale that had been taken away from me. But one thing I never regretted was beginning, and continuing, life as a journalist. I could really never have been anything else.

2

FROM LUSAKA TO LIVERPOOL:
EARLY DAYS

I ONCE HEARD OF A PARATROOP COMMANDER WHO CONFESSED that he hated jumping out of planes and never did so without feeling queasy. Why, then, had he pursued the career he had? 'Because I like being with the kind of people who like jumping out of planes.' I became a journalist because I wanted to write. I became a political journalist because I am fascinated by the political process and by the interplay between personality and policy. I have remained a political journalist for over thirty years because I like the kind of people with whom the life brings me into contact. A few journalists can be self-important; many are cunning. We are all a bit inclined, like politicians, to think that we have found a solution when all we have found is a phrase. But most journalists are questioning, non-hierarchical, unstuffy and fun.

My political instincts were first stirred as a boy in Zambia by seeing a white man hitting a black man who was offering no resistance, a sight which haunts me still. They were stimulated further when I was a boy at a British public school, Wellington College. In 1959 the school held a mock election, and nobody wanted to be the Labour candidate. Although I lacked even the most basic political knowledge, this too shocked me; so two of us wrote off to Transport House, acquired some material and ran a campaign which saw Labour limp home in fourth place – behind the communist, who happened to be a star of the school rugby team. Don't try to persuade me that personality doesn't matter in politics!

Journalists are always interested in the world about them, and the joy of our trade – I hesitate to call it a profession – is its variety. Journalism has taken me most of the way around the world; and I have never ceased to feel privileged as I walk into the Palace of Westminster and think 'This is my workplace.' But it would seem, on the face of it, an unlikely career choice for the son of Joe Oakley, a civil engineer who had a healthy contempt for both journalists and politicians – two breeds, he used to insist in his days as a director of the Wimpey construction company, who never got anything right.

I might easily have opted for a more outdoor life. As a child I lived for some years in Lusaka, Zambia (then Northern Rhodesia) while my father built bridges, airports and hospitals. This time bred in me a love for Africa, with its velvety night skies, its untamed bush and its fascinating bird life. Early memories include the days it literally rained frogs which had been sucked up by wind columns from the swamps around; helping to beat out bush fires with besom brooms; and wading barefoot up streams, shooting fish with bows and arrows. I still shiver at the memory of being struck at by a snake as I shinned down a well on a rope to retrieve a Wellington boot thrown there by a friend. I recall, too, a birthday party in metal barges on the Kafue river amid crocodiles and hippos. And my parents have not forgotten the time I went missing for twenty-four hours, sleeping with a friend in a grain shed alongside the railway line.

I also remember more than once coming home from school with black eyes and a bloody nose, having been beaten up by Afrikaner boys who had jeered that we, the British, put people in concentration camps. Ignorant at the time of Boer War history and believing them to be comparing us with Hitler, I would always hotly deny the accusation and be pummelled for my pains.

Back in England at ten, I fitted awkwardly into the prep school system at Aldro, near Godalming in Surrey. These were the days of compulsory boxing, corporal punishment and domineering matrons. We swam in the muddy school lake and played rugby on pitches shared with defecating geese – not much encouragement to the sliding tackle. My only distinction was holding the school record for throwing the cricket ball. I don't quite know why, but my parts in school plays included both Queen Elizabeth I, and Juliet in *Romeo and Juliet*. I could have been fitted for life as a drag artiste.

I always enjoyed acting, and maybe that was some kind of preparation for the TV news screen. Michael Brunson was a keen student actor and John Sergeant, for a long time my number two as chief political correspondent and then Michael's successor at ITN, was a star of student revues who then began his working life as an actor alongside Alan Bennett. Playing Juliet, however, might have put me off public performance for good. I could not understand why my passionate rendition of the balcony scene ('Romeo, Romeo, wherefore art thou Romeo?' and all that) was causing such merriment in the audience. It was only afterwards I learned that my long conical hat had early on developed a definite list to starboard which became more and more pronounced as the scene wore on.

I persevered with the acting at Wellington College, but

continued to be dogged by mishaps. Once, playing a scene on board ship in *Seagulls Over Sorrento*, I accidentally threw my hat through an open porthole instead of onto the bunk. A stage hand helpfully, but not very thoughtfully, threw it back. And I doubt if my old headmaster Graham Stainforth would have thought me cut out for a career as a TV correspondent compelled to reduce, say, the latest controversy over the single currency to a succinct two minutes thirty seconds. He once wrote on my report: 'Oakley must learn to give the examiner the cream from the top, and not the whole bottle.' I may, however, have been drawn towards a writing career by picking up a few of the well-endowed essay prizes which the school's benefactors had provided – in contests that usually required writing against the clock.

On at least one occasion I showed the rat-like cunning always said to be required of a successful journalist. At a fete held in the school grounds I persuaded a florid-faced vicar who was operating the roll-a-penny stall that he could make much bigger profits if he let me roll sixpences rather than pennies down the chutes and onto the board. The coin had to land entirely within a square to win; and it was, of course, much easier to fit a small sixpence than a large old penny inside the square. Before he was on to my racket I had won enough to keep me in Mars Bars for the rest of term.

I have inevitably had my moments of mortification in a business where mistakes are very public property; but none has ever caused me the misery of my worst moment at school. Playing for Wellington in the third round of the Schools Rugby Sevens tournament at Rosslyn Park, I had burst clear of the opposition and had only to run to the line when somehow, inexplicably, I tripped over my own feet. The communal, spontaneously gasped '*Aargh!*' that rang around the ground as I fell and saw the ball go rolling away from me will be with me until I am six feet under.

In my tutor at Wellington, Robert Storrar (called a 'house-master', although we lived in 'dormitories', not houses), I had my first encounter with enlightened authority.

'Oakley,' he said, early in my last year, 'I've seen the smoke curling from the window of your room. I do understand that senior boys like you may occasionally need a cigarette. So in future when you feel a real urge for one I would be grateful if you would come down and have your smoke in my flat – just so juniors don't get a bad example.'

What I could not tell him was that, as a fanatical athlete with the promise of £25 on my twenty-first birthday if I hadn't smoked before then, I was actually not the culprit. It was my best friend, a diplomat's son, who had been puffing in my room.

The first commercial journalism I ever produced was an article for my local newspaper – the *Surrey Herald*, I think – about a scholarship trip to Ghana, Nigeria and Sierra Leone before going to university. From 1960 to 1963, I was at Brasenose College, Oxford, where I did a few pieces for university newspapers and magazines. One entitled 'The women of Oxford' I remember researching with particular thoroughness. Again there was some acting, with a part in a college production of Tennessee Williams's *Camino Real* at the Oxford Playhouse. That was in my 'trendy' period when I tried to look cool by sporting dark glasses almost permanently – a period which ended after I fell rather uncoolly down the steps of a trendy Fulham coffee bar, the Café des Artistes, because I couldn't see where I was going.

But to succeed as a student journalist, actor or politician you really had to devote yourself to one particular clique or another;

and I preferred to dabble in many fields, doing a little acting and writing alongside a minor involvement in politics and a good deal of sport. My one natural talent in life seems to have been an ability to throw things (some might call that an appropriate talent for a journalist). At Wellington I had been three years on the athletics team as a javelin thrower, a sport I had taken up after being sacked from the colts' cricket squad for what the master in charge described as 'an irreverent attitude to batting'. It had been my hope before going up to Oxford that I might win an athletics blue, having at one stage trained with a national juniors javelin squad. Sadly, a series of back injuries forced me to abandon the event – although not, unfortunately, before the night in a college beer cellar with the OU Athletics Club at which I rashly said to a girlfriend new to the game of darts that I would indicate with my fingers where she should aim. Her first throw proved so accurate that with a sliver of skin it pinned my finger to the board.

Oxford also enabled me to develop an interest in horse-racing, a sport which had intrigued me since the days when my family lived close by the old Hurst Park racecourse in East Molesey, Surrey (a track, sadly, long lost to the housing developers). As a child I used to ride my bike to the end of the road, prop it against the fence and stand on the saddle to peer over the top and watch the horses flash by. The approaching thunder of hooves, the jingle of bits and creaking of saddle leather, the jockeys in their bright colours shouting for room and then the roar from the distant stand as the horses approached the finish filled me with an excitement at the spectacle which has never left me. I used to cycle round, too, to watch the crowds going in, some stopping on the way to play 'Find the Lady' on an upturned orange box with the shifty-eyed three-card-trick merchants or to buy wisdom from the tipster 'Prince Monolulu' in his tatty feathered head-dress as he shouted 'I gotta horse . . .'

There was one other way to get close to the Hurst Park racing action. The old Upper Deck swimming pool beside the course on the banks of the Thames overlooked the seven-furlong start. Many a jockey missed the break because his attention was diverted by bikini-clad lovelies parading themselves on the Upper Deck.

It was from Oxford that I first visited the Holy of Holies in jump racing at Cheltenham and was driven in awe through the training centre at Lambourn, later to be the subject of my first racing book. I also supplemented my grant income (or convinced myself that I did so; not many bookies ride pushbikes) by betting. To my shame as a student of the form book these days, I remember going to a point-to-point and backing a horse called Everything's Rosy because my then girlfriend had left me the night before. But it did win, and at 33–1.

I have never been a heavy gambler, but I have always enjoyed a punt, just on the horses. One of Kipling's female characters once said that kissing a man without a moustache was like eating an egg without the salt. As a lifelong follower of racing I have always felt much the same about betting. I like that extra little spice which it brings. At Oxford, with a few friends I developed a system based on the midday edition of the *Evening Standard*, which listed the selections in each race of the top tipsters from all the newspapers. I kept records of their performance, and we began doubling up on the selections of any tipster who had reached his previous longest losing run, say fifteen selections without a winner. The basic idea was that we would be backing the selection of somebody who knew far more than we did and who was, moreover, by that time pretty desperate for a winner. Gus O'Donnell, a leading Treasury economist, one-time Downing

Street press secretary to John Major and a man with a reputation for his prowess on the roulette table, once told me that it was as good a system as he had encountered. The syndicate was, I seem to recall, about £120 up when I was taken into hospital with glandular fever, at which point somebody else managed to lose the records and the whole thing foundered.

I have always found an interest in racing a passport to social acceptance in almost any field. Joining my fellow labourers in two-shilling yankees, patents and each-way trebles stood me in good stead as a student working on building sites every summer to supplement my grant. At the other end of the scale, racing topics have never left me short of conversation when encountering the Queen and her entourage at Commonwealth Conference drinks parties. But around the House of Commons, where some MPs aware of my other life were inclined to seek inside information, I was always rather cautious. Being in the contacts business I could not afford to become like Damon Runyon's Seldom Seen Kid, rarely on the scene because he had to avoid the many people to whom he had handed on duff tips.

I was able to develop my racing interests early in my journalistic career, which I began as a graduate trainee on the *Liverpool Daily Post*. I had been offered a job by the Thomson Group, but they did not initially specify where; and, as a home counties boy, I wanted to get experience away from London. Liverpool, still humming with the aftermath of the Beatles era, did, of course, have for me the added attraction of Aintree racecourse, home of the Grand National.

Going through my papers for this book I came across the script of a piece I recorded for Grand National morning in 1996. In this, the only sports item I ever did for the BBC, I tried to explain what the National meant to me. My feelings have not changed since I delivered it. For those who have not had the Aintree experience, it goes something like this:

Forget the ebb and flow of an Ashes test. Forget even the awesome crunch of the English and Scottish packs coming together for the first scrum of a Calcutta Cup match. For me the Grand National sucks you in like no other sporting event.

As the horses fiddle and fidget waiting for the tapes to go up I share their jockeys' butterflies, their adrenalin surge. As they charge, always far too fast, for the first fence where a few dreams are buried instantly by nervous over-jumping I am mentally there in the pack jostling for room.

Streaming towards Becher's for the first time the cautious find space on the outside, the patient hunt along for the first circuit and the hapless and the headstrong surge ahead. Spruce flies at the fences, tumbles are taken and whips are beaten into the ground by frustrated riders whose hopes of fame have gone for another year. Potential disaster is rarely more than a stride away and I can only marvel at the sheer guts required of horse and rider alike.

It's excitement all the way from the moment you prop the *Racing Post* against the marmalade pot to comb through the form. There's the wizened figure who marks your racecard with a grubby ballpoint in a jostling bar, the hum of expectancy around the parade ring as pale-faced jockeys swing into the saddle. The lists of past winners, trainers and riders stir the blood like hymns from your childhood – Neville Crump, Fred Rimell and Fulke Walwyn, Dave Dick, Pat Taaffe and Brian Fletcher. Back come memories implanted over the years. Those grainy black and white films of poor Devon Loch's collapse only yards short of the finish. The bravery of the front-running Crisp, leading all the way with 12 stone on his back only to be done at the death by Red Rum, later to become the supreme

Aintree hero of them all. And, of course, the 23rd fence carnage in 1967 when all others were brought down and the outsider Foinavon picked his way through the stricken from behind to win. The riderless horse which caused the chaos by running down the fence? I remember it well. Popham Down. I'd backed him.

I've had the winner sometimes – Lucius at 14–1, Specify at 28–1, both two and a half milers who came again over four miles to pick off the plodders. But it isn't the winnings you remember with the National, it is the stories.

Jockey Bob Champion and Aldaniti triumphing over cancer and breakdown respectively in 1981. Jenny Pitman's first training win for a woman with Corbiere. And the brave old amateur rider the Duke of Albuquerque. He broke both legs riding the National. He cracked vertebrae. By the early 1970s the bookies offered 66–1 against him getting round. But in 1974, having broken a collar bone the week before, he did so at last, at the age of 56.

Some though aren't so lucky. Never, ever will I forget Paddy Farrell's crashing fall at the awesome Chair fence in 1964. It broke his back and helped to generate the Injured Jockeys' Fund. May they all come back safely today.

For life experience, Merseyside in the 1960s could not have been bettered. I lived initially in Hope Street, Britain's only street with a cathedral at either end (the modernistic Roman Catholic one with its tube-shaped centrepiece being irreverently dubbed 'The Mersey Funnel'). My one-bedroomed flat had a combined bathroom/kitchenette with a letterbox in the bathroom door. The decorator had been heavily into off-cuts: there were seventeen different wallpapers visible from the single sofa. The basement below was frequently an inch deep in water and the ramshackle property was owned by a red-haired Polish lady who bred chihuahuas and whose husband was said to have disappeared in mysterious circumstances. I woke one morning to find her sitting on the end of my bed. It may just have been a reminder about the rent, but as far as I was concerned it was 'Hello, Mrs Robinson, but no thank you.'

The *Liverpool Daily Post* and *Liverpool Echo* group, which produced the city's morning and evening newspapers, ran their graduate trainee scheme to maintain a steady supply of reasonably literate sub-editors. These are the people who process reporters' copy and put together the newspaper pages, which in those days were still printed by the hot-metal process, with every letter cast by a typesetter and the pages assembled on a metal 'stone'. Most of the trainees, they knew, would be off to Fleet Street as soon as their four years were up. Contemporaries among my fellow novices included the late and much-missed Tony Bevins, later political editor of papers including the *Independent* and the *Express*; John Sergeant, who went straight off to broadcasting; the film-writer and pop culture icon Ray Connolly; and Malcolm Bruce, now an MP and one of the leading figures in the Liberal Democrats in recent years.

The great advantage of the scheme was that, provided you showed some aptitude, you were given considerable responsibility very quickly. After a mere year in journalism I found myself on occasion acting as the late-night 'stone sub', seeing the later editions of the paper to bed and literally able to say, 'Hold the front page!' You did absolutely everything, from processing City page figures like the 'Chicago lard and hogs' or 'pork belly futures' to writing book reviews of learned tomes by the statesmen of the day. You started, however, in the newsroom as a reporter, beginning with 'weather and temperatures' and progressing through the highlights of the Liverpool Show and gold watch awards to local workers – and hoping that you were on duty one day when a truly big story broke.

General reporting like this is an experience no journalist who is ever to hold command over others should be without. It included such duties as calling on suddenly bereaved families to collect the mantelpiece photograph of the husband or father killed in an accident in the docks. Invariably we were received with tea and courtesy, even on occasion being invited to view the corpse. Alf Green, one of the experienced local reporters, used to say of the local predominantly Catholic community that in any family tragedy they would call first for the doctor, then for the priest and then for the *Liverpool Echo*.

We all did our stint as 'subs' gathered together round a huge wooden table, nine or ten of us wise-cracking and ad-libbing the night away, sharpened pencils at the ready, copy boys shifting the subbed copy out of wire baskets in front of us. Of the older hands, one was an expert on boxing, another a rugby union referee. Another used to save up two years' holidays at a time and then go away on a cargo boat to South America or China for a couple of months, loading a crate of John Jameson on board before he did. Among this motley crew the humour was usually of a schoolboy variety. 'Here's one about a human torso found in a ditch. Put a head on that, Robin' ... 'But John, this story's got no legs' ... 'What size do you want for the body type?'

In addition to my main employment as a sub-editor for the *Daily Post*, the morning paper, I used to boost my basic income by writing articles on a freelance basis for the *Post* and for the evening paper, the *Echo*, under a variety of names. Should anybody still possess a faded yellow paper or two I was also Robert Leigh, James Edgar, Robert Frank, Francis Leigh, Frederick Pye,

Peter Godot and even, when I was writing for the women's page, Susan Germaine and Geraldine Fortescue. Much of this was the typical output of a young journalist who had seen one too many productions of *The Front Page*. Endless articles appeared under challenging headlines like 'Time to scrap the coroner' and 'Do we really need another Poet Laureate?' I wrote exposés about how easy it was to get hold of a shotgun, challenged local artists at an avant-garde exhibition to pick out my work from theirs and deliberately stirred controversy ('Come off it, Aberystwyth') by accusing the Welsh of arrogance over a demand that the Prince of Wales should go to a Welsh university (the *Post* had a strong circulation in north Wales).

There was an early piece on a visit to the then sensationally new experience of a sauna, and an interview, gleaned when on attachment to the paper's London office, with writer Laurie Lee in his favourite pub in Chelsea, where he warmed his barley wine by sticking in it a red-hot poker taken from the open fire. I was not coy at that stage about revealing any political opinions: one piece under my name was entitled 'A first-time voter picks Labour'. Early signs of my other abiding interest in life were also apparent. In 1964 came my first article on 'The crisis in British horseracing'. It would appear to have been in one ever since.

I was the original hack. In a variety of styles I wrote feature articles, leader columns, book reviews, humorous sketches, women's page features, and, before too long, a racing column under the pseudonym of Mandarin, my favourite racehorse, who, in the hands of Fred Winter, won the Grand Steeplechase de Paris in 1962 despite the bit having broken in his mouth before the fourth fence. I used to visit the stables of local trainers like Eric Cousins, the Tarporley handicap expert, and Colin Crossley, whose string used to train sometimes on the sands at West Kirby

– a glorious sight in the early morning light, silhouetted against the sea as their hooves flicked up the spray along the shore.

Amid all this activity I was summoned one day by the proprietor, Sir Alick Jeans. Perhaps, I thought, there was to be some praise for my diligence, even a promotion or a rise. Not so. The wispy-haired figure, more like a university don than a business tycoon, kept me standing and remained on his feet too, his long, bony hands twitching nervously at his sides. He did not have much to say.

'Oakley, you are earning far too much money for a young man of your age.'

Then I was dismissed back to the newsroom. I was, it is true, virtually doubling my salary with all the extras. But since the salary at that stage amounted to the grand sum of £950 a year, my total income hardly amounted to a fortune.

Much of this effort was motivated by the attempt to put together enough money to get married. At the end of my first year in Liverpool I had joined my family on a holiday in Italy, at the Hotel Villa Balbi in Sestri Levante. There I met Carolyn, who was to become my wife, my best friend and my guiding light through life. I cannot say 'my constant companion' because it simply would not be true. Carolyn always says that the reason we have been happily married for nearly thirty-five years is that I have worked such long hours and been away so much that I have retained a curiosity value. We have not spent enough time together to get bored with each other.

Spotting the glorious blonde vision across the hotel dining room and fancying her like mad was one thing. Engaging her interest in me was another thing altogether. I trailed her round the Italian resort and the local market trying to contrive a meeting, but she always seemed to be looking the other way. In the end I had a stroke of luck; and I owe my happy marriage to a dead sardine. Reading my book on the beach one afternoon, I heard a squeal of alarm and looked up to see Carolyn in a brown bikini stepping fastidiously around a seagull's supper floating belly upwards at the water's edge. Guessing where she might be headed, I dashed into the water, swam out to the raft in the centre of the bay and was there to help her up as she arrived.

'Grazie.'

'It's nothing.'

'Oh, you're English!'

'Yes, I'm sorry if that's a disappointment . . .'

I knew from the first moment that she was to be the love of my life. We started talking that night, and I have never lacked for advice ever since. But she must have had some explaining to do to her mother after our third evening, most of which we had spent amorously entwined on a wooden seat overlooking the Bay of Silence. Unfortunately, it had been redecoration day, and as she walked back into the hotel ahead of me I noticed that Carolyn's pink dress had a row of paint stains all down the back, matching the slats of the wooden bench.

Our honeymoon in the same spot two years later was something less than a success. Our car, a Rolls-Royce borrowed for the day from my father's company chairman, broke down on the way to Heathrow. Bad weather diverted us to a different airport in Italy. There was a rail strike which made it even harder to get to our destination. On the second day of our honeymoon I was taken ill. It turned out to be a severe ear, nose and throat bug which nearly cost me my hearing. The Italian doctor merely said 'English? Too much sun,' and prescribed suppositories. Carolyn was left to amuse herself for five days while I languished, eating little more than a few fragments of white fish. We still have a photo of me propped up against a palm tree looking like death. On the return journey our baggage was lost. If we could survive that lot, we reckoned, our marriage could survive most things.

The Italian doctor's comment and curling lip still rankle after all these years. So I took a special satisfaction in the summer of 2000 when, at Ascot to report on the Shergar Cup, an international challenge event, for my Turf column in the *Spectator*, I was able to write about an Italian jockey who had to give up one of his mounts because he could not stand the heat.

It's possible that I fell prey to that bug on my honeymoon because for the previous two years I had really been doing two jobs, working all the hours God sent for ten-day stretches. At the end of the ten days I would then drive down to London in my second-hand Mini. (It was once stolen by joyriders and abandoned in Bootle; but the thieves did me a favour. All they stole were the hideous leopard-skin seat covers I had inherited from the previous owner.) I would pick Carolyn up from work and we would go out for a meal in Soho, often to the Trattoria da Otello, where in those days a scooped-out orange full of coloured sorbet was real sophistication. Then we would drive on to Brighton, where Carolyn lived with her mother. On Monday we would be up before cock-crow for me to drop Carolyn in London and head on back to Liverpool to get there in time for my afternoon shift. And there wasn't much motorway in those days. No wonder my lovely mother-in-law used to wonder why I looked washed out and pasty-faced whenever she saw me.

My bride's reaction, when we arrived back in the north-west and I carried her over the threshold of our rented flat in Neston, on the Wirral, was not the best of omens. Carolyn took one look at her new home and burst into tears. 'You should have seen the other seventeen I looked at,' was my rather unsympathetic response. As we saved for a place of our own, I gave her house-keeping of £5 a week and we lived mostly on sausage flan. Our landlord was an amiable widower who enjoyed his drink and was edging his large kitchen garden with upturned wine bottles, making his progress through the vintages. He had a regular drinking companion who, when on holiday, used to send him postcards addressed to Pistus A. Newt Esq. or Mr Wun Tu Meni.

We lived more soberly. I may have made up for it since with the Sunday Times Wine Club and the Wine Society, but in those days of early struggle, with Carolyn working as a secretary/PA and me toiling all hours on the *Liverpool Post*, a pint at the Parkgate pub and a few prawns were the height of luxury. The only liquor in our cupboard was a bottle of sherry for visiting vicars.

3

LOITERING WITH INTENT:
THE LOBBY LIFE

IN 1967 I GOT THE BREAK I HAD BEEN HOPING FOR AND WAS moved to London. I began work in the House of Commons press gallery as assistant to the *Liverpool Daily Post*'s then London editor and political correspondent Norman Cook. Soon I was given the political job in my own right, and since then I have remained in political journalism as a member of that strange fraternity known as 'the Lobby'.

I learned rapidly that 'the lobby' was a shorthand term for several different things. The lobby is first of all a place – the cool, marble-floored Members' Lobby in the House of Commons, situated between the Central Lobby, where members can meet their constituents, and the House of Commons chamber. From here, one door leads off to the Commons library corridor – an escape route for MPs wanting to slink off for a snooze; another leads down a corridor to the Members' Car Park and New Palace Yard; and just off the Members' Lobby, where 'badge messengers' in white ties and tailcoats slip envelopes into MPs' pigeonholes, are the whips' offices, where parliamentarians quite literally get their marching orders. It is, therefore, the Piccadilly Circus of the Commons, where you have the best chance of encountering the maximum number of MPs – or at least, you did before they had new offices built and all went off to spend hours in front of their computer screens.

A little like the entrance halls of the posher London clubs, clustered with statues (including one of Churchill, whose toe Tories are reputed to rub for luck) and with a supply of free snuff still available to MPs, the Members' Lobby is part bazaar, part political bus-stop and part rumour factory. And even in these days of big majorities it comes buzzily alive with gossiping groups before a big vote.

The term 'the lobby' has also come to be applied to the corps of journalists officially listed by the Commons Serjeant at Arms as accredited representatives of their media organizations. Only MPs and accredited lobby journalists are allowed into the Members' Lobby; and journalists have to leave when a 'division', or parliamentary vote, is called. There is also a nearby bar, known as 'Annie's' after a former barmaid, which is restricted to MPs and lobby journalists. I made little use of it, because most of the members you found in there were unlikely to have stories that mattered or, if they did, were inclined to tell them to half a dozen others.

The Members' Lobby is where we political correspondents loiter with intent to pick up our passing trade and snatch conversations with ministers and whips. Conversations 'on lobby terms' mean that you may use the information but you are not allowed to identify the source. The Members' Lobby is also the place where the more publicity-minded MPs can grab us for a word. Some, however, are best avoided when time is short. There is no such thing as a brief conversation, for example, with the amiable Tory Eurosceptic Bill Cash, who always has some new Brussels monstrosity to excoriate or some new scheme for frustrating the Europhiles to outline. Murdo Maclean, private secretary to a series of chief whips of both complexions, once told me of an occasion when Richard Ryder, a former Tory chief whip, saw Cash approaching at the other end of a corridor and, in order to avoid him, walked purposefully through the first door he came to. It turned out to be a broom cupboard – and Ryder had to stay within for some time, hoping that Bill would not pursue him.

There are plenty more like Bill Cash, some of them reminders of Churchill's definition of a fanatic: a man who can't change his mind and won't change the subject. I escape such longer-winded MPs when necessary by grabbing the pager from my belt, studying the last message as if it had just come in and excusing myself with the pressing need to phone the newsdesk.

Confusingly, 'the lobby' is used also to refer to the twice-daily briefings at which those journalists on the Serjeant at Arms's list meet with the Prime Minister's press spokesmen. The morning session is held in Number Ten Downing Street, the afternoon one in a garret room in a tower in the Palace of Westminster. These sessions have been seized upon by journalists who do not work at Westminster to represent political correspondents as a group involved in some sort of cosy conspiracy with politicians. The idea is that we are all a bunch of lazy layabouts who simply take down the words that fall from Alastair Campbell's lips and re-cycle them as news. If this were so, one wonders, why would Campbell need to indulge so frequently in diatribes against political journalists? What the conspiracy theorists forget is that we are in a highly competitive business. Everybody wants to be first with the story, and everybody wants to have an original angle. Lobby briefings are for the most part a convenience for both sides; a chance to run through the nuts and bolts of the upcoming political agenda, to hear the government's reaction to the latest events and to save a few hundred separate calls to Downing Street in the process.

I regard the lobby system much as a plumber regards a monkey wrench – as a useful tool; certainly not as a mystic freemasonry. Sometimes the spokesmen do try it on; but we know where they come from. We are employed to interpret and to aim off where necessary. We talk to alternative sources. For the past twenty years I have not lacked access to senior politicians under different administrations. But they cannot always be reached, and when they cannot we need media spokesmen who reflect their views faithfully and who can answer our questions knowledgeably. I am content that by talking to them sometimes on lobby terms I have been able to give readers and listeners better information than if I had insisted on on-the-record conversations only. Every group of specialist correspondents, from transport to snooker, finds that it pays on occasion to talk to regular sources on protected terms. Basically all conversations between politicians and lobby journalists are assumed to be on lobby terms – not for attribution – unless stated otherwise.

There are snags in the lobby system, of course. It gives the government first run on a breaking story and increases its chances of being able to manage the news on a quiet day. There is a danger, too, in the intimacy of access when you travel with political leaders: it can lower your guard. Unscrupulous politicians in all parties can and do exploit lobby terms to fly kites and then blame the media when they tumble out of the air. But if they try it too often and abuse the system then we leave an obvious fingerprint or two on the stories they inspire, and they soon desist.

Critics of the British lobby system, with its quotes attributed to 'government sources' or 'government officials', tend to allege that the Americans do things more honestly, with named spokesmen on the record and on camera. Not always, they don't. Often, only the opening section of a briefing is on camera. And after an open, on-the-record, on-camera session in Washington, a favoured few are invited in for a further word with the briefer – off camera and off the record. As for having named spokesmen on the record, enthusiasts for the US system should have attended the background briefing at the Rizzan Sea Park Hotel at the Okinawa G8 summit in 2000, following the bilateral talks between Presidents Clinton and Putin. Here there was an exchange which began with remarks from a source identified only as 'Senior Administration Official'. He then suggested: 'Why don't I turn it over to my colleague, and then we'll take a few questions. My colleague 1-A.'

Second Administration Official: 'I was going to be Colleague 2, but I negotiated with Lockhart for 1-A.'

That simplifies and improves our system about as much as it does calling a lift an elevator. The idea that the Americans have a pure and unsullied system is about as realistic and convincing as a bird flying backwards.

Some people are fussed by the notion that spokesmen in Downing Street undermine ministers and others who have fallen out of favour. This does happen occasionally, as when Bernard Ingham in Margaret Thatcher's time as Prime Minister likened the Foreign Secretary Francis Pym to the radio character 'Mona Lott' and described John Biffen as a 'semi-detached' member of the government. We saw it happen again, spectacularly, in January 2001 with the fall of Peter Mandelson over the Hinduja passports affair, with Alastair Campbell consciously or unconsciously echoing Ingham's turn of phrase. As it became clear that Mandelson, having resigned, was already regretting being bundled out and was beginning to fight back, Campbell used a Sunday paper lobby briefing to suggest that the former Northern Ireland Secretary had been losing his former skills and becoming 'slightly detached'. Again, it was a case of weak politicians struggling against the power of a media which they had helped turn into a monster.

Mandelson, the renowned master of spin, blamed the media for his downfall, arguing that he was rushed into resignation on incomplete evidence because of their hue and cry. On the day he was forced to resign he met the Prime Minister at 10.15 a.m. 'Already the media pressure was mounting,' he recorded three days later.

> The 11 o'clock press lobby was assembling and a decision from me was required. For the first time, and I hope the last time, in my life the fight suddenly went out of me. I felt isolated. I knew I hadn't done anything wrong, but I had no time to prove it. I agreed to resign and the Prime Minister – understandably given the present-ation of the facts – did not try to dissuade me. I should have fought for time to allow a fuller examination of the facts.

He did not get the time because, with an election approaching, the Prime Minister and Alastair Campbell wanted to draw a line as quickly as they could: the eleven o'clock lobby had to be fed.

In fact, character assassination is a rarity at lobby meetings. I cannot recall a single instance, with the exception of the Mandelson affair, when Alastair Campbell bad-mouthed a minister at a lobby briefing. More often, the character assassin-ations come elsewhere in the system, as ministers' political advisers or parliamentary groupies joust on their patrons' behalf. Treasury sources were quick to insist in 2000, for example, that the Prime Minister had 'slapped down' the Foreign Secretary, Robin Cook, and forced him to withdraw pre-released remarks from a speech on the single currency. The battle between Gordon Brown and Robin Cook will, as they say, run and run. But even these episodes are not daily occurrences; and they would happen with or without a formal lobby system. A government can always find a few compliant journalists with whom to plant ideas, and Downing Street briefers do not need to use the full lobby sessions to indulge in such exercises.

There is no doubt, though, that a lobby system can be advantageous to governments. A typical example of how government can benefit came in March 1995, when the American administration granted a visa for Sinn Fein leader Gerry Adams, despite strong lobbying in Washington by the British government against such a move. On the *Nine O'Clock News*, presenter Peter Sissons asked me how annoyed the British government was about the granting of a visa. I replied:

Outwardly, Downing Street is saying nothing except the diplomatic nicety that it is of course a matter entirely for the United States who they give a visa to, how and why. But behind the scenes, ministers and senior officials are hopping mad, particularly because Sir Patrick Mayhew [the then Northern Ireland Secretary] has been in Washington this week insisting that Mr Adams should not be given a visa that allowed him to go in for fund-raising, because the British government doesn't believe that there can be any sensible differentiation between fund-raising for the political activities of Sinn Fein and fund-raising for the other activities of the IRA. Sir Patrick was insisting that the IRA is still targeting, recruiting and training and that kind of activity can only be increased if it has access to funds from the United States.

In what was obviously a well-briefed reply following conversations with ministers and with the Prime Minister's press secretary, I was clearly serving the government's purpose, enabling it to get across to an audience of over five million exactly why ministers were arguing against a visa for Gerry Adams – and to indicate its anger with the US government without fear of a comeback. No minister would have dreamed of prejudicing future relations with America by saying such a thing on the record. And if anybody in the US administration had objected, the British could have said, 'Well, you know these bloody journalists. They'll make up anything.' At the same time, the government knew that the US embassy would have monitored my live exchange with Peter Sissons, would have been well aware that I would not have reported as I did without foundation, and would have reported back on how the Washington decision was playing in London.

On such occasions we journalists are useful pawns in the diplomatic game. Should we allow ourselves to be used in that way? Absolutely. It was quite true and newsworthy that the British government was 'hopping mad', and it was interesting to know the arguments Sir Patrick had used in Washington. On such occasions I was happy to be 'used'. So long as there is a genuine story there, I see no problem.

There is one extra factor we have to take into account now that Number Ten makes a potted version of the Downing Street briefings available on the internet. The Prime Minister's office is playing to a wider audience too. When William Hague was pumping up the issue of asylum-seekers with proposals for detention centres in the summer of 2000, I persisted with a series of questions at a morning lobby about the government's own actions in this sphere. We obviously needed to do that to balance the story. But Downing Street did not want the story to develop any 'legs' and had little to say.

Lance Price, then number two to Campbell on the political side of the office before he moved to Labour headquarters, attacked me for my line of questioning. Pursuing a familiar Campbell theme, he said it was a 'typical example of the BBC taking up the tabloid agenda'. Before going to work in Downing Street (a move which had the Tories crowing 'We told you so' about the political views prevalent in the BBC), Lance had been a very calm and effective member of the team of BBC political correspondents. Angered by his charge, I told him in the meeting that if he really thought the Hague line on asylum was not a political story then he had let his instincts as a journalist fade pretty fast in his new role. Afterwards he came up to me with a grin. 'I was asked to be sure of working that line in,' he said. It was a message Number Ten was keen to spread; it had to be uttered in the meeting so that it could be put out on the internet afterwards.

I am an agnostic about the lobby operation. As political editor of *The Times* and of the BBC I could have lived easily enough without it. My calls would mostly still have been answered. But, although I have had to swallow hard occasionally at the odd pomposity which the lobby breeds, I do not forget what an asset it was in a provincial journalist's life back in 1967. Senior figures did not answer my calls then, and in those days I blessed the lobby system for helping to put me in some aspects on equal terms with the top political writers for the nationals. To us junior correspondents, men like Francis Boyd, Bob Carvel, Harry Boyne and Harold Hutchinson were grand, magisterial figures. You did not sit down beside them uninvited at the press cafeteria table. But at lobby meetings it was open to any of us to ask questions.

Entering the lobby back then was a huge step-change in my life. Instead of being limited to the local politics of Liverpool City Council, my brief now included the national political scene. But there was still, of course, the pastoral aspect with local MPs and their constituency concerns. Woe betide the provincial lobby correspondent who failed to report in full detail the efforts of his regional band of MPs in respect of allotments, school crossings or factory fumes on their local patch.

It was a hectic life. I had to write heavyweight features about the key issues of the day and personality profiles about local figures, and for the *Liverpool Daily Post* in those days that meant Wales as well as Merseyside. The editor wanted lively political gossip and a full news service. I had to cover the national and local political scenes and write think pieces on major controversies. So busy was I that I rarely had time to tap out my news stories on the rackety old upright typewriter. I simply grabbed a telephone, asked for 'Copy' and dictated my story off the cuff. Although I did not know it at the time, this was a good training ground for live work on television. Having to dictate my copy instantly forced me to concentrate on the essentials. As I was to discover later, more time to deliberate only increases hesitation. First instincts were usually proved right.

But the rush and the grind were accompanied by a heady excitement. Suddenly I was where I had long wanted to be: at the heart of national politics. Of course, as a provincial lobby correspondent I was not immediately on terms of intimacy with

Cabinet ministers. To begin with it was more a case of a few beers with Liverpool backbenchers than lunches with the great and the good. But there were fractious and fascinating debates long into the night with other politically besotted young correspondents like Frank Johnson, later to be the sketch-writer supreme and editor of the *Spectator*. There was Peter Rose, who went on by way of *Sun* leader-writing to become an author and history lecturer. And there was music expert Hugh Macpherson, who for many years combined a column for the left-wing *Tribune* with a well-paid job in the higher ranks of the John Lewis department store chain.

Two of us queried Hugh's socialist credentials one day when we had all been at a think-tank lunch and emerged to find it snowing hard. As Peter and I trudged along the slushy pavements, coat collars turned up against the raging elements, the *Tribune* columnist drew alongside in his chauffeured limousine, his thoughts no doubt turning to his next bout of invective on behalf of the underprivileged. Was he going to offer us a lift? Not on your nelly! As he waved to us in lordly fashion his car sped past, spurting slush into our turn-ups. Norman Lamont, also at the lunch, had raised an eyebrow over Hugh's car as he left, but *Tribune*'s columnist was unabashed. 'Why should the Tories have all the best chauffeurs?' he countered.

I enjoyed, too, the regular exchanges with the parliamentarians on my patch. You build your contacts as a lobby correspondent by starting with those in your region, and for me there was plenty to admire about men like Labour's Dr Edwin Brooks, a bearded academic who managed to combine a heavy constituency workload in Bebington with an eye for the big issues. I also liked the independent-minded Tory Tim Fortescue and Eric Ogden, the chirpy Labour member for West Derby. The ex-paratrooper

Colonel Dick Crawshaw, who used to fast one day a week, was a far from stereotypical Labour member, and Sir John Tilney was an ever-courteous Conservative of the old school: born to a sense of service, constitutionally loyal but prepared to defy his party on a point of principle.

Not all local MPs treated you as they would the big names on the national papers. Left-winger Eric Heffer, a self-important figure who once declared of himself, 'Jesus Christ was a carpenter too,' would be on to my editor with a complaint if I missed a question from him about public lavatories in his Walton constituency, but he could not spare the time to talk to me about the latest machinations of the Tribune Group. He would go and talk to the *Guardian* about that.

But never mind. I was at Westminster. I was where I wanted to be. As a junior correspondent I had to pay heed to the curious little leather-bound rulebook on lobby practice which warned me not to run after ministers in corridors or to interrupt conversations between politicians and lobby colleagues. I had to go along with the mumbo-jumbo of notices which went up on the board in an instantly penetrable code, announcing a briefing session with 'Red Mantle' or 'Blue Leader'. But I had the precious access to the Members' Lobby. Though not all would respond, I had the excuse to approach any figure in national politics who strolled through. I may not have been in the front rank; but I was, at last, on the inside track.

4

A PRIME MINISTER ON MY PATCH

ON MY VERY FIRST DAY ON THE INSIDE TRACK, I WAS BROUGHT TO a shuddering halt by a national figure who accosted me.

September 1967 saw me not at Westminster but at the Labour party conference, which that year was being held in Scarborough. Somewhat apprehensive about how to begin approaching MPs and wondering where I might start looking for an original story, I was standing with a colleague in the foyer of one of the main hotels when the famously bibulous Foreign Secretary George Brown came up to us. He poked me in the chest with a pudgy forefinger.

'Are you from the Press?' enquired the great man, swaying slightly, owlish eyes bulging.

'Yes, sir,' I replied, noting that he had perhaps enjoyed an ice-lolly or two.

'Well, I've got a few things I want to say to the Gentlemen of the Press,' Brown told me pugnaciously.

Shortly before the conference he had been entangled in a fracas with press photographers on the passenger liner *Queen Mary* over his attempts at a then fashionable dance called The Frug. Always emotional, he was now full of a sense of grievance and had soon emptied every bar within shouting distance as, in his rich trombone tones, he unburdened himself of his feelings about the media. He went on and on. And on.

Eventually, to my great relief, his poor wife Sophie took him in hand. 'Come on George, you've had your say now, come on up to bed . . .' she pleaded, trying to drag him up the elegant curved staircase.

'No; I've got a few more things I want to say to the Gentlemen of the Press,' he insisted, standing his ground. I stood beside him, notebook in hand, scribbling furiously and wondering if life in the lobby was going to be like this every day. It wasn't. But, thanks to the likes of John Prescott and Peter Mandelson, both equally emotional in their different ways, it has had its similar moments.

I never got to know George Brown. I was too junior, although I was friends with his brother Ron, also a Labour MP, though he later joined the SDP. But for all his flaws and repeated resignations, George Brown was a big man of rare talent. And there was some real character in the Labour Cabinets of those days. Roy Jenkins made some of the best Commons speeches I ever hope to hear. Barbara Castle snapped my head off so sharply at my first press conference I should have loathed her for ever more, but I admire still the sheer professionalism of her public performances. No-one can make a pause count for more. She is physically frail now, but still all woman. I took her arm a little too briskly to guide her into the studio for a *Week In Westminster* interview earlier this year.

'Take me into dinner, don't march me to the scaffold!' she admonished me with a smile.

Mo Mowlam told me at one recent conference of another characteristic retort. Barbara had come to Mo's constituency to speak for her, and as Mo helped her into the car to drive her back to the station, she said, as she habitually does to passengers, 'Would you mind putting on your seat belt?'

'*Mind*, dear?' replied the one-time transport minister; 'I *invented* them.' She would have done a good Lady Bracknell had her career taken her onto the stage.

As a student I had been a great admirer of Tony Crosland's *The Future of Socialism*. I considered Crosland to be a future Prime Minister and was deeply sad when he died so tragically young. He was kind enough to write a foreword to an early political book which Peter Rose and I wrote together. But I may perhaps have been seduced just a little by the sheer glamour of his political style – the fiercely competitive tennis with Roy Jenkins, the broad canary-yellow braces and the massive whisky he poured me in his ministry one night after a reshuffle when I happened to be there by appointment for an interview about something else and he did a roll-call demolition job on his Cabinet colleagues, sadly off the record. Frustrated not to have got the job he wanted, he was sinking an equally large measure himself and letting off steam: 'Sometimes you'd think that Roy [Jenkins] was the only person in this government who's ever picked up a book. I know twice what he does about economics,' he declared.

On another occasion I went to Crosland's home for an interview. I have forgotten now what it was about. What I do remember – and it is a memory which still has the power to make me cringe – is the incredulous gaze of his lovely wife Susan at the apparition which presented itself on her doorstep as I announced my appointment. I was trying at the time to grow a version of the then rather trendy Viva Zapata moustache. It was, I have to say, a miserable failure, and it was Mrs Crosland's polite but obvious effort to control her mirth at the sight of the straggling, uneven growth that convinced me it was time to abandon the experiment. It was off within twenty-four hours. I have not followed fashion since.

One Cabinet minister of the Wilson days, the future Commons Speaker George Thomas, did become a friend, and a popular visitor with our children. As I have already noted, a strong Welsh circulation was important to the *Liverpool Daily Post*, and in his time as Secretary of State for Wales George was the first Cabinet minister to become a good contact of mine. I should have thought more carefully, however, before I took him to lunch for the first time. I chose a Soho restaurant, L'Escargot, to which we walked from some other function, and George was in a rare state by the time we reached our destination. A Methodist lay preacher, he was terrified that a press photographer might emerge as we strolled past a series of strip clubs, porno shops and girlie bars and snap him in such surroundings.

Not, it seems, that the fare on offer would have much interested him. The former Labour MP Leo Abse, to me an exotic nonentity in his own days at Westminster, has recently won himself some more of the publicity he always craved by 'revealing' – having waited until George was in his grave and unable to hit back before doing so – that George Thomas was a homosexual who was ashamed of his sexual orientation and who lived in a perpetual state of terror that he might be blackmailed or exposed in the media. I can only say that such a 'revelation' about a life-long bachelor who talked endlessly about his 'Mam' and who took regular holidays in north Africa came as no surprise to any in the Westminster community. I remember a slight sense of unease once in my very early days as a reporter when George Thomas chucked me under the chin and said, 'You *are* a good boy.' But then I saw him do exactly the same thing to a wizened backbench mining MP twice my age and relaxed. Most of us at Westminster had a pretty clear idea of where George's tastes probably lay. But I was interested in his politics and in his stories, not what he did with his spare Saturday afternoons. If he did work himself into a state of terror about possible exposure in the way that Abse describes then I am sorry. It is far healthier now that Cabinet ministers can reveal their sexual orientation without fear or fuss. In that small area at least, the tabloid terror has diminished.

George was a natural gossip, who would accompany his best stories with a grasp of your upper arm and the slightly camp exclamation, 'Oh, I am *wicked*!' One of the best tales he told me was of the wily Jim Callaghan when Callaghan was running for the Labour leadership contest. Jim and George, both Cardiff MPs, had never been the best of friends. Nor had Callaghan been famed for his religiosity. But with the leadership contest on, George told me, James Callaghan came to his room, got down on his knees and suggested they prayed together for spiritual guidance on whom to support! It beats kissing babies, I suppose, but only just.

A sense of humour really does help a politician, and my favourite story about George, who prospered by instinct rather than intellect, was of the time he was with a parliamentary delegation in the Middle East. Somebody slammed his finger in a car door; whereupon, instead of turning the air blue, the future Viscount Tonypandy impressed his hosts by uttering nothing more than a strained 'Hallelujah!' Complimented on his restraint, he responded: 'Ah, but I was thinking all the words that you might have used.'

*

My best piece of luck during those early days was that the MP for the Merseyside constituency of Huyton was one Harold Wilson. For a young political journalist seeking to make the grade, having a Prime Minister on your patch was a real help. Thanks to that geographical accident I gained a little more access to the top than a junior provincial correspondent might have expected. Wilson was perhaps Labour's cleverest ever Prime Minister in the academic sense; and if Tony Blair is accused of being excessively image-conscious and media-obsessed, watching Harold Wilson in action was no bad preparation for dealing with his later successor.

I followed Wilson for a fair bit of the 1970 general election campaign. In public he would puff his pipe and be photographed with a pint of beer: Wilson, the man of the people. In the privacy of the railway carriage with his entourage he preferred a brandy and a cigar. In private, the tone was Oxford English; on the public platform, the Yorkshire accent sharpened grittily and the supposedly non-political Mary Wilson was often vigilant in tugging his sleeve to point out a face to be welcomed or a placard to be taken up and commented upon.

On election night in 1970 Wilson was staying, as he always did, in the Adelphi Hotel in Liverpool, ready to travel out at an appropriate moment to his own count in Huyton. Along with a couple of other journalists I was invited to dine at the Adelphi that night with Marcia (later Lady) Falkender, the Prime Minister's close confidante and highly influential political secretary. Our host was the dome-headed, boffin-haired Will Camp, a talented novelist, the public relations guru for organizations like British Gas and British Steel, and in that election the Prime Minister's unpaid spin doctor.

Yes, even in those days there were spin doctors, though their role then was rather less prominent, being confined to advising the Prime Minister rather than strolling round the press gallery scrutinizing the opening paragraphs on a journalist's computer screen with an audible sucking of teeth and dropping a document or two in their wake. But there were considerable parallels. Just as Tony Blair has had former *Mirror* journalist Alastair Campbell as his press secretary, so Wilson had the equally professional and equally combative ex-*Mirror* man Joe Haines. Campbell regularly abused the lobby and latterly restricted his appearances as he heaped scorn on his former media colleagues; Joe at one stage broke off relations with the lobby journalists altogether and cancelled the briefings. I still have a copy of the letter with which he did so.

There is always a battle among the intimates for the closest position beside the monarch's ear. And if there have been tensions under Tony Blair between the court favourites Alastair Campbell, Peter Mandelson and Jonathan Powell (head of the Prime Minister's office), so there were spitting matches in those days between Joe Haines and Marcia Falkender, on whose lavender notepaper he alleged was sketched out the infamous honours list which was to wreck Wilson's reputation after his unexpected resignation as Prime Minister in 1976.

Labour was the strong favourite to win that 1970 election. At one stage they had enjoyed a twelve-point lead in the polls, and that night Will Camp was in buoyant mood, buying the most expensive claret I had ever drunk in my life. But Marcia was a little subdued. Over the meal she explained why.

'I had a terrible dream last night,' she told us. 'I dreamed that the polls had got it wrong and that we would all be carrying furniture out of Downing Street tomorrow.' But she soon consoled herself. 'It was, of course, ridiculous.'

After dinner we went up to Harold Wilson's suite to begin watching the early results. Things did not start well for the Prime Minister. As he and his chauffeur Bill Housden manoeuvred the sofa so he could see the television, the castors ran over Wilson's foot. But the drinks were on hand, the expectations were high. This was to be the election which fulfilled Harold Wilson's dreams and cemented Labour in position as the party of government, a claim he had made for his party in an interview with me just a few weeks before. They were no longer, he said, a party to be tried in desperation when things went wrong, but one to be trusted in ordinary times.

We few journalists would not have been there in the suite if the Wilson entourage had not been confident of success. But suddenly you could sense the chill as an exit poll from, I think, Gravesend, brought bad news. Then the first actual result, from Guildford, fell far short of expectations. As more unfavourable indicators followed, the atmosphere of heady expectation in the suite switched rapidly to one of puzzlement and then alarm. Wilson's face lost colour. Marcia Falkender's nightmare, we swiftly realized, was becoming a reality. The press were hustled rapidly from the room, and as I excitedly made my way round to the *Daily Post* office to begin writing I found time to wonder how Will Camp was going to justify that wildly expensive claret on his expenses.

Harold Wilson lost that 1970 election by believing the opinion polls, which he affected to ignore, and by carrying on with wise-cracking walkabouts depicting the Tories as the 'National Misery Party' instead of addressing the issues. He worked on the theory that the country wanted a quiet life after the two years of hard slog provided by Roy Jenkins's budgets, and that people would not listen to prophets of economic doom. But while personality is important in politics – and Harold Wilson had plenty of it – the 1970 election proved that personality and slick public relations could not do it alone. People, I have always believed, want a message too. They want to see the colour of your policies as well as hear the sharpness of your soundbites. They don't trust politicians who say 'Let us finish the job' and who ask for a blank cheque. The electorate want to be told what the job is, and how their politicians intend to go about it.

Labour's campaign in the sunny summer of 1970 was curiously short of content. In an election which has had many echoes in 2001, even if the result has been different, the Tories in 1970 were derided by their opponents as 'Yesterday's Men'. In the run-up to the poll a stern Chancellor, in the shape of Roy Jenkins, had concentrated more on winning his party a reputation for financial rectitude than on doling out tax cuts to win easy popularity. Wilson, who reckoned he had buried the image of Labour as a left-wing party whose policies were determined by wild-eyed zealots at party conferences, played things in a cosily presidential style. He was confident he had the Tories labelled as a harsh, uncaring alternative, for at that stage their leader Edward Heath was in his now often forgotten Thatcherite phase. At the Selsdon Park Hotel near Croydon earlier in the year, Heath and his team had agreed to reduce public expenditure, to make benefits more selective, to abandon incomes policy and to cut off state help for the lame ducks of industry. 'Stand on your own two feet' was the unspoken motto. Wilson leaped on it. The Tories, he proclaimed, were 'designing a system of society for the ruthless and the pushing', just as Labour in 2001 castigated the Tories for their planned spending cuts.

In contrast to Wilson with his amiable, cheeky chappie image, the Tory leader Ted Heath was wooden and buttoned-up, with no sense of how to use media opportunities. When we flew in with him to Cardiff Airport a group of labourers, stripped to the waist and displaying generous builder's cleavage, held out a foaming pint of beer and invited him to join them.

'No thanks, I've had coffee on the plane,' Heath said stiffly, marching on with the attendant cameramen groaning at a missed opportunity which would have made every front page. But for all the Tory leader's physical awkwardness, housewives in particular listened to him when he reminded them of the rising cost of living and insisted that it was the 'shopping basket election'.

It was, incidentally, a campaign in which we had a rare joke from Heath. I was with the Conservative leader the day we heard that Wilson, in another part of the country, had been hit by an egg thrown by a bystander. We asked the Tory leader for his reaction. Deadpan, Heath replied that since Harold Wilson's movements were not being announced in advance for security reasons this showed the state the country was in. People were clearly so desperate that they were travelling about with eggs in their pockets, merely on the off-chance of meeting the Prime Minister.

Harold Wilson was the first Prime Minister with whom I had any dealings, and he was unfailingly kind to me as a young correspondent. When I conducted my first interview with him, he asked me at the start if I had switched on my tape recorder, saying that an interviewer the previous week had failed to do so. In my nervousness, I hadn't, and I was grateful to him for the prompt. Not long before this, I had interviewed the racehorse trainer Eric Cousins for a BBC North sports programme. It was the first time I had used a sensitive piece of broadcasting equipment and I failed to notice Cousins's habit of rubbing a matchbox against his corduroy trousers as we spoke. When I played back the tape afterwards this had become a noise like a circular saw. The interview was unusable.

As a politician Wilson really was the first of the PR men, a short-term tactician who succeeded brilliantly in holding together a fragile, scarred party but who faced up to few of the big problems. Had there been focus groups in his day he would have followed them slavishly. The Wilson government came with a lot of gimmickry: the First Hundred Days of dynamic government (he had seen President Kennedy in action); the Winter Emergencies Committee; the beer and sandwiches at Number Ten. In composing his administrations he was obsessed with balance: north and south, Gaitskellite and Bevanite, trades unionist and intellectual. And he certainly surrounded himself with a court of cronies.

But Wilson was a lonely man. Having been the youngest minister since Pitt, he had had little time for fancy dinner clubs in fashionable restaurants, little chance to establish backbench friendships on the way up. He even used to play golf alone. And he was not as ruthless as he seemed. He was physically sick the night he had to sack the loyal Fred Lee to create reshuffle space. His ministers were suspicious of him, but he inspired true loyalty in those who served him as secretaries, drivers and aides, always finding the time for small personal kindnesses. A former don and civil servant, he was a genuine academic, but he shared the instincts of his party workers and he never lost the common touch. He was the scholarship boy at the end of the road whose success all could share. And whether or not he really preferred tinned salmon to smoked, he certainly gave that impression.

Wilson was smart at the Despatch Box in the Commons and

always a quick thinker. One of his ministers once told me of the reshuffle day when Wilson had looked up from his desk and got a shock. Entering the room was not J. P. W. 'Curly' Mallalieu, his old ally from the Bevanite left, whom he had been planning to appoint as a minister, but Mallalieu's elder brother Lance. Downing Street had somehow contrived to bring in the wrong Mallalieu for promotion. Wilson racked his brains as they exchanged small talk for a minute or two, recalled that the other Mallalieu was a religious man, and promptly offered him the non-governmental post of Second Church Estates Commissioner, a grand-sounding title which makes its bearer effectively the spokesman in the Commons for the Church of England.

Even today Wilson remains something of an enigma. Although he held the reputation of a sophisticated political trickster who was incapable of thinking beyond the short term, he was in many ways a plain man. As one of his colleagues told me when I wrote an article marking Wilson's ten years as party leader, 'The truth is that Harold does not really like London. He is at heart a provincial. And so too are most of the people in the country.'

As a provincial political correspondent I was grateful for that allegiance, and I benefited from it. And in our stamina-sapping game I learned his secret. It was the catnap. Harold Wilson could put his head back anywhere and be asleep in two minutes. I once heard him say that ten minutes' sleep in the day was worth an hour at night. It certainly kept him sharp enough to win four elections. In the years that followed, as I progressed up the journalistic ladder with the story pressures building and the hours becoming ever longer, I was to remember and occasionally act on Wilson's advice.

5

CROSSBENCHER:
THE LUNCHTIME YEARS

IF THE YEAR 1970 BROUGHT AN UNEXPECTED CHANGE IN fortunes for Harold Wilson and for Edward Heath, it did so for me too. Every provincial journalist at Westminster looking for a step up yearns for an invitation to join a news agency like the Press Association or to become one of the team of political correspondents on a national paper. My shorthand was never good enough to make me a news agency candidate, partly because I had not used it for three years while 'subbing' in Liverpool but also because, at the time I was supposed to be learning my Pitman's outlines in my first year on Merseyside, I had been much more concerned with the outlines of our startlingly pretty shorthand teacher in her pink twinsets and pearls. Nevertheless, I got my chance when I was approached by the *Sunday Express* to join their political team.

The idea was that I would be groomed with a view to becoming the next Crossbencher columnist in succession to Douglas Clark, a chirpy little bantam cock of a man who wrote like an angel, enjoyed his drink (and the next man's) and had the cheek of the devil. Douglas was the only man I know to have propositioned Margaret Thatcher, which he did once by telephoning her bedroom in a party conference hotel. The response was icily dismissive, but a large bouquet was sent the next morning and Douglas claimed she never held it against him.

Sadly, before I joined the *Sunday Express* Douglas had a severe illness, and so when I arrived I was immediately pitched into writing a column which had become an institution on the political scene under the eagle eye of *Express* editor John Junor, one of the most fearsome figures in Fleet Street and a former Crossbencher himself. I was thrilled to be taking over such a well-known column at only twenty-eight, even if I was buried behind a pseudonym. And, anyway, I told myself, all the politicians knew who wrote the column. But for a year I hardly slept on Saturday nights, wondering what telephone calls of complaint I might receive from the column's victims or their lawyers once they had digested my remarks over the breakfast table. Had I and 'Mac' – Henrietta McKay, my dark-haired, chain-smoking assistant – done enough to double-check the story that embarrassed a minister? Was the source of a wounding snippet really trustworthy? Worst of all, would there be some dénouement that would bring down upon me the fearsome wrath of my editor?

'JJ', as he was known on the paper, was a big, ruddy-faced man with large teeth, thinning hair, and a taste for cronyism and navy-blue suits. He loved to put people down in front of others and could be extraordinarily personally offensive. 'You grow a remarkable amount of hair in your ears,' I heard him say to one backbench executive.

But JJ also taught me a few basics about journalism. After our first few inquisitions (you could hardly call them conversations) I never came into the office without having read every paper on the Street. Following his edict, I never again threw away a reader's letter, even the idiotic ones in strangely coloured inks. His rule was that every one received a response. The rudest got his favourite reply, which I have adopted and used ever since for the green-ink merchants: 'It is always a pleasure to receive constructive criticism, courteously phrased.'

Carolyn and I had moved by this time from a flat in St Andrew's Square in Surbiton to a white-painted cottage by the duckpond and the Cricketers pub on Epsom Common. Since Junor was a man of rituals and since he lived just a little further down the same railway line at Dorking, he and I established a routine for the Crossbencher column, which I wrote for nearly nine years.

The column always consisted of a comparatively lengthy opener about a leading frontbencher whose career was advancing or retreating, followed by three or four shorter items recording curiosities, exposing embarrassments and errors, or generally having fun at a politician's expense. The victim for the top item was selected on a brisk Friday morning stroll. As the specified train rolled into Epsom from Dorking I would find John Junor in the first carriage. There we sat without communication for the half-hour journey, I finishing my newspaper while he muttered incomprehensible notes and instructions into a pocket dictaphone in a Scots accent conspiratorially thickened for the occasion to confuse any eavesdropping fellow commuters. From Waterloo we would then set out on a brisk walk, keeping south of the river and heading for Blackfriars Bridge, as I outlined to him my ideas for that week's Crossbencher.

'So, who's your lead this week then?' he would enquire as we stepped across the pedestrian crossing on York Road.

'Well,' I remember saying one January morning in 1974, 'I

think I should write a piece suggesting that Margaret Thatcher could be the next leader of the Tory party. I'm picking up quite a bit of talk about her prospects from the younger MPs.'

'Look, laddie,' he replied, holding me back from stepping into the path of a taxi as I warmed to my theme and we crossed another road, 'we're talking about the Tory party here. There's as much chance of them picking a woman leader as there is of the good ladies of the Auchtermuchty Women's Institute decamping en masse to join the chorus of the Folies-Bergère.' He really did tend to talk like his own column on these occasions. 'You need to be sounding out the real decision-makers, not a few gullible backbenchers in the Strangers' Bar. Let me tell you the most important thing that happened this week was Keith Joseph's drubbing of Michael Foot in the social security debate on Monday. I'm told he's going to be the next Chancellor.'

As usual on hearing such a claim, I wondered which friend of Keith Joseph's JJ had lunched with that week. I had long been tempted to try to bribe the head waiter at the White Tower and my editor's other regular haunts to send me lists of his lunch guests, confident that he would not have been over-tipping the restaurant staff himself. Junor was full of scorn for most politicians and wanted me to write about them in the most vitriolic terms – until he met them personally. Then he was a pussycat. His personal friendships always overrode his political prejudices. Thus, although he was essentially a right-wing Thatcherite, he was very friendly with the left-wing Tory Sir Ian Gilmour, a man described among those whose company Junor most enjoyed as being 'so wet you could shoot snipe off him'.

Persuading Junor to admit new figures to the small *galère* of politicians he considered worthy of a Crossbencher lead was a constant struggle. I used to try to get him to lunch with a wider circle because I was so often reduced to mind-reading party leaders like Edward Heath and Harold Wilson, other leading figures like Denis Healey and Roy Jenkins, and Junor's buddies like the Chancellors Reggie Maudling and Anthony Barber.

That particular week I had no success, although I tried again as we headed across Blackfriars Bridge, the river boats hooting beneath us.

'But JJ, Keith Joseph has twice before been touted for the job and not got it. Everybody calls him the Mad Monk. The significant thing about Thatcher is that she's winning support from people who don't even like her ideas, simply because she scores some points for the party.'

I tried a couple of alternative ideas but he was not really listening and, as we turned into Fleet Street and headed up towards the *Express* building known as the 'Black Lubianka', the column lead was settled.

'So you'll do Joseph then,' Junor decided. 'And remember he'll be a popular choice in the City because his father was a Lord Mayor.' So JJ had been at a boardroom lunch somewhere that week. The trouble was that all his opinions were uttered with equal vehemence, whether he had picked them up from lunch with a Cabinet minister or from a chat with the Walton Heath bar steward after a round of golf.

By 4 June 1974, however, he must have had lunch with Margaret Thatcher, for on that day, at long last, she made the grade with her first Crossbencher lead. It began with the glorious political incorrectness of those days:

Picture Mrs Margaret Thatcher serving up the Sunday lunch today to her husband Denis. You may be sure of one thing. Her mind is not entirely on the roast potatoes. For Mrs Thatcher is telling herself:

'Come October I could be Chancellor of the Exchequer. And if we should lose the election, why, I might even have a chance of a better job still. That of leading the Tory Party.'

JJ had still taken some convincing, because the item went on to enquire:

Do you fall off your chair laughing at the idea of Mrs Thatcher becoming Tory leader?

After all, he had done so, just a few months before. But consistency was never his worry and now the verdict, as always in Crossbencher, was clear:

There are hard, shrewd men in the Tory Party, I can tell you, who do not. Some of them indeed are wondering: might not a woman leader be the best possible hope of winning back the women's votes? Consider how Mrs Thatcher's star is rising. She is the one Opposition spokesman who carries real conviction in attack. Young MPs press to be included in her backbench team. The Tory ladies give her twice the ovation they accord to Mr Heath.

It was at about this time that Keith Renshaw, the *Sunday Express* political editor, told me that Ladbrokes were quoting 50–1 against Mrs Thatcher's becoming party leader. We both made a reasonable investment. I was not at that stage convinced she would necessarily win any leadership contest, but because I spent so much time on political gossip with MPs I was well aware, as some older lobby correspondents were not, how many young Tories who did not share her opinions were impressed with her ability. For that reason I knew her chances were a great deal better than 50–1. My wager paid for a very nice holiday when she won in February 1975, with 146 votes to Willie Whitelaw's 79 in second place.

The Crossbencher column, like much on the *Sunday Express*, was highly stylized and formulaic. It was all about the power struggle: who was up, who was down and why. The column assumed that every politician throbbed with every fibre of his or her being to become Prime Minister, and that every move he or she made was devoted to that end. It was personality politics pure and simple. Policy never got a look in.

I found myself writing between stylistic tramlines, with a typical opening going something like: 'How is Harold Wilson in Moscow this morning as that secretive eye flicks from onion dome to minaret?' or 'Picture Mr Denis Healey flexing his fingers at the family piano today. It is all he can do, you can bet, to stop himself from pounding out a victory march.' Leading characters were nearly always allotted their full collection of Christian names – Michael Roy Dibdin Heseltine was a typical example – and much energy was expended on getting right the little details which added an admittedly sometimes spurious authenticity. So the then Chancellor Anthony Barber would be 'dipping into his tangerine marmalade' and his Cabinet colleague Geoffrey Rippon would be 'pouring himself his pre-lunch Campari'.

Crossbencher in my time dealt in pithy opinion. Thus the column declared when Peter Thomas was appointed Conservative party chairman that 'The Tories need a bell-ringer. The only one he'll ever ring is the one to summon the Carlton Club waiter.' The column delighted too in vignettes, revealing for example that Edward Heath had slept late on the morning of an election victory, telling his housekeeper not to wake him. When he awoke he asked if there had been any calls. 'Only one,' his housekeeper replied, 'from America. A Mr Richard Nixon. I told him to call back.'

Tart remarks and witty put-downs found their way into the column, as when Professor Dorothy Hodgkin described Margaret Thatcher as 'such a loss to chemistry'; or when the Conservative shadow Cabinet, taken to see a demonstration by the SAS, were warned that terrorists might demand a minister in exchange for hostages and that they should think before coming to office how they would respond. In the minibus on the return journey somebody asked: 'Well, what would we do?'

'Send Heseltine,' came the spontaneous chorus in response.

Many years later, sharing a platform with Neil Kinnock and Michael Heseltine to pay homage to my predecessor John Cole on his retirement as BBC political editor, I recalled publicly how I had once stopped Heseltine being selected as a Tory candidate. Revealing in Crossbencher that he was among those being interviewed for a safe seat, having lost his own through boundary revision, I had suggested that since there were a number of military types on the selection committee he would be well advised to have his flowing locks trimmed before attending for interview. A week later I saw him and asked him if he had made the shortlist.

'No,' he said. 'And it's your fault, you bastard. I had been due for a haircut anyway. But when I saw your column I had to hold off. It would have looked as though I was crawling to the media. So I went there with hair curling over my collar and I didn't make it.'

Prefacing my story, I had described it as an episode Michael Heseltine had probably long forgotten. He came up to me afterwards. 'No, Robin, I hadn't forgotten. Nor have I forgiven,' he said, with one of those wolfish grins.

The Crossbencher column in those days would chivvy new MPs who were slow to make their maiden speeches, awarding a wooden spoon to the last of a new intake to do so. It would list peers who went to the House of Lords and collected their attendance allowance but did not utter. And it followed up MPs like Eddie Griffiths, one-time MP for Sheffield, who had promised when he was selected to go and live in the constituency but who proved exceedingly tardy in living up to his pledge.

Crossbencher also chronicled little human stories like the tale of Newcastle Tory Sir William Elliott. Having forgotten his glasses, when joined on the train to Westminster by Yorkshire Tory Wilf Proudfoot he was delighted to find that he could read his papers using Proudfoot's glasses. The pair alternated with the specs until they reached their London terminus. In the cab on the way to the Commons they realized that they had managed between them to leave the glasses on the train. They stopped the cab (no mobile phones in those days) to use a telephone box to alert lost property; but unfortunately, without the glasses, neither could read the number to call . . .

The *Sunday Express* lawyers always took a close look at my column. Luckily I never cost the paper any money with a libel, but one case which nearly came to court would have been truly bizarre. The Tory backbencher Commander Anthony Courtney, a bluff Monday Club right-winger, had enjoyed a colourful past before his parliamentary career and at one stage as a diplomat in Moscow he had been ensnared in a 'honey trap', when compromising photographs had been taken of him in company with a young lady of dubious morals. I had written a story about the promotion of a meeting which Courtney was to address for the Monday Club, in the course of which I had described him as a man 'whose proudest boast was to have had Reds not only under his bed but in it'. He and his lawyers took great exception to this. But they could hardly deny that he enjoyed boasting about his experience. I knew of too many MPs who had seen him do so for him to deny that. But the burden of their complaint was that I could not claim his amatory antics to have been the '*proudest*' boast of a man who had been commander of his country's naval intelligence services. It was a complaint which boiled down, therefore, to the three letters 'est' at the end of 'proudest'. Our lawyers held firm, and eventually Courtney's lawyers went away, but it would have made an interesting case.

Of course, some people didn't like what I wrote about them. But only one man ever tried to bribe me into not running a story. Inevitably it was 'Captain' Robert Maxwell, as he liked to call himself then, in the days when the man who was later to become infamous as the proprietor of the *Daily Mirror* was combining life as a publisher with service as a Labour MP. I have forgotten the detail, but he had got word that I was pursuing an unflattering story about him. He arranged to meet me in a bar at the Labour conference in Blackpool, where he bought me a large drink and wrapped a huge bear-like arm around my shoulders.

'Come on, young man, let's be sensible about this. We can come to some arrangement. I'm sure you've got a book you want to write and get published.' I was naïve, but not that naïve. I finished my drink, wrote the story and never heard another word.

The worst part of writing the Crossbencher column came on Friday afternoons. My work would be submitted to John Junor at lunchtime and I would then sit in some trepidation by the buzzbox intercom on my desk awaiting a response: a compliment, an OK – or the dreaded 'I'm afraid this just doesn't work' summons to his office for detailed deconstruction of a piece which had not pleased.

Working for John Junor was an experience. He was, in his way, a great newspaperman; but he was also a bully and an obsessive. Nobody could edit a daily paper the way he used to edit the *Sunday Express*. He used to read every dot and comma of every article and story before it went in the paper. To the despair of those trying to get the hot metal pages finalized and cast for the presses, he would still be revising phrases in his own column on the final page proof. Every Saturday lunchtime he would hold court for a favoured few over cottage pie, which he demanded and was given at a cheap rate at the Cheshire Cheese, an ancient pub down a flagstoned alleyway off Fleet Street. He was one of those men who always knew how to get anything you could think of cheaper than you could, and at one stage reprimanded me (inaccurately) for lunching politicians in more expensive restaurants than he was using.

The Cheshire Cheese lunches were eaten in wooden booths off sticky, varnished tables. As the occasional anoraked American tourist paced the sawdust-strewn floors, guidebook in hand, JJ would give full vent to his saloon bar prejudices.

'Never trust a man who wears a hat in a car,' he would say.

'*Chablis*, Robin? Only poofters drink white wine.'

Among those who participated in the rituals were Victor Patrick, the hefty, straightforward deputy editor, Keith Renshaw, the cheerily innocent political editor, and the leader writer Ronald Spark, a mysterious little man who used to go off for long lunches on his own in Soho and who wore in his lapel what we all took to be the emblem of the *Légion d'honneur* while fulminating furiously about most aspects of the European Community. Ronnie was a master of the direct, economical *Sunday Express* style and I suspect that Junor was in awe of him intellectually. Certainly he was permitted a latitude in his timekeeping that was not accorded to any other member of staff.

At the Cheshire Cheese lunches Junor's main sport was to draw the gullible Renshaw into venturing an opinion on some thorny topic. He would then utter an entirely contrary opinion and watch as poor Keith, fearful of displeasing him, struggled to reconcile the two views. But Junor was not an identikit right-winger. He frequently inveighed against the police, and it seems he did so with good reason. He used to drive the kind of sports cars usually driven by much younger men, and after an argument over a minor traffic offence which got him on the wrong side of one officer he suffered real harassment, sometimes being tailed home through the Surrey lanes, he insisted, by cars with no lights on.

JJ's mercurial nature once nearly did me serious damage on the road. He had decided to send me to Cyprus in October 1978 to write a political piece about the enmity between the Greeks and the Turks either side of the United Nations' 'Green Line' across the divided island. A day or so before I went he decided he did not want the political article after all but wanted instead two separate travel pieces, one on (Turkish) northern Cyprus and one on (Greek) southern Cyprus.

'But JJ, I'll be there less than forty-eight hours, and it can take half a day to get through the Green Line formalities,' I protested.

In response he merely growled a typical Junor challenge: 'If ye canna write a travel feature about a country in twenty-four hours, laddie, ye canna call yourself a journalist.' The more dogmatic he was being, the more Scots he seemed to become.

I duly hurtled round both sections of Cyprus, from Kyrenia in the north to Paphos and the beaches in the south, taking in the Troodos mountain ski spots and the wine-growing districts. Signs on the mountainside warned 'roads slippery with grape juice', and you could actually see it dripping from the backs of high-piled, tilted donkey-carts. Late at night, heading back into Limassol and absolutely dog-tired, I was forced off the road while duelling with an aggressive local motorist as we approached some road-works. With a sickening rending of metal beneath the car I hit a concrete kerb, bounced over some poles and ended up amid gravel and cement bags, facing the wrong way. Shaken and bruised but luckily not badly hurt, I remember wondering as I waited for the police to arrive what the local drink-driving laws were. I had stopped in a taverna earlier for a kleftiko and a couple of glasses of wine (red, of course, for a *Sunday Express* travel feature that had to survive the Junor inspection). But I need not have worried. The cheery officers arrived on their motorbikes and helped me and a few locals to lift the car back on the road. There they pronounced it a write-off and, having phoned the car-hire firm for me, departed with a handshake, nothing more said.

A couple of years earlier, in 1976, Junor had sent me for a while to cover the terrorist troubles in Zimbabwe under Ian Smith. That too might easily have proved the end of my career. As I went about the country interviewing farmers and others about their experiences, I was warned to look closely at the dirt roads ahead for signs of disturbance to show that mines might have been planted. While I might have had reservations about some of those farmers' political opinions, I was full of admiration for the courage of their wives, who drove their children to school along such roads every day without turning a hair. Some would have been up much of the night too, doing duty on the local radio network, coolly calling up reinforcements while their own husbands were pinned down under terrorist fire.

I was provided most of the time with an armed escort carrying an Uzi sub-machine gun. One night as I drove back towards

Salisbury, now Harare, he asked me to drop him off as he wanted to spend the night with a girlfriend.

'You'll be fine,' he said. 'Just remember if you come to a road-block manned by troops to look at the magazines on their rifles. If they're curved magazines then they're "terrs" [the then Rhodesian Army term for terrorists]. In that case you duck your head, put your foot down and drive like hell through the road-block, swerving as much as you can. If the magazines are straight they're our side and you stop and do what they tell you.'

All was fine until, in the gathering dusk – not a long period in Africa – I saw a roadblock ahead. I panicked, completely. In a cold sweat I tried to recall which side had which kind of rifles and I could not. There was nothing for it but to slow down and hope for the best. Fortunately for me it was not a terrorist road-block, or mine could have been a rather short career. As it was, I decided definitely that I was not cut out to be a war correspondent.

Despite doing Crossbencher duty for most of my time at the *Sunday Express*, I did have my coups. I predicted, for example, that when Anthony Barber ceased to be Chancellor he would walk off the Tory front bench, which he duly did. He never made any secret of his intentions to me. I also learned the ways of national politicians as I steadily filled my little black contacts book.

One week, doing the political news as I did in Keith Renshaw's absence, I learned most of the details of a forthcoming reshuffle from one of the Tory whips. Seeking some corroboration before going hard with the story, I made the mistake of contacting Peter Walker, formerly a City whizz-kid as part of the Slater Walker partnership and one of the key up-and-coming ministers in the

Heath government. Walker, who was in his time trade secretary, energy secretary, environment secretary and, under Margaret Thatcher, who couldn't abide him, Welsh secretary, denied my story completely, saying that I was not up to date and that things had changed.

I pulled my punches and wrote only half the story. A few days later everything happened as I had been told it would originally. I confronted Walker with his denial.

'What could I do? You had me by the short and curlies,' he protested.

He could, I pointed out, have simply said 'No comment.' I never trusted him again, and after that I was inclined to believe the stories about him fostering the family man image by taking a child from a waiting nanny each time he went to the front door to greet a journalistic guest.

The Crossbencher years of 1970 to 1979 also taught me the delight which politicians take in lunch and in gossip. Much of my business, inevitably, was conducted over meal tables, mostly those days at L'Epicure, the Soho restaurant with an ever-burning gas jet above the door. It has been a relief to me and, I suspect, to my doctor that the political lunch has changed shape over the years. When I was on the *Sunday Express* my lunch guest would frequently take a couple of gin and tonics before the meal. At least a bottle of wine would accompany the food, and there would probably be at least one brandy or port afterwards.

First to go over the years were the pre-lunch drinks. The one-time *Guardian* political editor Ian Aitken, one of the shrewdest in our trade and a man who coped better than most with the liquid lunch, once declared that the saddest five words in the English language were 'Shall we go straight in?' Next, the guests whose tongues I was keen to loosen gave up the post-prandial brandy.

Finally, in recent years, even the wine has been limited to 'Well, just a glass, if I may.' Nowadays the most taxing decision as the wine waiter approaches tends to be 'still or fizzy' for the seemingly obligatory mineral water. The drink-driving laws were one vital influence; greater health consciousness another. But it is also true that the House of Commons has over the years become a much more professional place and much less the best club in London.

No longer is it true, as the socialite MP Chips Channon, father of Paul, noted in his diaries in 1937, that 'There is nowhere in the world where sleep is so deep as in the libraries of the House of Commons.' Some of the people who left my Crossbencher lunches were not fit to walk across the street, yet I would see them on their feet in the Commons later making perfectly articulate speeches. But most in those days could do that in their sleep. The late Sir Douglas Glover, member for Ormskirk, once confessed that he was called by the Speaker as he awoke from a slumber in the chamber and got up to head for the gents – whereupon he made a twenty-minute impromptu speech on the Forestry Commission.

I used to encourage my guests to drink in the hope of eliciting indiscretion. Some knew the game and were careful. The most elegant refusal I ever had with the wine waiter hovering was from the then Lord Chancellor, Lord Hailsham. As I pressed him to take another glass he demurred, with what was probably a well-practised reply.

'No, thank you. The House of Lords is sitting in its judicial capacity this afternoon, and while I may be drunk as a lord I must be sober as a judge.'

The snag was that you had to imbibe a fair bit yourself to make them feel comfortable. This may account for what my wife finds my most irritating habit, that of clutching and cradling my glass throughout a meal – a habit probably inculcated as I sought to conceal from my guests my own rate of consumption. But when the conversation flows it is easy to misjudge one's intake and capacity. I once had to interview the Northern Ireland politician Gerry (nowadays Lord) Fitt, a lovely man and the father of Eileen, one of my favourite *Nine O'Clock News* editors, in a Westminster pub. After five rounds of gins he had not turned a hair. I was virtually incoherent.

We all let our hair down occasionally, though, even these days. When I was with the BBC, John Sergeant and I used to entertain together at party conferences. One year not too long ago he and I and Clare Short had a late-night end-of-conference dinner which – thanks to our efforts entirely, I am sure – became a four-bottle affair. We heard some wonderful stories. But sadly, by the time we met at breakfast the next day, neither of us could remember much about any of them!

Political lunches are intriguing affairs and are generally conducted on a bartering system. MPs know very little of what goes on in other parties or, often, at the top of their own. Senior political journalists see a lot more of ministers than they do, and they are interested to learn what they can. So we trade informally in information. It is a kind of futures exchange. Sometimes ministers or opposition frontbenchers, especially those not worldly-wise in the ways of the media, say to you rather awkwardly, 'I'm sorry, I haven't got a story for you.' But that, I explain, is not the point. There may be no such thing as a free lunch, but you do not always pay in direct coinage, arriving with a 'story' instead of the thank-you note so few politicians bother any longer to send afterwards. Lunch is often a getting-to-know-you affair, so that the next time the minister's department does figure in a story you are not a stranger when you come on the phone.

I once had accidental confirmation of how seriously the politicians themselves take lunches with journalists. In the late 1980s, when on *The Times*, I was sent an employment department minister's briefing for his lunch with me. Clearly some outer office secretary had misunderstood instructions. I did not send it back, thinking that would cause more embarrassment: it was better for them just to assume the material had got lost. But I have kept it as a souvenir of the lobby life.

The documentation included my original letter inviting the minister, John Cope, to lunch. On it were six different annotations, including his instruction to accept my invitation. Observations from other officials included: 'Robin Oakley is an influential journalist who also writes the occasional leader. This is a good opportunity for Mr Cope to expand on his general philosophy.'

The confidential briefing typed out for the minister included the comments:

Robin is a senior journalist of management status on *The Times* [news to me!] and has many contacts in the Government ... so far he has not built up a relationship with ministers in our department since the election and has not yet met the Secretary of State. In the past he has been on private telephone conversation terms with ministers including Secretaries of State.

Robin Oakley is not averse to small firms stories [I was supplementing my earnings at the time with an occasional article for a small business journal] ... a good 'Sunday for Monday' contact ... Mr Cope has a chance of making an extremely valuable friend here who can be relied upon implicitly and will not harden a story more than it deserves ...

It was fascinating, and even a little alarming, to discover how much effort and research had gone into the lunch preparations in John Cope's department. We had, as far as I remember, a civilized exchange, but he and I never became intimates – despite the departmental encouragement.

Over lunch, some politicians talk about nothing but themselves and are desperate for reassurance and career advice. They treat you over the Caesar salad and Dover sole as if you have invited them to lie on the psychiatrist's couch. Norman Lamont was one of those. I kept trying, given the positions he held, but I don't believe I winkled a real story out of him in fifteen years. Others take time to relax. The earnest Gordon Brown spends the first twenty minutes of the meal (usually breakfast in his case) giving you what amounts to a potted version of his last four economic speeches. He then winds down and becomes the most delightful of companions, enjoying the usual 'who's up, who's down' political gossip. I take some credit, with my racing interests in mind, for persuading him over a series of breakfasts to stop unveiling his budgets in Cheltenham Festival week.

One of the more bizarre invitations I had over lunch came from the then Tory health secretary Virginia Bottomley. She was insisting that her policies were much more popular than I thought, and that people were always coming up to her in public places to say so.

'Tell you what,' she said, 'why don't you bring a camera crew along next time I'm buying my knickers in Marks and Spencers and you'll see how people respond.'

I declined politely. Where would we have looked? And I am afraid that on another occasion I did her, unwittingly, less than a favour. There was a controversy at the time about smacking in children's homes and Mrs Bottomley, who was sometimes mocked in the papers as 'Nanny Bottomley', conversationally sought my opinion, declaring that she was in favour of the occasional smack. Lightheartedly I said that, given the clear delight Tory conferences took in corporal punishment, she would probably do herself no harm by saying so publicly. Two days later she did. And I opened a paper the next day to see she had been re-christened 'Spanker Bottomley'. A journalist's advice is clearly best ignored.

The trick of the political lunch is to give the impression that you know more about something than you do. If you talk knowledgeably enough about the fifth of an event that you do know about, with luck your guest will assume that you know nearly all the story and will fill in much more of the uncompleted jigsaws you are always carrying with you in your mind.

One thing I would certainly avoid if I were a politician is the 'group lunch' with a number of journalists. Ministers and senior politicians will in general lunch singly with political editors. More junior correspondents often find they have greater pulling power if they combine in twos, threes and fours to invite a senior politician who might not reckon them worth his or her time on their own. But there is no safety in numbers for the politician: quite the contrary, in fact. The groups will often leave asking each other, 'What was the best line out of that, then?' They will bid each other up, and all will finish up writing a stronger version of the story than their exchanges with the politician truly merited, knowing that if there is a comeback they will be able to tell a querying editor or newsdesk, 'Well, the *Express* and *Mail* had it too.'

I was involved in one or two celebrated lunch stories over the years. One was during the years of John Major's premiership when I was eating with Frank Dobson, then a shadow minister and later Labour's official candidate against Ken Livingstone for the London mayor's job. We were at Chez Nico in Park Lane – and before licence-payers worry about the effect on the BBC's finances, let me reveal that the set menu, to which I confined my guests, was then the best value in town at £25.

At a nearby table that day Kenneth Clarke, then Chancellor of the Exchequer, was being lunched by two of my BBC political correspondent colleagues, Mark Mardell and Jon Sopel. Amid a Cabinet row about the single European currency, Clarke was on good form. He revealed to the two that he had urged party chairman Brian Mawhinney to 'tell his kids to get their scooters off my lawn'. This was a deliberately disparaging reference to Harold Wilson's demand to union barons Hugh Scanlon and Jack Jones to 'get your tanks off my lawn', shortly after the uprising in Czechoslovakia which had given birth to the phrase. In his lunchtime chat Clarke also revealed that he would not be part of a Cabinet which ruled out the possibility of participation in a single currency.

After a day's pause Jon Sopel used the story on the lunchtime news, without identifying Clarke as the source. Listening to it, Frank Dobson realized exactly where it had come from and called Tony Blair's office to say so. Within hours Blair was exploiting the row between the Prime Minister and his Chancellor. Soon the papers were full of stories about the political lunch, some going so far as to publish maps identifying my favourite restaurants and those of the other political editors. For the record, my other favourite haunts were, and are, the elegant Le Caprice in Arlington Street, the bustling Orso in Covent Garden, the Great Gallery dining room at the RAC, presided over by the incomparable Hans Jahns, and, for more casual encounters with backbenchers, moles and researchers, Joe Allen's in Covent Garden.

Lunching with the great, the good and, as often as possible, the wicked, I stayed in the Crossbencher role for far too long. It had its advantages. For a young family man it offered stability. The hours were predictable, and there was not too much travel away from home. I was given regular salary increases and a company car. But the Sunday paper life has its own strains. On a daily paper the newsdesk will accept that there can be a quiet day. If you produce a story which disappoints, you can rescue your reputation within twenty-four hours with the next day's edition. On a Sunday paper, with Saturdays turning up little on the news conveyor belt, you are under real pressure by the end of the week to produce an exclusive. If somebody else runs even half of your story on Friday or Saturday, you are scrabbling frantically to recover. And if you do draw a blank there is a whole week of waiting before you have the chance to redeem yourself. You have to work on Saturdays too. I missed so many of Alex's school matches that other parents must have believed my children came from a single-parent family.

I was lulled into staying at the *Sunday Express* as long as I did by promotion to assistant editor. I fell for Junor's hints, dropped when he sometimes gave me a lift home late on a Saturday night after a game of snooker, that he saw me as an eventual successor. Only later did I realize that it was a technique he used with several of the up-and-coming journalists on the paper, including the diarist Peter McKay and the books editor Graham Lord, to keep us there for longer than we might otherwise have been inclined to stay. In truth, Junor never wanted any of the talents on his paper to blossom so far that they became any kind of threat to his own position. He believed in total domination.

In fact, for my last two or three years I was chafing at the bit, desperate to get back to a less stylized form of journalism and to full-time political reporting. I had some degree of status and a bulging contacts book. I saw plenty of the top players in politics. But when the political editorships elsewhere came up, I was not being considered for them. It dawned on me that I had become trapped behind the Crossbencher pseudonym.

6

THE BIG BREAK: HIRED GUN
ON THE *DAILY MAIL*

EVERY JOURNALIST NEEDS A LUCKY BREAK AT SOME STAGE, AND mine came in 1979. I have never been good at touting for jobs. From my first position on the *Liverpool Daily Post* to the end of my days at the BBC, every job I obtained was the result of somebody approaching me to join them. On this occasion the approach was from Tony Shrimsley, the editor of the new magazine *Now!* offering me the chance to escape from behind the Crossbencher pseudonym. He recruited me to become the political editor (and an assistant editor) of Jimmy Goldsmith's intended British rival to such weekly news magazines as *Time*, *Newsweek*, *Le Point* and *L'Express*.

I had been planning to get back on a daily newspaper. But this was exciting and different, and since Tony was luring some of the big names in Fleet Street and in the process lifting journalistic salaries into a new range, it was an offer not to be scorned. Carolyn, Annabel and Alexander strongly approved, too, of the snazzy pale blue Granada which came with the job: it was much the most capacious and luxurious car we ever owned.

I found myself on a lively magazine among a battery of

right-wing columnists. Editor Tony Shrimsley, who sadly fell victim to cancer not long after *Now!* closed down, told me before he died that Jimmy Goldsmith had reckoned me 'a bit of a lefty' (which in his terms I was, being a natural centrist without allegiance to the Thatcherite ideology he embraced so enthusiastically, or indeed to any other). But fortunately Jimmy liked my writing style and rated my judgement. Before the end, he and Tony had even promoted me to associate editor with wider responsibilities.

It seems to have been my lot to work for most of Fleet Street's tigers. There was John Junor on the *Sunday Express*, Goldsmith as a hands-on proprietor of *Now!*, the feline Sir David English on the *Daily Mail* and then Charlie Wilson, the tough Glaswegian with a reputation for typewriter-throwing, as editor of *The Times* – although I am bound to say that Charlie never threw anything at me. Perhaps it helped that he and I had 'legs' together in the racehorse Sunday For Monday, and that I knew, when his wife did not, that he had shares in another horse as well.

Jimmy Goldsmith was an extraordinary man, one of those rare individuals who seem truly to exude life force and energy. I shared few of his opinions, but I rather liked him. He would occasionally bound into my office, sleeves unbuttoned and pushed up his arms, restlessly puffing on a cigar. His eyes gleaming, he would pace about, firing out questions and opinions at the rate of one of those ball machines used by tennis coaches. Although he was a right-winger he did not expect everybody else to agree with his opinions; in fact, he quite liked a challenge. What mattered was whether you had ideas or information which interested him.

Now! was probably doomed from the start, first because news magazines flourish best in countries which do not have truly national newspapers and second because, even as he started the venture, Goldsmith's other commercial energies were beginning to focus more on the continent and on America. There was also the distraction of his time-consuming battle with the satirical magazine *Private Eye*, which founded the 'Goldenballs' fund to raise the money to fight off his legal actions. I always wondered why a man with the chutzpah to parade a lovely wife in England and an elegant mistress in Paris while managing to be a courtier of Margaret Thatcher was quite so thin-skinned about *Private Eye*'s attentions. Goldsmith spent far too much time obsessed with *Private Eye*, and *Now!* suffered as a result, I believe, because smart advertising people liked to join in mocking him rather than to be seen pushing clients his way.

But we turned out some lively journalism. I did one big feature which attracted a lot of attention by revealing the membership of the top Tory dining clubs, Blue Chip and Guy Fawkes, whose members were to provide most of the leading lights in the Conservative party through the 1990s. I see that the list I picked out as the young politicians to watch in 1979 did not fare so badly either. They were: Neil Kinnock, John Nott, Jack Straw, Leon Brittan, Cecil Parkinson and George Robertson. All made it to the Cabinet; one became party leader, two have been European commissioners and one, Lord Robertson as he now is, is secretary-general of NATO.

Edward Pearce, who wrote a 1991 biography entitled *The Quiet Rise of John Major*, was kind enough to record one other piece of prediction in what he called the 'glossy, bright and fashionable *Now!* magazine'. 'Very soon after the [1979] election Robin Oakley, bought from a national for hair-starting money, justified the fee with a piece about "The New Boys" which said that the consensus among the intake about themselves was that the one man among them with the makings of a Prime Minister was John Major. Mr Oakley's case rests.'

One curious thing was that *Now!* looked so substantial that people appeared not to want to cut up their copies for the coupon sales which are so important to the flimsier Sunday paper colour supplements. For years after it closed I used to meet people who told me they still had every copy of *Now!* in their attics. And I believe that it might have gone on to success if Jimmy had persevered longer. So many people, again, told me that if they dropped *The Economist* or the *New Statesman* on the table at home it would lie there ignored, but when they brought home *Now!* the family squabbled over it. The students and late teenagers of the 1980s were used to seeing the news on television in colour, but they had to read it in black and white in their newspapers. We gave them news and comment with top-quality colour photography. They would have stayed with us.

The first two or three editions of *Now!* sold around half a million copies. Sales then plummeted to 70,000–80,000. But that had been the pattern too with the continental equivalents *Le Point* and *L'Express*, which had then steadily built up over another couple of years to sustainable sales figures. Goldsmith had talked to us of their example, and we thought we were working on the same sort of timescale. But suddenly, after just eighteen months, he ended the experiment. I was on a driving holiday in America at the time, and learned that I was without a job as I picked up the papers at Heathrow on my return. Goldsmith, incidentally, behaved entirely honourably, paying us out in full on our contracts. The family and I ate for years in what we called the 'James Goldsmith Memorial Kitchen', purchased with the proceeds. But they were sorry to lose that smart blue Granada.

That day at Heathrow, fearful of what the future might bring, Carolyn and I and a strangely quiet Annabel and Alexander went back to Epsom by bus, not taxi. But morale lifted a little when we arrived home; for waiting on the doormat were two job offers.

While I was still on *Now!* the *Daily Express* had asked me to go to them as deputy editor. I declined because I wanted to see through the experiment on *Now!*, where I had been well treated. Had I accepted, I suppose that I might in due course have then become editor of the *Express*. But even if I had, given the turnover rate of *Daily Express* editors since the 1940s, it is even more certain that I would soon have been an ex-editor of the *Express*. To adapt a phrase, the paper had lost an empire in the 1950s and never quite succeeded in establishing a role thereafter, as readers leached away to the zippier, classier *Daily Mail*, and proprietors and editors came and went.

Now the Goldsmith venture had foundered, Arthur Firth, the then *Daily Express* editor, came back with another less specific offer to join his team. I talked to him, but made no final commitment. The other serious approach (there was also someone who wanted me to edit a scaled-down, cheaper *Now!* – a project which never got off the ground) was from David English at the *Daily Mail*. After our talk he put pressure on me by sending down his chauffeur with a contract which he insisted must be signed within twenty-four hours or the deal was off, because he was going abroad.

I decided to go for the *Mail* job, and telephoned Arthur Firth to say no to the *Express*.

I had not reckoned with what happened then. I received an extraordinary telephone call from the irascible Jocelyn Stevens, then managing director or something similar at the *Express*. For something like ten minutes he hurled abuse at me, screaming:

'You'll never work this side of Fleet Street again!' Of course, the one thing the *Express* could not bear in those days was to lose anything it wanted to the ever-rising *Mail*; but still, it was a bizarre performance – and a worrying one, too, for someone with a family still to educate. What if things did not go well for me at the *Mail*? How many options had I closed off?

Working for the *Mail*, and for David English, was daunting: sometimes exhilarating, sometimes terrifying, sometimes infuriating, but never boring. The *Mail* wanted everything first, and everything right. It was swift to pick up trends, both social and political. Often, for me, it was uncomfortably extreme in its views, and at times it had me knotted with nervous frustration, engaged in a constant struggle to report stylishly on the things which I wished to report without having too many of the more extreme parts of the *Mail* agenda loaded onto the page beneath my byline. But it was and remains the most skilfully edited of the tabloids, in tune with Britain's middle classes to a degree that forces every political spin doctor, friend or foe, to read it and every Prime Minister to defer to its views. The *Mail* is a supremely professional newspaper, and generous exposure in its columns helped me to make my mark as a political commentator.

David English hired me as Assistant Editor (Politics), partly to produce, as he hoped, some creative tension between me and the political editor Gordon Greig, a lovely, humorous but disorganized man and an intuitive reader of the political scene who would disappear for hours at a time pursuing a complicated private life, but who somehow would always be there when the big story came up. Gordon and I struck a deal. I would do the political features, the by-elections and the 'specials' on issues like unemployment. Gordon would do the political news. We would split the summits and the foreign trips with the Prime Minister, and we would cover each other's roles when either was absent. I do not ever recall our having a cross word in working things out.

Writing the page six political features was the most testing part of my role. I remember David English being much taken with the first I did, about John Nott, then a coming man in the Tory party. 'He shoots, fishes and farms without a hint of tweed or the merest whiff of retriever coming through as part of his Westminster persona,' I wrote. Nott was an excitable character, best remembered for tearing off his microphone and stalking out of the studio in the middle of an interview with Robin Day, and in the end did not stay the course in politics. I remember him arriving for lunch one day absolutely brimming with joy. When I asked him why, he told me that the Cabinet had that morning agreed to abolish exchange controls. That meant, he insisted, that never again would a Labour government be elected in Britain. The mere prospect of Labour being in contention at any point in the future would be enough, he suggested, to begin such a run on the pound that the public would reject the idea immediately.

David English's theories on creative tension were allowed full play over page six. Two or three pieces were written in competition for that slot every day. You had to go in after lunch to face the 'hanging jury', normally consisting of David English and his deputies: Peter Grover, a schoolmasterly figure with thick glasses, and the irrepressible Stewart Steven, a man who wore vividly striped shirts and opinions to match. He was later editor of the *Mail on Sunday* and remains a pungent columnist. Usually all three had lunched well, and they would be scoring points off you and off each other as they read through what you had written.

I operated, we all knew, at the heavier end of the paper, and the choice of what would run had as much to do with whether or not the rest of the paper was 'light' or 'heavy' that day as with the merit of what you had written. Often English would go through a piece saying, 'This is fine, but it is rather held up by this point here.' *Slash*. 'There are too many figures here.' *Slash*. 'And it goes on too long here.' *Slash*. 'Otherwise that's good stuff . . .' Reading it in the paper the next morning I could agree that the flow had been improved, but what had been a reasoned piece with supporting facts and arguments had become instead a scream of opinion.

Sometimes I had to ghost pieces for politicians to appear in the page six slot. Most seemed to care little what the piece said, provided the cheque was prompt and the byline picture flattering enough. One exception was the SDP leader Dr David Owen, who had said something on the *Today* programme one morning which had caught David English's ear. I was deputed to call him and ask him to write us a feature saying the same thing. Owen said he had no time to do so, so I offered to write it for him. He did not want words put in his mouth, but eventually we struck a deal: I would write an article based on his comments that morning. I would then meet him in a car at Westminster at 2.00 p.m. to take him to the flight at Heathrow he had to catch; he would read the piece on the way and make any corrections he felt were needed. If he was not satisfied, we would not run it. I duly wrote the article and picked him up. During the journey my respect for him only increased as he proceeded to negotiate the whole way to Heathrow, arguing over every adjective, preposition, dot and comma in the piece. Only as we arrived at the terminal did we conclude.

My five years on the *Mail*, from 1981 to 1986, coincided with the rise of the SDP. For me, the launch of the Social Democratic Party in March 1981 was one of the most fascinating developments of my years covering politics. Many other journalists felt the same; after all, we in the media are always inclined to be excited by something new, and the SDP was the first new and truly national party to emerge since the early 1900s. Many of us believed that the country was yearning for a new style of politics, less confrontational, less ideological, less class-based than was on offer from either Margaret Thatcher or Michael Foot. People found her too strident and him too scatty.

There was much to be said, too, for a new party which was financed neither by the City nor by the trades unions, and which therefore did not seem to owe allegiance to any kind of establishment. But just as important to the SDP's appeal was its moderation and rationality. Its leaders did not insist that everything its opponents did was either malevolent or idiotic. It would, many of us hoped, offer politics something better than the old slanging matches. People were refreshed to hear David Owen, asked on the *Today* programme what the government had done wrong, reply calmly that on the topic under discussion they had got it pretty nearly right.

There was a heady excitement about the potential realignment of the left in British politics, the feeling that the SDP was sketching on a fresh canvas. When David Owen was accosted by a Southampton woman on launch day and asked what was in the SDP manifesto, his unapologetic if somewhat patronizing response was: 'If you want a manifesto, love, go off and join one of the other parties.'

The founding of the SDP provided constant drama with the regular peeling away of Labour MPs – eventually, nearly thirty of them – disillusioned with the extremism of the party they had previously served. The original Gang of Four had a curiously effective chemistry: Roy Jenkins provided the polish, Shirley Williams the warmth, Bill Rodgers the organization and Owen the backbone. They brought a new range of people into politics, political virgins who had been alienated by the structures and the tribalism of the older parties. And let us remember that at one stage the SDP/Liberal Alliance even stood at 51 per cent support in the polls.

The SDP were, of course, easy to mock. It was done best of all by my old friend Frank Johnson. In their history of the SDP, Ivor Crewe and Anthony King quote Frank's dissection of the party's factions:

> The Owenites, the Jenkinsites, the Elisabeth Davidites; those who want a successor to Polaris; those who want a successor to their Volvo; militant Saabs; supporters of Tuscany for August as opposed to the Dordogne; members of those car pools by which middle class families share the burden of driving their children to the local prep school; owners of exercise machines; people who have already gone over to compact discs . . . readers of *Guardian* leaders; and (a much larger group) writers of *Guardian* leaders.

But the SDP-ers could take a joke against themselves. I remember one night – probably over a stripped pine table, although we drank burgundy rather than claret – plotting the outlines of the 'Social Guide to Social Democrats' which Bill Rodgers' wife Silvia and I planned to put together. We had trouble, I recall, deciding what was the typical SDP dog. Golden retrievers were undoubtedly Tory, terriers were Labour. We were about to settle for Weimaraners – sleek, trusting, European and just that little bit different – when somebody else pointed out that they were hunting dogs too and that wouldn't do.

Many of the SDP political virgins were unduly earnest. While aiming to be classless, they tended to be preponderantly middle-class. And they provided an early lesson in the power of the media to make and break. In a way, they were as much the creation of the media as they were of the Gang of Four. The new party had an inherent appeal for many media people, particularly those in broadcasting organizations like the BBC professionally imbued with notions of non-partisan balance, and this was partly why the SDP, to begin with at least, earned huge media attention.

Encouraged by David English, who could see the new party's appeal to many of his middle-class readers, I wrote copious amounts about the SDP. I had good contacts among its leaders, who were pleased to be getting good coverage in such a Tory bastion as the *Daily Mail*. Roy Jenkins's second place in the Warrington by-election in July 1981 was greeted by a huge *Mail* headline declaring 'Well done, Roy' over a piece in which I wrote, 'Never again will they be able to say that the only thing he is capable of fighting for is a corner table in a good restaurant.'

But when another of my leader-page articles, this time bearing the headline 'The night the safe seat died', celebrated Shirley Williams's victory in the Crosby by-election, there were strong rumblings from Downing Street as Conservative Central Office began complaining about the attention I was giving to the SDP. And soon, David English told me, senior figures in the Tory party were pressing for the *Mail* to get rid of me. Fortunately for me, David usually put his instinct for a story ahead of his political sympathies.

One thing I used to enjoy especially on the *Mail* was covering by-elections, a fruitful source of big stories during those early heady days of the SDP. You had the fun of writing daily sketch pieces on the campaign as well as the excitement of the result on the night and the challenge of writing rapid political analysis of a fast-changing scene to get the feature follow-ups into the next morning's paper. For me, the sheer pace of the media life has always been an addictive drug.

Most papers had their regular contributors to what became a travelling corps of by-election specialists. The team included sketch-writers like the *Guardian*'s Simon Hoggart, who has always had a wonderful turn of phrase. I remember him writing of Edward Heath's flecked tweed country ensemble when he arrived in Hillhead: 'Mr Heath was wearing what had been a perfectly good suit until somebody had thrown a pizza at it.' It was Simon, too, who captured that wrist-rolling gesture which is part of Roy Jenkins's occasionally orotund speaking style by saying that he looked 'like some medieval baron exerting his *droit de seigneur*, cupping the breast of an innocent young peasant girl'.

Along with Simon, there were the *Telegraph*'s Godfrey Barker and the *Express*'s Keith Raffan. Raffan later became in turn a Tory MP at Westminster and a Lib Dem member of the Scottish Parliament, a conversion he would have lacerated in his writing days. But we always knew he was going to be a politician. Nobody used the personal pronoun more often in his copy. The star of the travelling caravan, though, was the bumptious and irrepressible Vincent Hanna of *Newsnight*. I will always remember the film he made of the Hove by-election in which a series of 'shall I go this way or shall I go that way?' hesitations down garden paths by the Tory candidate Tim Sainsbury were devastatingly set to music – to 'The Dance of the Sugar Plum Fairy'. Vincent's early death took a lot of fun out of politics.

Early on I formulated Oakley's Five Laws for By-election Coverage:

(1) Always canvass on your own, not with the parties. People do not like to tell enthusiasts the truth and confess they will not be voting for them. They tell journalists the truth more often. Having nodded quietly to the candidate and his helpers, earning a tick in the canvassers' 'possibles' column, they would turn to me and tell me their real feelings. 'I wouldn't vote for that shower if they came down the street with a barrowload of fivers and dumped it on my doorstep,' I was told by one old boy who had been marked down as a 'yes' by the local Tory team.

(2) Always buy a street map. Politicians' street directions are hopeless. I don't know how some of them ever find their way to Westminster.

(3) Check out the public loos. You are normally a long way from base, you drink endless coffees with candidates and it is usually perishing cold. I used to say map the phone boxes too, but now we all have mobiles.

(4) Beg, borrow or steal to find a guaranteed parking spot near each party headquarters. You are dashing pell-mell from one press conference to another, and don't want to miss the visiting bigwigs who might be putting their foot in it – as when Norman Lamont famously told us at the Newbury by-election, 'Je ne regrette rien.'

(5) Never, ever, believe parties' canvass return figures. The Tories claimed to be running second at the Bermondsey by-election. I backed Liberal Simon Hughes at 10–1. He won and the Conservatives finished fourth.

I gave up political betting, incidentally, when I joined the BBC, for fear that people would accuse me, with the large BBC audience, of trying to rig results. It was a pity, especially as I usually did rather better with my political bets than on the horses. But when racing friends in 1997 sought my opinion on the best election bet I urged them to go long on the Liberal Democrats, with the spread betting firms then expecting them to get around thirty seats. Paddy Ashdown's team came home with forty-six, and I got a drink or two from grateful friends.

My biggest coup in by-election terms while I was on the *Daily Mail* was not a bet but an article I wrote which was later much copied. Early in Shirley Williams's attempt to overturn a Tory majority of nearly twenty thousand in Crosby I joined the early morning commuters, solicitors, accountants and top secretaries on the platform of Formby station. I then wrote an article which the *Mail* ran on the leader page under the heading 'The revolution now gathering steam in Crosby', in which I predicted her victory. It was not a piece lacking in conviction.

In the mist-laden morning air the commuters on Formby station were an impeccably prosperous bunch. These were settled people. Men who would go down to the pub every Sunday morning wearing blazers getting just a little bit too tight. Women with the places in their plastic-covered paperbacks neatly recorded with tasselled-leather bookmarks. As well-groomed wives decanted their overcoated husbands from Rovers and Cortinas and as vivacious secretaries, adjusting their earrings, clattered down the steps for the line to their Liverpool offices, they did not look the stuff of revolution. And yet political history is probably being made. Sociology students of the future will be analysing Crosby Man as they once dissected and tabulated Orpington Man.

I had spoken to thirty people on the platform and found nineteen votes for Mrs Williams, four for the Tories and one for

Labour. And my conviction was not misplaced. Mrs Williams eventually took the seat with a majority of more than five thousand.

The other key victory for the SDP followed soon after when Roy Jenkins won Glasgow Hillhead. What he had warned might be an experimental plane which could come to grief a few fields away from the runway was now soaring in the sky. Hillhead had not seemed natural territory for the SDP, and I recently came across a guide to Glasgow *patois* which the Scottish Nationalist candidate George Leslie produced at the time for SDP-ers up from the Home Counties. '*Whituryeswantin?*' was to be interpreted as 'May I be of assistance?' Then there was '*Gonnigiesabreakjummy*': 'Sorry, old chap, but you have called at a rather inopportune moment.' '*Wurbroonedaffwirralotoyis*' meant 'My family is somewhat despondent at the current political situation,' and '*Nawmamawsnoinranoo*' indicated 'The head of the household is not available for the moment.' And, rather cheekily, Mr Leslie suggested that if things were going well the SDP canvasser could take '*Havanurraglesashatolannyjummy*' as 'Do join us in another glass of this rather naughty little claret.' Candidates with a sense of humour were always welcome, and one could see why they say that in Edinburgh breeding is good form and in Glasgow it is good fun.

Another place I visited on the by-election trail in 1982 was Peckham, where in 2000 the schoolboy Danilola Taylor was murdered. It is depressing to realize how little has changed in nearly twenty years. My piece back in 1982, when Harriet Harman won the seat for Labour, began:

So long as there are places like Peckham the corrugated iron manu-facturers will not starve. Much of it is the kind of territory which even the guard dogs patrol in threes. Anything you want to keep, you keep padlocked. Backyard businesses deal in secondhand car parts. Listless young mothers with middle-aged faces push pramfuls of toddlers home to blocks of flats where it can take three years to get a broken window replaced. Luxury in Peckham, south east London, is an unvandalised telephone box, a lift that works five days out of seven. On the stairways of the huge council estates you can meet old men who have been mugged twice in a month.

Sometimes we are right to be angry with our politicians and our urban planners.

It was in south London, too, that we saw another of the spectacular by-election successes of the 1980s, this time for the Liberal Simon Hughes in February 1983. I have never seen a politician perform better on the doorstep, before or since, but he was helped by the split which saw two Labour candidates running: gay activist Peter Tatchell as the official candidate, and John O'Grady as an independent 'Real Bermondsey Labour' candidate backed by the previous MP, Labour's former chief whip Bob Mellish. The split, I wrote then, typified Labour's generation gap, 'across which old sentimental Labour and theory-stuffed new polytechnic Labour stare at one another in bitter incomprehension'. Underlining the party's difficulties, the Labour leader Michael Foot dithered. First he sought to stop Tatchell becoming the candidate; then he went down to support him. At the nadir of its fortunes, Labour lost a seat it had held for sixty years. Just when people were beginning to query the staying power of the SDP/Liberal Alliance, it was given an enormous boost with the Liberal candidate's demonstration that it wasn't just Tory seats that it could pick up.

In the end, of course, the SDP itself failed. Unlucky with the timing of the Falklands War, it suffered from its lack of funding and organization, from personality clashes and from fading fashions. When the Liberals and the SDP started to squabble over who should fight which parliamentary seat, and when the tensions between Roy Jenkins and David Owen began to show, it looked like just another old party. And, as the media had played a crucial part in its launch and rise to popularity, so they did also in its decline and demise. As the novelty value wore off, the SDP secured little coverage. Junior correspondents were sent to cover its conferences and few attended its briefings. The media lost enthusiasm for a party whose lack of weight in Parliament meant it could not initiate events or in any real sense make the political weather. And without sustained media interest and enthusiasm, political survival becomes a problem.

Looking back now, I have to say that the SDP failed in its immediate ambitions. The SDP–Liberal Alliance never either attained power on its own or held the balance of power in the national Parliament. It did not succeed in changing permanently the whole style of politics, nor did it achieve electoral reform at Westminster. But we have seen the introduction of PR for the Scottish Parliament, for the Welsh Assembly and for the European Parliament; and the elements of the SDP which merged with the Liberals have continued to give third party politics a boost in Britain. The Liberal Democrats are now a significant force in local government, consistently holding around five thousand council seats and running many town halls. They are coalition partners in the Scottish Parliament and Welsh Assembly, and an enduring element in calculations at Westminster.

Labour returned to power in 1997, I believe, only because Tony Blair created in New Labour a party in which returning Social Democrats would feel comfortable. But the Liberal

Democrats were not the only force which helped to reforge the Labour party. Margaret Thatcher's success had much to do with that as well, forcing Blair and Co. to adopt the language of the market and to turn their backs on old-style socialist nostrums. The Alliance politics of the 1980s helped to refashion the mould of British politics. By demonstrating the appeal of the centre ground and by splitting the anti-Conservative vote, the SDP also helped the Tories to stay in power for so long that Labour grew hungry enough to overhaul its programme and to acquire the discipline needed to win elections.

The exposure which the *Mail* gave me certainly helped my career – not least with a leader page article in 1981 headed 'Who's on Mrs Thatcher's chopping list?' Aided by some good contacts, I went through her options in full and made twelve predictions for the forthcoming changes. Ten were proved right and one half right, including the departures of Lord Thorneycroft and Lord Soames and the surprise appointment of Cecil Parkinson as party chairman.

I had to take some flak when I wrote a piece in 1981 suggesting that Tony Benn could actually win Labour's deputy leadership. The *Mail* executives were nervous about it, but I was vindicated when he came within 1 per cent of doing so. For this was a period of political change. As Benn entered the contest, I wrote:

What Tony Benn woke up to as a practical politician long before his colleagues was that there are two Labour Parties. There is the old traditional Labour Party of the miners' social – a party of broad bottoms, brimming glasses and warm Welfare Statism. Coming up alongside it has been the new Labour Party of the polytechnic generation – a lean envious party owing everything to Marx and nothing to Methodism, a party of white collar unions and half-baked social theorists. The old party rubbed along with a constitution which gave party conference delegates the appearance of power but which in practice allowed the leadership to run things the way they wanted. The new party, Benn saw, was not going to be fobbed off that way. Step by step the militant activists, many of whom would not have been allowed into the Labour Party in the days of Attlee and Ernest Bevin, have won control of constituency management committees and of the majority of NEC seats. By pressing year after year they have won a say in the election of the leader and the right to sack MPs of whom they disapprove. Benn saw it all coming and pitched his appeal over the heads of the MPs to the constituencies.

In one sense, I developed a good deal of sympathy for the Benn brigade and the young activists of the Campaign for Labour Party Democracy. I wrote a piece for the *Mail* in October 1981 – which I was a little surprised they printed – analysing their effectiveness and his appeal. It was an appeal from which senior politicians in all parties should have learned their lesson in an age when so many young people turn their backs on party politics for single-issue pressure group campaigns or charity work instead. 'Mr Benn and the CLPD', I wrote,

> have enabled young people to march straight out of university or polytechnic or even school onto the stage of national politics. They are made to feel involved. What they say and do actually counts for something . . .
>
> Ten years ago youngsters cutting their political teeth were strictly slave labour in local parties. Now they can swing the votes in general management committees. Ten years ago at conference they would be

lucky to be allowed to fetch a drink or earn a nod from the party stars. Now they find themselves at 1.00 a.m., sitting in the crowded hotel bedroom of a national figure helping to draft resolutions and plan tactics.

Not for the new generation the pleasures of heady rhetoric. The Benn generation goes for power first. They go into a CLPD meeting where they are instructed just which minute amendment has a chance of getting through. And they can see the results of their efforts on the party constitution or on conference practice within days. 'We've proved that the rank and file can achieve things,' says CLPD campaigner Pete Willsman, a researcher with the public employees' union NUPE. 'The bigwigs are clueless really, despite all the attention they get from the Press. Nowadays they're coming to ask us what the vote is going to be.'

The young are energetic and idealistic. It is they who troop off to a series of fringe meetings every night on worthy causes like world hunger, Gay Liberation, women's rights and racial discrimination while their elders go off for a good meal. Only one senior party member can keep up with them – the unstoppable Mr Benn.

Of course some of the causes adopted by those young activists were crazy. Of course there was entryism and manipulation of the Labour party by Militants and others which had to be fought. Of course there was mixed up in the CLPD's efforts some crude demonology of the World Bank, the City, the IMF and the multi-national corporations. But democratic parties need to find a way of harnessing the enthusiasm of the young and making them feel involved in the way that groups like the CLPD did. I used to enjoy their meetings more than I did hearing some careerist merchant banker or play-safe union official spouting their respective party lines as he or she manoeuvred for a safe seat.

Although he was one of the best debaters in the Commons, Benn had one flaw as a politician. He was simply too obsessed with politics, as was revealed to me once by his fellow left-winger Dennis Skinner. When they were together on Labour's national executive one year Dennis, a keen athletics fan, told Tony just before a key race: 'I won't be there for the next vote. I've got to go and see Coe and Ovett.'

Benn was blank-faced. 'Oh?' he said. 'Are they your constituency delegates?'

Tony Benn's bottom-up democracy had a heady appeal through those years of 'accountability' when the Labour leadership was scorned by its class-conscious, anti-capitalist activists for selling out the interests of the party's rank and file. But things went too far. The demonology grew rampant, the focus become too internal and the policies lost touch with the public. As some sought to turn it into a sect, Labour was bitterly divided through the 1980s. That precipitated the breakaway by the Gang of Four and the emergence of the SDP–Liberal Alliance, which in turn split the anti-Conservative vote, giving Margaret Thatcher a clear run. By forcing leaders like Michael Foot to listen more to his own activists than to ordinary voters in the centre ground of politics, the 'democracy of the activists' made Labour unelectable through the 1980s, producing in 1983 that election manifesto which was condemned by Gerald Kaufman as 'the longest suicide note in history'. If Tony Blair and New Labour are now accused of becoming control freaks, you can see why they wanted to create a centre-left party (with the words in that order) and to return to top-down control. The trick is to harness the enthusiasm of the young and the activists without losing touch with less-political Middle Britain, but it is not an easy one to bring off.

Parties, it seems, do not learn from history. William Hague is a capable politician. But, having seen what splits did to the Conservative party under John Major, he chose to make his appeal to the party's activists rather than to the centre ground; and he paid for it at the polls and with his job.

As well as the early Thatcher years and the zig-zag rise and fall of the Liberal–SDP Alliance, my period at the *Mail* also included the Falklands War and the report of the inquiry by Lord Franks into the conduct of ministers and the intelligence services in the period leading up to the conflict. Reporting on the Franks inquiry proved an illuminating experience for me in more ways than one. When I was viva'd for my degree at Oxford, the dons involved had some fun with my special subject paper on Cromwell and the English Revolution. They had clearly realized that in my revision I had only had time to mug up the views of Hugh Trevor-Roper, then the Regius Professor of History, on the origins of the Civil War. I had gone heavily for his book on *The Gentry 1540–1640*, and had therefore neglected the counter-case made by other historians like Christopher Hill, which they put to me with some relish. I did my best, but was forced to wriggle. As I left, the final comment was very Oxford: 'Mr Oakley, you may now go. You have borne the stripes of the Regius Professor with manly fortitude.'

Having literally sat at Trevor-Roper's feet as a student, I regarded him with some awe, and was intrigued when Lord Dacre, as he had by then become, was recruited by the *Mail* to share with me the task of reviewing and reporting on the Franks Report; but my exaggerated respect for academic figures almost entirely disappeared as we toiled in adjoining cubicles. Every fifteen minutes Dacre popped his head round the partition to ask what I thought, scarcely venturing an opinion of his own. Finally he came up with a verdict remarkably similar to mine. His brain would have enveloped mine several times over; but academics, I suppose, even academics who become directors of Times Newspapers, are not as accustomed as journalists to working against the clock.

The use of Lord Dacre on the Franks Report was a typical David English wheeze. He would always come up with a new slant, a new way of doing things or a fresh but appropriate face in the paper. And while I shared few of English's prejudices, I found it easy to share his enthusiasms on the big days. He was, for me, the supreme newspaperman. On the day of a big story he would emerge from his office and take the main chair on the back bench, immediately communicating his excitement and generating a buzz across the newsroom floor. He would sweep the first few pages clear of advertisements and scribble away at the page layouts himself, chuckling with glee as he did so. 'Oh, don't you love it. Isn't this just *marvellous*,' he would declare to all around him. All the while he would be swivelling in his chair and firing commands at the newsdesk as new angles occurred to him. The best headlines were often his.

The only time I ever saw him slightly discomfited was when Frank Chapple, the right-wing former union leader, was in the office discussing a piece and there was passing reference to somebody's recently acquired knighthood. 'Being a knight is no effing good to man or beast,' said Frank. 'It's neither one thing nor the other. You need to be a proper peer or nothing.' Chapple, who had been ennobled for his services to Labour, was forgetting himself. David English, although he would certainly have acquired a peerage later had he lived longer, was merely Sir David.

Whatever his rank, English was a man of style and occasional generosity. After the rather predictable 1983 election, in which he left much of the political coverage to me and during which I worked virtually non-stop for a month, late into each night, he called me in for a thank-you. His gratitude took the form of a trip to Venice on the Orient Express for me and Carolyn, followed by a long weekend in the Hotel Danieli. It was the most generous gesture ever made to me as a journalist.

I worked on the *Mail* for five years and learned much from doing so. But I knew that I was steadily allowing myself to be pigeonholed as something I was not. The *Daily Mail* really wanted journalists committed to the Conservative cause. I had developed plenty of friends and good contacts in the Conservative party. It made sense to do so. They were in power for a good proportion of the time that I was a senior political journalist, and news comes mostly from governments. But while I respected heart-on-the-sleeve pro-Labour journalists like Alastair Campbell and the *Guardian*'s Michael White, who made no secret of where their sympathies lay, and while I had been fascinated by the SDP phenomenon, I resolutely shied away from any party allegiance. I always voted, but not always for the same party. I felt that I could not sign up with anybody, and that I could do my job better if I didn't.

As an uncommitted writer working for a very committed paper I was under strain. What tends to happen in such a situation is that on the issues where you do agree with the paper you go right over the top in your relief at being able to chime in with the prevailing view. Where you disagree, you have to wait for the big issues to take a stand. David English would be perfectly reasonable, for example, if he asked me to write a leader on a 'conscience' issue like capital punishment and I refused because I was opposed to it. But you could not quibble over every little item where you disagreed with the paper's line, or life would rapidly become impossible.

After five years, I realized, I had made so many small compromises that they were adding up to something quite big. I was becoming perceived as something I was not. The day I decided to get out was the day when Patricia Hewitt, formerly Neil Kinnock's press secretary and now one of Tony Blair's new 2001 Cabinet, said to me, entirely without rancour and quite matter-of-factly on an issue we were discussing: 'Well, some of us would take a different view on that to the *Mail*'s hired guns like you and Paul Johnson.'

When she bracketed me in that way with Paul Johnson, the ex-editor of the *New Statesman* who was now displaying all the zeal of the convert to Thatcherism which he had become in fulminating against the *Mail*'s chosen targets, I knew it was time to move on. Paul is a fine journalist and writer, a great professional who delivers to the word, and on time. But I was not a fellow marcher for his adopted causes.

Once again, fate intervened. Within weeks of that conversation I was invited to take one of the best jobs in British journalism. I accepted, and resigned from the *Mail*. At this point, sadly, David English displayed the lesser side of his nature. He stayed away from my *Daily Mail* leaving party. And because he did so, all his executives boycotted it too.

7

THE TIMES – AND MARGARET THATCHER, A LADY WITH HER OWN 'ISM'

THE JOB I DECIDED TO TAKE IN SEPTEMBER 1986 WAS THAT OF political editor of *The Times*. I discovered later that a number of people, including some leading politicians, had been sounded out about my suitability. Friends had reported to me some weeks before a flurry of rumours that I was to succeed Julian Haviland, the current incumbent; but I had heard nothing. What stimulated action, I suspect, was that I had received an approach from Peregrine Worsthorne about becoming political editor of the *Sunday Telegraph*. I said no to that, partly because the money on offer was a great deal less than I was getting at the *Mail*, and partly because I did not really want to go back to the Sunday paper schedule. I craved daily stimulation. Within days the editor of *The Times*, Charlie Wilson, who must have heard something on the grapevine, invited me to breakfast at the Waldorf and offered me the *Times* job. I had little hesitation in accepting, even though his offer too involved a drop in my salary. It was to become a repeating pattern. When six years later I left *The Times* to go to the BBC, I had to take a salary cut once again. I am sure it does not happen like that in the City.

Charlie's offer was manna from heaven. If every soldier carries a field marshal's baton in his knapsack, I had always carried a notebook with that byline on it in my battered briefcase. I had dreamed of being political editor of *The Times* since my starting days on the *Liverpool Daily Post*; but I had never dared voice the thought, or expected that I would make it. Nevertheless, over the celebration meal which Carolyn prepared for me that night and the best bottle of wine we had in the house I uttered just one warning. Fearsome things, after all, were being said at the time about Rupert Murdoch and his papers. Following my time on the *Mail* I was worried that there might be a heavy shadow looming over my typewriter.

'This time,' I told her, 'I am going to make my own mistakes. I am going to tell it as I find it, full stop. If there is too much pressure to toe a line then we'll go off and run a smallholding in Wales or something. We're young enough to start all over and I'm never going to tear myself apart again.' Bold words, and I do not know if I would have lived up to them. Fortunately, the test never came. I was left pretty well free at *The Times* to do my own thing. The shadow never loomed over my typewriter, or over the word processor which soon replaced it. During the six years I was political editor there I met Rupert Murdoch only four or five times, usually at dinners when he would throw a few conversational stones into the pool and sit back to watch his executives jostle. I only had a single row each with Charlie Wilson and his successor Simon Jenkins, neither of them life-threatening. With Charlie, it was because I had shouted at one of his backbench executives over his treatment of one of my stories. With Simon, it was over a set of directions issued to the political staff along with others on the paper which I considered an insult to their professionalism.

I always preferred national politics to office politics, and spent as little time as possible attending meetings at the Wapping head-quarters of News International. At the splendid Garrick Club dinner which Simon hosted in my honour when I left for the BBC, he told the assembled executives wryly that I had always considered it my duty to represent Wapping at Westminster rather than Westminster at Wapping. Among a political editor's other functions, he said, was the Jeeves-like one of, as it were, brushing down the editor's overcoat before a meeting with the Prime Minister, murmuring, 'Sir should find it profitable to enquire about electricity privatisation. But it might be wise this week to steer away from the poll tax . . .'

For all of my time with the *Daily Mail* and for most of my period at *The Times*, Margaret Thatcher was at Downing Street; and, as Prime Minister for eleven years, she was of course the single most dominating figure of the political scene on which I was reporting. Like most of her Cabinet ministers, I never particularly liked her – with the exception of a chosen few ideological disciples, she was not cosily available to correspondents, preferring to deal with proprietors and editors – but I respected her hugely, and enjoyed reporting on the zesty years during which she led her party. With Margaret Thatcher life was never penny plain, always twopence coloured, which is why the media in general so thrilled to Britain's first woman Prime Minister.

Thatcher was well equipped to cope with an age of strong media. The media barons were with her because of her strong stand against trades union power, and in her time the bulk of Fleet Street was firmly on the side of the Conservatives. But she was good copy, too, both because of her novelty value as the first female premier and because of her combination of strong views with a quirky personality. She was in a sense the political equivalent of the tabloid news editor, seeing the world in sharply contrasting black and white, with no intervening shades of grey. Few in private life would have dared to call this rather forbidding figure 'Maggie', but she was happy to be Maggie for the tabloids, riding on a tank with her scarf streaming in the wind. She played up shamelessly to the image created for her, as with her conference declaration 'The lady's not for turning,' or when she told a Cabinet committee, 'I've only got time to explode and have my way.'

There was a familiar joke in Tory circles at the time of a lunch Margaret Thatcher held at Chequers for the Cabinet. Asked by the waitress which meat option she would take, Mrs Thatcher replied: 'Steak.'

'And the vegetables?'

'Oh, they'll all have steak too.' It was a joke she probably told herself on suitable occasions.

Conviction and determination were the keynotes of Margaret Thatcher's premiership. Edward Heath, in his 'Selsdon Man' incarnation, had at first seemed to promise the rigorous market-based Toryism of which she approved, but had then shied away from it; so, her mentor Sir Keith Joseph having shown himself unwilling and tactically unfitted to seek the Tory crown, she had resolved to go for it herself. She won the job on the basis of strong performances in economic debates in the latter days of Heath's leadership, but then found herself presiding over a shadow Cabinet dominated by those she came to call the Wets. Not one of those at her top table had voted for her.

After she came to power in 1979 many of her colleagues were

aghast at the tough Budgets she and Geoffrey Howe drove through, exacerbating the effects of recession as they sought to curb government spending and to institute in Whitehall the 'good housekeeping' she had learned from her Grantham grocer father. Some of her ministers felt she moved too fast on trades union reform as she and Norman Tebbit sought to cure the 'British disease' of industrial unrest. To test her mettle there were huge early battles on the industrial relations front, with the miners, the steel workers and the civil servants, and she did not win all of them. It is not generally known that at one point in June 1981 her Cabinet urged her almost unanimously to settle the civil servants' pay claim at 7.5 per cent. She would resign, she declared, if such a deal were struck. Some weeks later the strike was settled, with the civil servants getting – 7.5 per cent.

As time went on, Thatcher purged her Cabinet of Heathite moderates and other doubters, producing from Heath a grumpy response which I labelled rather cruelly in a *Mail* article as 'the endless sulk', a label which stuck. She quarrelled with strong figures like the Chancellor Nigel Lawson, whom she alienated by preferring the counsel of her economic adviser Sir Alan Walters, and, famously, with Michael Heseltine over the Westland Helicopters episode. She pushed ruthlessly for a compliant Whitehall machine, enquiring before key appointments were made, 'Is he one of us?' By the time she came to sack Sir Geoffrey Howe, ideologically a loyal lieutenant, provoking a backlash on Europe which was to prove her undoing, he was the last survivor of her first Cabinet. All the rest had gone.

The media adulation fed what became in the end Margaret Thatcher's greatest weakness: her belief in her own invincibility. Time and again she was told by her advisers that what she wanted to do could not be done, and time and again she succeeded in proving them wrong. They told her that she could not hope to tame the unions and that this was best left to a Labour government; but she chivvied her employment ministers into pushing through a whole new raft of laws on industrial action. They told her that even with her handbag-swinging style she could not secure a rebate on Britain's contribution to the Common Market budget; but she won back a significant slice of what she insisted on calling 'our money'. They told her after the Argentine invasion that she could not possibly hope to mount an expedition so far away and win back the Falklands; but she did.

Thanks in part to the relationships she developed with her ideological soulmate Ronald Reagan – you could see her return with her batteries recharged each time she went to visit him – and with the Soviet Union's President Gorbachev, the 'Iron Lady' became a world figure, lifting Britain's profile. That 'Iron Lady' label, pinned on her by the Soviet press and intended as an insult, became a badge proudly worn, as with the Desert Rats in the Second World War. The same thing happened with 'Thatcherism', a term coined by her opponents and happily adopted by her supporters. From time to time the media, notably the *Daily Mail*, tried to make her more cuddly than she was. But, abroad as at home, she won respect rather than affection, making few friends in the Commonwealth, for example, with her stand against sanctions on the apartheid regime in South Africa. Nevertheless – and this was part of the excitement for those of us who covered Thatcher's daily doings – she became a real force and a widely recognized personality internationally. No-one could have accompanied her and Lech Walesa into the Solidarity church in the Gdansk shipyard in 1988, or watched her the year before being mobbed by the babushkas from Moscow high-rise flats after she had lit her 'candle for peace' at the Zagorsk monastery, without realizing what a potent symbol she had become for so many.

The newspapers lapped up her 'conviction politics', the slogans about Victorian values – OK if you don't have Victorian sewers as well – and her declaration that 'there is no such thing as society'. But in consequence she became careless of the need to take the people, and many MPs in her own party, along with her. This led, for example, to the political disaster of the poll tax, an attempt to find a replacement for the much criticized domestic rating system which became hugely unpopular when people realized that a street-sweeper could end up paying the same poll tax as a duke. Many Tory MPs came to believe they could not be re-elected while it existed and that it would not be scrapped so long as she was in Number Ten. Thatcher's restless, almost Maoist revolutionary march through the institutions of British society made her enemies, and at a time when the national and Conservative party mood on Europe was different from that happening now, many became convinced that her strident Euroscepticism was becoming a liability for Britain.

For all of this, Thatcher has been one of the dominant political figures of the past half century, a testament to the abiding force of personality in government – despite the fact that opinion polls show that the country as a whole never actually subscribed with enthusiasm to her 'Thatcherite' values. A MORI poll in June 1990, the year she left office, showed that the nation still preferred 'a mainly socialist society in which public interest and a more controlled economy are most important' to 'a mainly capitalist society in which private interests and free enterprise are most important'. Asked if they wanted a society which 'emphasizes the social and collective provision of welfare' or one in which 'the individual is encouraged to look after himself', 54 per cent opted for the former view, only 40 per cent for the latter. What people appeared to respond to was not her free-market economics or her creation of popular capitalism, with more home-owners, more privatized industries and lower union membership, but her strong personality, her populist streak and her perceived raising of Britain's status in the world. Margaret Thatcher succeeded in spite of her views rather than because of them.

Thatcher won the respect and the votes of people who would never have invited her home to dinner because she persuaded them that Britain's future did not need to be the management of steady decline. She restored a sense of authority in government and optimism in the general public by dealing in simplicities. The simple moralism of saying that you should not spend more than you earned, and that this applied to governments as well as to individuals, struck a chord even while Denis Healey was denouncing her as the 'La Pasionara of middle-class privilege'. She was lucky in facing a divided Labour party for most of her years in power; but with the aid of Fleet Street she did reach out for a while to parts of the electorate long untouched by other Tories.

'Forget that I'm a woman,' she said once, early on, to her Finchley constituents. 'Forget the accusations that I am a right-winger demanding privilege. I had precious little privilege in my early years. I am trying to represent the deep feelings of those many thousands of rank and file Tories in this country – and potential Conservative voters too – who feel let down by our party and find themselves unrepresented in a political vacuum.'

The greatest tribute one can pay to Thatcher is that she changed parties other than her own. No major party in Britain these days seeks significantly to reverse the privatization of the old state-owned industries, the sale of council houses, or the acceptance of the free market. Labour has repealed little of her trades union laws, designed, as she put it, to give managers back the ability to manage. Few prime ministers have their own 'ism'. Margaret Thatcher did.

I first encountered Margaret Thatcher when she was education minister in Edward Heath's government, and I remember just one thing about the first time I took her to lunch in that role. She had, at that stage, only one criterion for judging anybody, and it came into play whenever I sought an opinion on another MP or a civil servant.

'Smith? Oh he's a second-class mind I'm afraid . . . Jones? He's pretty intelligent . . . Brown? Not blessed with much of a brain.'

When I said something about an aspect of policy which interested her, there was only one immediate follow-up.

'Do you know a good academic on that?'

She had an exaggerated respect for sheer brainpower, and other more political qualities like oratory and organization simply did not come into the equation. In a sense this explains some of her later ministerial appointments. She gave Cabinet jobs to people like Ian Gilmour and Chris Patten, despite regarding their political views with suspicion, simply because she respected their intelligence. It was always said that she particularly prized chartered accountants. Her son Mark having failed to qualify as one, she had an exaggerated respect, her intimates told me, for ministers like John Wakeham and Cecil Parkinson who had. But there was another route to Thatcher's favour: she was feminine enough to appreciate the good-looking and the natural charmers. Cecil Parkinson, who was no slouch at the politics either, was one whose looks were no handicap to his advancement in her inner circle. Her one-time chief whip

Humphrey Atkins scored on sheer elegance, as did Willie Whitelaw and Lord Carrington with their old-style courtesies.

Unlike some women politicians, though, Margaret Thatcher did not use her femininity as a weapon. She was always intent on being the best man in the Cabinet, and she never wheedled colleagues with brimming eyes as Barbara Castle had been known to do. And, although she was acutely aware of her appearance, when the two of them shared a hairdresser it was reported that it was Mrs Castle who had the private cubicle and Mrs Thatcher who was out on public view in her curlers.

There were certainly tears on occasion, as when Mark Thatcher, never a public relations asset to his mother but always a cherished son, was found safe in the desert after disappearing on a car rally in 1982. Undoubtedly, she did have a softer human side. Calling in for a late-night interview once, I was impressed by her fussing to ensure that staff with young families got off home. Few of those present in one of the Commons bars the day her parliamentary private secretary Fergus (now Sir Fergus) Montgomery was acquitted on a shoplifting charge will forget the scene when the doors burst open and in swept Thatcher to plant a great smacker of a kiss on his cheek.

'I'm so happy!' she exclaimed.

More significantly perhaps, the night he was charged she had made a point of having Fergus escort her around the Commons corridors, after which she sat with him publicly in the Members' Tea Room for an hour.

There was feminine flair, too. Willie Whitelaw received a public kiss once, during their contest for the Tory leadership. Never one to shirk a photo-opportunity, she willingly gave in to the entreaties of the photographers. As poor Willie squirmed, she embarrassed him further by enquiring why there should be such a fuss.

'After all,' she explained, 'we've done it before – in hotels and halls, on staircases and in the streets.'

I had written much about her when I was on the *Mail*. But along with the celebration of her anniversaries and achievements and the 1983 election landslide, I had not hesitated to criticize her excessively abrasive style, urging in 1985 that she should stop lecturing and start persuading. People had had enough stridency, I argued. 'They don't want every issue tackled as if it were the storming of Bluff Cove, every doubter roasted as if he were the Argentinian leader General Galtieri.' In May that year I reported on the development of the 'TBW Factor', the declaration by voters on doorsteps to Tory canvassers that they were not prepared to support the Tories so long as 'That Bloody Woman' was in charge. Intimates in the Thatcher entourage claimed that the first time she encountered the expression, to her fury and amazement, was in a Saatchi and Saatchi election advertising presentation in 1987. Clearly her press secretary Bernard Ingham had been filtering my *Daily Mail* pieces in the summary of press cuttings he passed on to her daily. Interestingly, when her one-time PPS Sir Archie Hamilton asked Lady Thatcher why she did not read the papers, she replied: 'The press make such hurtful remarks about me and my family that if I read the papers every day I would never get the job done that I am here to do.'

In July 1985 the *Mail* ran two consecutive double-page spreads entitled 'The Thatcher Factor' in which I presented the findings of an NOP poll on why former Tory voters had gone off Margaret Thatcher. A common response from those questioned was that her self-confidence and arrogance 'get up my nose'. People complained of her inflexibility. Typically, she responded by insisting that she would continue to be a strong leader. The

Mail may have been regarded as firmly in the Thatcher camp, but I see that I was allowed to chide her in January 1986 for being 'just another minister shoved around by events' and for making a speech which was 'a failure on every front' over the Westland Helicopters crisis which saw Michael Heseltine walk out of her Cabinet. That leader-page article was headed 'The day even the faithful told Maggie she'd failed'. By 10 May I had written another, after a Tory flop in local elections and in the Ryedale parliamentary by-election, setting out 'What Maggie must do before it's too late'.

While giving praise where it was due and acknowledging her as the dominating political figure of the decade, I continued to report the growing criticisms of Mrs Thatcher when I moved to *The Times*, especially after her performance at the G7 summit in Paris in 1989. There she seemed to be abrasive for abrasiveness' sake, picking an unnecessary row with President Mitterrand by scorning the French Revolution whose bicentenary the French were celebrating. In a *Times* piece entitled 'Let's have tact instead of attack' I pointed out that she seemed to have difficulty adjusting to a more consensual period in world affairs, and that the cinematic image of the 'battling granny' which she had become was something of a comic figure. Diplomats, too, were beginning to say, 'She thinks she knows it all,' or 'She's gone too far.' In November that year she certainly went too far in an interview she did with me for *The Times*, implying that she was planning to fight not just the next election in 1992 as Tory leader but even the one after that in 1997, which would be her fifth.

I had pursued the question because Mrs Thatcher had clearly blundered some two or three weeks before when talking to the *Sunday Correspondent*'s Donald Macintyre. Don had asked her if it was likely she would fight a fifth election after the next one.

This is a sucker question for a Prime Minister, a question you should always duck unless you want to become a lame duck. The moment you acknowledge that you have a date in mind for departure, your power starts to ebb away. But she had fallen into the trap, saying, 'No, because I would think that it was time for somebody else to carry the torch.'

Going into a wide-ranging interview, a journalist is always looking for the line that will produce the added bonus of a front-page story; and, reckoning that Mrs Thatcher would be sensitive about the speculation which had followed Don's interview, I decided it might be worth probing her further. She did not disappoint me. When I questioned her about how long she would go on, she said that she had only spoken to the *Correspondent* in the terms she did because people might think that six years more was rather a long time. But she had changed her mind.

'The question the *Sunday Correspondent* put to me was "Was it likely that I would fight" . . . was it likely? And I have had so many protests about my answer that by popular acclaim I am quite prepared to carry on.'

Feeling assured of my front-page headline, I sought confirmation. Did that mean, I asked, fighting not just a fourth but a fifth election as leader?

'Quite prepared to carry on, yes. But let us get the fourth one over first. I am quite prepared to carry on,' Mrs Thatcher replied.

She did not leave any room for doubt.

'But, you see . . . "Was it likely . . ." and I thought people will think maybe that is a bit long. But by popular acclaim – the number of complaints that I have had – they all thought it meant I was going after the next election. So let me make it quite clear, I am very happy to carry on.'

Now we had a different story: a sixty-four-year-old party leader with three election victories behind her saying that she intended to contest two more general elections, the second of them possibly when she was seventy-two. The 'on and on and on' attitude alarmed even her own supporters in the Tory party and made a challenge to her leadership that much more likely. I had my story.

In the same interview I also raised with her a matter which irritated many people. Why did she so often use what appeared to be the royal 'we' as her personal pronoun, instead of saying 'I' like other people? The most notorious example had been her confirmation that her son Mark and his wife had produced offspring, phrased in the particularly confusing announcement: 'We are a grandmother.' Neil Kinnock had mentioned the Thatcher 'we' only the day before. So why did she use the expression?

'I can tell you exactly why,' she informed me. 'I am not an "I" person. I am not an "I did this in my government," "I did that." I have never been an "I" person so I talk about "we" – the government. I cannot do things alone so it has to be "we". It is a Cabinet "we". That is the antithesis. It is a silly, stupid thing and it just shows the smallness of mind. Do they [meaning Kinnock] not talk about "We"? If they do not it is a very revealing factor. Yes, you can lead very firmly but in the end the point of leadership is that you get a lot of other people with you, so is that clear?'

Frankly, it wasn't; but there was something about the gleam in the Prime Minister's eye which made me feel that 'We' had better be encouraged to talk about something else if the interview was to last the course.

In the ensuing leadership election she did well enough, beating off the 'stalking horse' candidate Sir Anthony Meyer by 314 votes to 33, with 27 not voting. Of those participating in the election,

58 were ex-ministers whom she had sacked and 97 were back-benchers to whom she had not offered a frontbench job in ten years, so you could say that to be denied the votes of only 60 Tory MPs was good going. But the result was a warning, and the combination of her shilly-shallying over her future and the staging of a leadership contest took an edge off her authority which she never regained.

Her growing tendency to go over the top was demonstrated again at the Commonwealth Conference in Kuala Lumpur in 1989, where I earned my fifteen seconds' worth of fame in the anthologies. There was a big row going on over South Africa, with virtually everybody else at the conference supporting the idea of sanctions against the apartheid regime.

'Don't you worry that you could just be wrong, being so completely isolated on this issue?' I asked Mrs Thatcher at a press conference.

'If it's forty-eight against one then I'm just sorry for the forty-eight,' she declared shrilly in response, fixing me with one of those glacial stares which used to shrivel junior ministers at twenty-five paces.

You had to marvel at such self-assurance. And you could certainly be impressed by the showmanship. On a visit to Seoul in South Korea around that time she planted a tree to mark the opening of a university. It was out in the blazing noonday sun and she was the wrong side of sixty. In such circumstances most visiting dignitaries offer a limp-handed pat or two with a silver-handled trowel and have done with it. Mrs Thatcher instead seized a large implement and sent seventeen spadefuls of earth flying into the hole. She then thumped it back into the ground with a grunt of 'There you are: there's a bit of British productivity for you.' Pure manufactured theatre. And as she walked past me down the path I saw her wagging her finger at the bemused chancellor of the new institution.

'Just make sure you water it too,' she instructed him.

That wagging finger could be a danger. Mrs T was every bit as vehement in private as she was in public, and one day she was hectoring a group of us at the back of her RAF VC-10. I think it was the *Guardian*'s Ian Aitken who was unwise enough to challenge her. 'That is absolute, complete, utter, unadulterated nonsense,' she declared, accompanying each adjective with a finger prodding into his upper arm. When he came down to breakfast the next day in a short-sleeved shirt you could see the bruises from shoulder to elbow.

One wondered at times how her husband Denis, or 'DT' as she calls him, put up with it; but then, he was sometimes more influential than he appeared. An ambassador in the Far East told a few of us once how Mrs T had arrived the night before a key meeting full of fire and brimstone as she talked about how she was going to deal with the country's Prime Minister. Seeing that she was on a collision course that at the very least would scupper a series of contracts for British firms, he pleaded with her to take more account of local styles and susceptibilities. But she stumped off to bed adamant that she was going to give the host country a piece of her mind. Seriously worried, the ambassador confided his worries to Denis, who had stayed down for another drink or two before retiring.

'Don't worry,' he said, 'leave the old girl to me.'

Next morning Mrs Thatcher came down to breakfast first.

'Ambassador,' she began, 'I've been thinking we might approach today's meeting in a different way . . .'

I cannot resist one story of 'DT''s directness told to me by somebody who worked closely with Lady Thatcher over many years. One night when the Thatchers had come to dinner, the men were strolling ahead of their partners, Denis suffering somewhat from aches and pains.

'What I need,' he told his host, 'is two new knees and a new pair of balls.'

His host raised an eyebrow. 'Oh, Good Lord, no,' Denis added, reading his mind. 'We haven't done *that* for years.'

Travel with Margaret Thatcher was extraordinary. So was her stamina. In my *Daily Mail* days we once did twenty-six thousand miles with her in six days, taking in Bahrain, Bombay, Beijing, Hong Kong, Guam, Honolulu and Washington, and spending forty-seven hours in the air. It was just before Christmas 1984, and on the final home leg of such a remarkable trip we were all in relaxed mood. She pulled crackers with Bernard Ingham and with the US ambassador Charles Price, and showed us her Christmas present from Ronald Reagan: a Cartier plaited gold basket filled with enamelled wild strawberries. The media party laid on a cabaret on board for which I wrote a few lyrics – bowdlerized carols really – and I still have the Prime Minister's note of thanks for my contribution to the festivities. She fully entered into the spirit of things, doing her own impression of Janet Brown doing her impression of her.

We arrived back the day before Christmas Eve and I went to a party with friends in Epsom, only to be phoned with news that the *Mail* wanted me desperately. It turned out that the on-board photographer, who had taken a few shots of the party which we all thought were for private use, had sought Downing Street's permission to use them, which was duly granted. The best shots were of Margaret Thatcher and me, drinks in hand, and would I please supply copy to go with them urgently. Luckily I still had the notes of my cabaret songs, and I reworked them for the paper. David English was so tickled with the whole thing that for the first day's publication after Christmas he demanded a leader page feature entitled 'It's the headiest cocktail in the world'. This, after a fair bit of tickling from him, began

> I've seen Margaret Thatcher when she was down, though never out. I've seen her grim, determined, combative and all the things she's famous for. I've also seen her on occasions thoughtful and I've even seen her a little indecisive. But I've never seen her as high as a kite before until last week. Believe me, it was quite some experience. The lady was over the top with a Christmas cocktail which was one part very good Scotch and eight parts diplomatic triumph. And she took me with her, which is how I got my picture on the front pages of the world's Press, bringing its own form of fleeting Christmas prestige, though I, of course, had only had the Scotch.

With typical *Mail* brio, others had been airbrushed out of the photo so that it appeared that I and Mrs T had been alone together in celebration!

In September 1989 when we were coming back from Japan we stopped off at Bratsk in Central Siberia to refuel and Mrs Thatcher was entertained by local dignitaries. This time there was no pool photographer aboard, and one of the Downing Street staff dashed into the room where we were queuing for the only usable phone to dictate our stories, enquiring if anybody had a camera. I did, and was duly pressed into service to record the occasion so Mrs Thatcher could sign the prints and send them off to those she called 'my chums in Siberia'. I waited with some nervousness for the Boots developing service to return my film. There was a little more at stake on this occasion than promising your neighbours a copy of the shots taken at the road party. But fortunately I had not kept the lens hood on this time.

Going to interview Mrs Thatcher was always a risky business because of the ever-present danger that you might press the wrong button by accident – upon which she would be off and unstoppable on the latest hobby horse, using up half of your interview time with a single reply. It happened to me at the G7 economic summit in Toronto in June 1988. I was called for the first question of what we had been warned could only be a fifteen-minute press conference. In response to my rather general enquiry she launched a rampage about litter which lasted fully five minutes. My colleagues wanted to lynch me. We had been relying on the press conference for a story which it did not provide.

The *Times* deputy editor John Bryant telephoned me a few minutes later.

'Robin,' he said, 'we're desperate for a lead story. We've got nothing and the front page goes in twenty minutes. What can you do?'

'Don't worry,' I told him. 'Put me on to Copy.' Working on a few motherhood and apple pie paragraphs about drugs and crime in the communiqué, I wrapped them up with a few scrappy gleanings from earlier talks with briefers and officials, and the paper got its story. Does that make me an old hack? Probably. Sometimes you have to be one, and I have enjoyed every minute of such challenges. Much of the time, newsdesks and programme editors run down politics and complain that it is boring. But news is comparative, and in politics you can always find a story of some kind.

Although there was always that worry about what direction

Margaret Thatcher might take, you knew too that if you were granted an interview with her you would have a story. The coinage of prime ministerial and party leader interviews has become severely debased since then. John Major and Tony Blair have been too eager to win friends and have given too many interviews when they had nothing to say. Yes, of course I have been among those pressing for such interviews; but a journalist always hopes that he or she will be the one to strike lucky.

Margaret Thatcher may have been Scary Spice at times, but she was also the total pro. Working for *The Times* in the 1987 general election, I had been promised interviews with all the party leaders, and they had been advertised in the paper. As we approached the last few days of the campaign, all bar Margaret Thatcher's had been done. I pressed again – and suddenly the Tory campaign managers said she could not do it. She had been ill with toothache, they told me, and her schedule was too tight. Over the final weekend of the campaign I cashed every outstanding cheque I had at the top of the Tory party in my efforts to secure the interview. Finally I persuaded David Young, the employment minister and one of her favourites, to go and see her to press my case. 'David', she once said, 'brings me solutions when others bring me problems.' I hoped Lord Young might do the same for me; and so he did, finally winning agreement that she would see me on the Monday before polling day.

In the early hours of Monday morning, however, I nearly lost even that concession. Along with the other papers, the first edition of *The Times* was brought into Downing Street. The main election headlines on the front page were: 'Labour piles on pressure in marginals', 'Gould in appeal to waverers' (frontbencher Bryan Gould was the highly effective co-ordinator of Labour's campaign), 'Thatcher keeps summit waiting' and

'Customs men start election week disruption early'. To cap this, as far as Tory campaigners were concerned, the main front-page picture was of a happy-looking Neil and Glenys Kinnock waving to crowds.

When Mrs Thatcher returned after midnight to Downing Street, having done fourteen 'takes' of a many times rescripted party election broadcast that night, she and Lord Young were hopping mad. Lord Young telephoned me and my editor Charles Wilson to complain that we were trying to win the election for Labour and to say that the interview was off. The arguments went on, and eventually it was reinstated, after a fashion, a day or so later. I was allotted just twenty minutes between her press conference and her departure by helicopter for her next appointment.

With a combative gleam in her eye, Mrs Thatcher came in to the small room we had been allotted in Smith Square with its cheap pine-style yellow desk. I asked her the first question and she rabbited on for four minutes with an unusable non-answer. I had sixteen minutes left and I had to gamble.

'Prime Minister,' I said. 'We both have a job to do. I have half a page of *The Times* to fill. You have an election to win. We have fifteen minutes. We can't go on like that. I need concise forty-second answers to a dozen questions, otherwise we will never get this done.'

She looked ready to explode, and as she pushed back her chair I thought I had blown it. But then, suddenly, she smiled. 'All right then. Shoot away.' From that point she fired out short, pithy answers with total discipline, and we got through every question.

After all the trials and tribulations of the previous days, I would not have liked to have had to go back to my editor

Charles Wilson and say that I had no interview with the Prime Minister in my notebook and tape recorder. But it had been a close call.

Margaret Thatcher managed the media by sheer force of personality; and she forced other parties to reshape themselves. But she left her own party with a problem. She had led the Tories to great success, but in the process she had turned them from a pragmatic party interested in the getting and holding of power into an ideological party interested in winning arguments. The Euroscepticism which she engendered with her famous Bruges speech in 1988 spawned the Tory divisions on Europe which dogged the party all through the Major years and do so still. Miscalculation over Europe led to her downfall, and many of the zealots in her party have never forgiven those responsible – or themselves – for letting it happen. Their collective guilt complex, and the mistaken belief that unadulterated 1980s-style Thatcherism, even without Thatcher herself, would miraculously bring British voters back to the Tory cause, hog-tied John Major and has continued to handicap the Tories ever since.

But politics moves on. The ending of the Cold War removed many of the traditional demons; Arthur Scargill and the other union chiefs who used to roam the land have long ago been locked up in trophy cupboards or industrial theme parks; and the Labour left huddles for warmth in neglected corners while the party leaders stuff their task forces with business chiefs. Yet any attempt by the Tory hierarchy to escape the Thatcher mould and to rebrand the party brings trouble within. William Hague and his then policy chief Peter Lilley tried in 1999. With all parties agreeing that the market rules, they sought for a while to refocus the Tories as the party of the public services and to remove common fears that the Conservative answer to everything was to privatize it, a solution not exactly regarded as an automatic recipe for success with Britain's railways in a shambles. Admittedly the Hague team's timing was appallingly clumsy: Peter Lilley made his keynote speech insisting that the market was not the solution to every problem on the same night the Tories were celebrating the twentieth anniversary of Mrs Thatcher's first stunning election victory in 1979. But that was not the only reason the party was immediately up in arms. So strong remained the force of Lady Thatcher's personality that nobody was prepared to comb through the careful text of Mr Lilley's speech. Within weeks he had paid the price: he was dumped in a reshuffle and a chastened Hague took personal responsibility for policy direction.

As for Thatcher herself, little changes. Jeffrey Archer helped to organize one of her speaking tours in Japan a couple of years into her enforced retirement. She was ushered in for drinks at a university, on what she thought was a social occasion with some senior academicians, and greeted by the university chancellor.

'Lady Thatcher, we have the senior students all gathered in an adjacent hall and we wondered if you would be kind enough to come in and say a few words to them?'

'This is a disgrace,' Thatcher declared, rounding angrily on Archer. 'Who is organizing this programme? Why wasn't I told about this in advance?'

A chastened Archer apologized profusely and said that there had been no knowledge of any such engagement. 'But don't worry, Margaret, there's no need to do it. I'll go in and talk to them myself for a bit.'

'Oh, no, you won't,' said Thatcher, who immediately swept into the other hall and gave the graduates forty minutes at full pitch on capitalism, privatization and the perils of socialism worldwide. Nobody else was going to get a look in when an audience had been assembled for her. She was and is political show business, and she knows it.

8

'AH, RED, NOW YOU'RE TALKING': PARTY CONFERENCES

THE NIGHT OF 12 OCTOBER 1984 AND ITS AFTERMATH SHOWED THE very best of Margaret Thatcher: her courage in a crisis, her resolve when up against it. It was the night an IRA bomb ripped apart the Grand Hotel in Brighton during the Conservative party conference – and I could so easily have been one of the victims. Having broken all my resolves to get to bed at a sensible hour, I had stayed for one more drink and chat after another with ministers, MPs, contacts and fellow journalists. Among those with whom I had had a drink early in the evening had been the Enfield Southgate MP Tony Berry.

About 2.30 a.m., just twenty minutes before the bomb went off, I had left the Grand and gone back next door to the Metropole Hotel, where I was staying. Having just gone to bed, I was stirred rather than woken by the blast; within minutes a colleague was hammering on my hotel door to tell me what had happened. I threw on some clothes and joined the milling throng of politicians, journalists and rubber-neckers on the esplanade gazing at the shattered hotel as rescue efforts intensified.

Most of those I encountered were in dressing-gowns or what few garments they had been able to grab as they left their rooms in the Grand. Emma Nicholson, then a Tory member, was in a rather fetching shade of pink. Another MP, Michael Spicer, with whom I had been at school, was in borrowed clothes; he had left his room naked as the day he was born.

At the time I was still working for the *Daily Mail*, and one of my colleagues, Bob Porter, kept open a phone line to the paper as the rest of us dashed about gathering what information we could about victims and survivors to feed through to the news-desk. Poor John Wakeham, we soon learned, was desperately injured; it was hours before he could be extricated from the wreckage, his legs badly crushed. His wife was dead. Held back behind the police cordon, we watched from afar as Norman Tebbit, his face contorted with pain but still apparently managing to crack jokes with his rescuers, was lifted clear of the wreckage. His wife Margaret was crippled by the blast. It is little wonder that he has been a hard-liner on terrorism ever since.

It was a stunning, numbing sight – that great black hole gaping in the centre of the hotel. Occasional slippages of broken brick-work, plaster and masonry would send little clouds of dust into the air. Luckily for those staying in the Grand, many of the lights had stayed on. Soon sirens sounded as the injured were whisked to hospital. Policemen wound black-and-yellow tape round street lamps to cut off access, and somewhere, incongruously, a burglar alarm was ringing.

Question, rumour and counter-rumour swept through the bizarre assembly. Was Thatcher alive? What about Denis? Were there ten dead, twenty dead? Thirty? How many of the Cabinet had survived? I worked my way through the seafront crowd, gleaning what I could and surreptitiously ticking off a list of survivors I could see or whose identity I had had confirmed. Soon we heard that Mrs Thatcher herself, who had had little idea at first of the extent of the damage, had been taken out of the hotel down a back staircase. After talks with other rescued colleagues at Brighton police station, she emerged to make a brief statement before going off to snatch an hour or two's sleep at Lewes Police College. Still with no news of casualties, she knelt to pray by her bed with her faithful aide 'Crawfie', who had brought some spare clothes for her.

As the hours wore on, politicians and journalists alike felt that the conference should continue despite the four deaths by then confirmed, among them that of poor Tony Berry, whom I had seen so recently in such good spirits. Whatever our individual political views, all those participating in or reporting on Westminster politics share a belief in democracy and a detestation for rule by bomb and bullet. There was something very British about the conference opening on time at 9.20 a.m., albeit in front of a smaller than normal audience, many having been held back by extra security searches. Cabinet ministers and party apparatchiks alike were in unfamiliar clothes; unable to get back to their rooms at the Grand Hotel, they had been fitted out at the local Marks and Spencer store, which had been opened privately for them thanks to an initiative by Alistair McAlpine, the deputy chairman of the party. The American ambassador Charles Price was in Denis Thatcher's spare pair of shoes, having lost his own in the confusion of leaving the Grand.

There had been some moments of incongruous humour. At one stage I was beside Sir Henry (now Lord) Plumb, the former National Farmers' Union president who led the Conservatives in the European Parliament. As a crane was lifting vehicles clear of the wreckage I heard him say, 'That looks rather like my car. Dammit, it *is* my car.'

For me, the most bizarre aftermath of the blast was my encounter with Nigel Lawson, the Chancellor of the Exchequer. I bumped into him, then a well-upholstered figure in his traditional blue dressing-gown, on the seafront at about 4.00 a.m. I had been sending him messages all the previous day because David English, who had asked me before the conference to line up a prestige lunch guest for the Friday, had cried off at short notice and I felt I had to give Lawson the option of cancelling now that he would be lunching only with me. I had received no reply.

'I presume in the circumstances you would like to cancel lunch,' I said to him now.

But this was in pre-Lawson Diet days. 'Good Lord no, dear boy,' he replied. 'Of course we must still have lunch.'

And so we did – at Wheelers on the seafront. My mind was full of the half-dozen stories we were pursuing in the aftermath of the bombing as my guest, decked out in his Marks and Spencers togs, sauntered his way through four courses. It is the only time in my journalistic life when I have been anxious to get away from a lunch with the Chancellor of the Exchequer.

Late that evening, after we had finished work and sat down for a meal and a drink, I suddenly found one of my arms twitching uncontrollably. It was, I think, a kind of delayed shock. I had been so busy finding out about others that it was not until that moment that I realized just how close I had come to being a victim of the Brighton bomb myself. I have never protested at a security search since.

Party conferences are not always, thank God, as dramatic as that. But they have often been colourful, story-filled, obsessive and slightly mad occasions. They are the great opportunity for the rank-and-file envelope-lickers and subscription-collectors of politics not just to see the high and mighty on the platform but to watch them let their hair down off it too.

I remember being at one of Jeffrey Archer's Krug and shepherd's pie parties in the early hours of an October morning which was later to see Kenneth Clarke make his first speech to the conference as Chancellor. For the moment he was planted here, glass in one hand, cigar in the other, locked in furious argument with Norman Tebbit over Europe. As the party broke up, Tebbit indicated a curtained alcove behind Clarke: 'There you are, Ken,' he urged. 'There's the way out.' The only problem was that we were three floors up and it was a window, not a door. So chummy, those top Tories.

Every conference, too, brings its lighter relief – as when Lord Holme, Liberal Democrat guru and negotiator, was attending his party's gathering in Torquay. Pyjama-less, he had slipped across from his room to the loo opposite in the early hours, only for his door to slam shut behind him. There was no night porter, and he spent the night in the lounge with only a prayer mat found on top of a chest of drawers in the lounge to protect his modesty.

At a much earlier conference, in the early days of the 1970 Heath government – although the beneficiary probably has no recollection of the incident – I may have saved the career and later knighthood of a young Tory MP and later party vice-chairman, David Knox. He did not approve of the government's line on South Africa and, a little emotional after an area reception, had announced to the group in which we were talking that he was going to tell the Prime Minister exactly what he thought. As Heath swept in I positioned myself in front of Knox and shoved him back into the deep leather armchair behind us.

Once during Heath's brief 'doorstep' he struggled up behind me with a squawk of protest. Once again I shoved him down, and by the time he had got to his feet again the Prime Minister had passed.

At another Tory conference I became a rumour myself, and very nearly a rich man too. In October 1995 I had been due to go to Blackpool as usual on the Sunday before the conference, but had had to stay in London to cover the defection to Labour of the Tory MP for Stratford-upon-Avon, Alan Howarth, for the late news. I booked a car to take me to Blackpool afterwards, arriving at 1.00 a.m. at the Imperial, the main conference hotel. At that hour, of course, the security pass office was not open, and the police would not let me into the cordoned-off hotel without a pass. I was due on air for *Breakfast News* within the precincts at 7.00 a.m. and, appreciating my problem, a senior officer suggested a compromise: if I went to Blackpool central police station, they would try to arrange for me to have a police technician's pass to get me into my hotel.

I spent an interesting hour or more in the nick as I waited for the paperwork to be done. I was alarmed by the number of children who were brought in after being found wandering the streets, often in nothing more than tee-shirts and jeans. They were half cocky, half scared; perkily streetwise, yet some of them sucking their thumbs. I was struck by the kindness of the police, who were using their own money to buy them cans of Coke from the dispensing machines while they sought to track down their addresses and their sometimes feckless parents. Eventually, I acquired my pass and got to bed for three hours.

There was much amusement all round the next day at the BBC's political editor having spent part of the night in Blackpool police station; and the story began to be confused with another which was also doing the rounds. Apparently a couple of junior journalists, one from the BBC regions team, had been apprehended in the early hours, having been caught *in flagrante* having sex in a flight simulator on Blackpool Pleasure Beach. In consequence the next afternoon the *Sun*, according to one of my friends on the paper, had in preparation a front-page scandal story which was to bear a heading on the lines of 'BBC political editor in Blackpool sex romp scandal'. If only they had not checked further and spiked the story I could have sued and holidayed in the Bahamas for years.

Party conferences are tribal occasions where the faithful salute their elders, icons and battle-scarred warriors like Lady Thatcher or Barbara Castle, both of whom know how to milk every second of adulation. The assembled tribe members conduct war dances against common enemies and listen to incantations from their spin/witch doctors. Some, of course, make dreadful mistakes amid the conference exuberance as they seek to ingratiate themselves with their party's activists. Michael Portillo's 'Who dares, wins' invocation of the SAS in an attempt to underscore his Eurosceptic credentials was one example which raised big question marks about his judgement. Former social security secretary Peter Lilley, much respected by Cabinet and shadow Cabinet colleagues for his cogent contributions to top-table debate, used to make a spectacle of himself year after year at Conservative conferences by inserting in his speech cringe-making little ditties modelled on Gilbert and Sullivan. One year he even broke into song. Nor was it seemly for Margaret Thatcher to have joined in treacherous hand-clapping under the table as a Tory representative demanded the return of the rope during a debate in which her loyal Home Secretary Willie Whitelaw had told the activists he could not and would not seek to bring back hanging.

But the party activists love conferences; and it is not always the ideology which grips them as much as the quality of performance. The same people will cheer both the Eurosceptic Tebbit and the Europhile Heseltine if they deliver, and as a media animal even I find I need my annual seaside fix. I can still thrill to the memory of Michael Foot in full flow on a Labour platform, glasses gleaming, finger stabbing, stresses randomly distributed throughout his sentences. In cold print the next day his speeches had little impact, but at the moment of delivery they were gloriously effective as he tore into the Tories of his time. I can see Michael Heseltine, his blond mane flowing as he delighted Tory activists with his battle cries and word pictures, evoking a socialist army marching 'Left, Left, Left' towards all that they held dear. You had to admire, too, both the silken skills of Douglas Hurd, quietly pressing the right buttons to defuse a Tory conference roused to flag-burning, foot-stomping anti-European intensity by Norman Tebbit, and the sheer theatricality of Margaret Thatcher and her 'U-turn if you want to. The lady's not for turning.'

Few of us who saw it will forget Neil Kinnock in Bournemouth in 1985, turning his vituperative scorn on Liverpool's Militant Tendency. 'You end in the grotesque chaos of a Labour council – *a Labour council* – hiring taxis to scuttle round a city handing out redundancy notices to its own workers,' he stormed. The council leader Derek Hatton, a leading member of the Militant Tendency, leaped to his feet shouting 'Liar! Liar!' after which both he and the left-wing MP Eric Heffer walked out. It was a symbolic moment, the start of Labour's rebirth as a moderate centre-left party determined to contest the middle ground of British politics. I remember Kinnock a few years earlier, then a man of the 'soft left' himself, turning white as he conducted the fund-raising spiel at the Tribune rally and one comrade sent up an envelope enclosing 'thirty pieces of silver'. It was the year that Tony Benn, the voice of the left, was fighting the right-winger Denis Healey in the contest for Labour's deputy leadership, and Kinnock had refused to support Benn. Neil has never been given the full credit he deserves for beginning the process of modernizing Labour.

Although the left has its own brand of dry humour, in the early 1980s – the days of Bennite 'accountability' and the advance of the hard left – there was little space for laughs at Labour conferences. Indeed, there were fisticuffs in some of the bars. We had Healey himself promising to 'squeeze the rich until the pips squeak', ministers being booed from the floor, and Arthur Scargill and Dennis Skinner in full rant, roared on by hundreds, at the fringe meetings. Both Scargill and Skinner are marvellous, witty speakers with a timing any Palladium comic would envy, but what tends to be forgotten now is the chill which went with such views from some of their comrades. In those days if you sat in the hall among chums in the Labour MPs' pen you experienced a real sense of physical menace as you watched the contorted faces of some of the clenched-fist constituency delegates and felt the waves of hate wafting across the floor.

One of Labour's problems as a party created initially to be the political embodiment of the trades unions has always been how best to maintain the right relationship with the unions without frightening off those middle-class voters who see militant unionism as a threat. Public support for Labour tended to suffer when unions were involved in high-profile industrial action, and so Labour leaders always needed to keep abreast of industrial developments. During one fractious public service dispute, Neil Kinnock told me later, he was keeping in close touch as opposition leader with the gruff rail union leader Jimmy Knapp.

Knapp rang him one morning with an important message. 'It's all right, Neil. I've done a deal with British Rail. We'll be settling at lunchtime today.'

In the early afternoon Kinnock took another call from Knapp. 'Hello, Jimmy, all over then?'

'Er . . . not quite, Neil. You see, the thing is, I had to get up to get some documents out of the briefcase behind my seat to announce the agreed terms, and as I did so one of the other lads drew the wrong conclusion. He got up and said, "If this deal isn't good enough for Jimmy Knapp, it's not good enough for my members either, and we're walking out too." Unfortunately, we haven't got them back yet.'

Such lighter moments aside, Labour politicians then had to be tough to cope with the brutalities of block vote politics and national executive manoeuvring. David Blunkett, a highly effective education secretary in New Labour's first term and a former national executive member, had an extra resource, allegedly put to good use at the time when he was in the process of turning from leftish local government boss to fully paid-up Blairite. 'Every time a tricky vote comes up he takes his dog out for a pee,' Dennis Skinner complained of his colleague's performance on the national executive.

In Labour conference politics, you had to know where the bodies were buried, and you had to be prepared to bury a few. One of the few surviving Labour politicians who can and did cope with that world is John Prescott. One night in the 1980s the *Daily Mail* team were entertaining John and Pauline to dinner at the Town and Country, the restaurant run by John and Judith Jallal which was a long-time conference favourite in Blackpool. A transport workers' delegate somewhat the worse for wear came up to pick a fight with Prescott – who excused himself, had a furious and detailed shouting match about transport technicalities and union tactics with the man for ten minutes, and then came back to pick up his gin and tonic and the social chit-chat as if nothing had happened. There aren't many made like that in the Labour party any more.

Prescott endures a lot of mockery for his habit of tumbling over his words, and in his less chip-on-the-shoulder moments he knows what his weaknesses are. I commiserated with him once after he'd been taken in for a head X-ray following a taxi accident. 'I asked them if they could do anything about the syntax while I was in,' he confessed with a grin. Yet he can feel the pulse of the Labour movement, and he knows where its soul resides. It has been John Prescott's presence at Tony Blair's side, as much as the silkier skills of wordsmiths like Peter Mandelson, that has helped Blair to modernize the Labour party.

Before the 1997 election Prescott had a session with several union leaders, including such key figures on the left as Rodney Bickerstaffe of Unison and the firemen's leader Ken Cameron. He was faced by a number of challenging questions, and he was honest about his own dilemma and how he had resolved it.

'I am spending my life dancing on the head of a pin,' he told them. 'I am compromising myself out of existence to get Labour elected, buttoning my lip on things like Harriet Harman's choice of school for her kids because I am not going to let the chance of election victory slip by or be blamed for allowing it to do so.'

Prescott used to complain privately that Mandelson and Kinnock had sanitized Labour to the point where the party had lost all belief, but under Tony Blair he has learned to live with the remake in exchange for a certain degree of licence to speak out. Old Labour activists and union barons had their guarantee, so long as Prescott was deputy leader, that things would not be taken too far, that their voices would still be heard at the top table. For them he held the line on proportional representation and on co-operation with the Liberal Democrats. And in one of the greatest conference dramas we have seen, he saved John Smith's leadership with his passionate speech urging the unions to accept his leader's reforms of the party constitution – the one member, one vote controversy – in 1993. I know that Smith, had he gone down in the vote, which was a close-run thing, had been planning to 'do a Gaitskell' and go back to the conference telling them he would fight and fight again to reverse the policy they had voted for. Prescott told me later he was determined to stop him doing any such thing, and that Smith might well have destroyed his leadership if he had.

I had great admiration for John Smith, one of the best parliamentary debaters of my time and a man who truly relished the cut and thrust of Westminster life. Glass in hand, he was tremendous, zestful company and a grand teller of tales. His personal probity made him a truly effective scourge of the Tories over sleaze, and his moral indignation at the poverty and lack of opportunity bearing down on some in our society could be lacerating. But he did not have a clear vision of 'the Project' for reforming the Labour party later shared by Tony Blair, Gordon Brown and Peter Mandelson, whom Smith could not abide and whom he sidelined as an adviser. Nor was Smith a nimble-footed tactician. Certainly he had not prepared for the task of carrying through his reforms at the 1993 conference as well as he might have done. That, I like to think, is why in Brighton that year I glimpsed a rougher side to him which I had not seen before.

The essence of the Smith plans was to reform the union block vote and to make trades union levy payers pay an extra annual subscription and become full Labour party members in order to have a vote in the selection of Labour candidates. It was a significant loosening of the union link. At the conference the day before the key vote Smith had scored well with his leader's speech, backing full employment and a national minimum wage, and castigating a directionless, sleazy Tory government obsessed with privatization. Typical of his style was his invitation to John Major.

'Find a quiet bathroom in Downing Street,' he advised, 'look into the mirror, take a deep breath, repeat the words "rail privatization" and then ask this question: "Mirror, mirror on the wall, who is the barmiest of them all?"'

But while they applauded his Tory-bashing, union leaders were taking a lot of convincing about his proposed reforms. So were some Labour MPs, even frontbenchers. Deputy leader Margaret Beckett, sponsored by the transport workers, was pointedly cool, and economic spokesman Dawn Primarolo voiced her opposition openly. There was a frantic series of meetings with union leaders in hotel rooms to try to win round their delegations, but the prospects for the Labour leadership of being able to pull a rabbit out of the hat did not look good.

'This rabbit,' said the GMB's John Edmonds, 'is a non-runner.'

With the decision due on Wednesday afternoon and tension building, I reported on Tuesday night that the votes were not there for the leadership. Smith supporters were lamenting that he had not staged the contest a year earlier when he was on his honeymoon as party leader, and worried that he had not done enough to make union leaders feel wanted. At lunchtime on Wednesday I told BBC viewers that the votes were still not there for Mr Smith, and that some of his supporters, although they applauded his courage in opening the debate, believed he was heading for the ground without a parachute. But then there were two developments typical of the old-style blood-and-guts Labour conferences. In the first, just hours before the crunch, the MSF union, in return for assurances of backing for linked reforms on women candidates which it was seeking, agreed to abstain rather than vote against Smith in the key vote. The second came in the final debate itself.

'I say to this conference that the changes I propose today are vital, absolutely central to our strategy for winning power, and I ask you all to unite behind them,' Smith implored, laying his leadership on the line.

But union leader Edmonds was equally blunt. 'John, you ask too much of us,' he declared.

Finally Smith sent John Prescott, a man whom nobody would suspect of being a union-basher, to the rostrum for one last appeal. Prescott warned his leader that if his speech worked he, not Smith, would be the conference hero and that it would reflect badly on deputy leader Margaret Beckett, but Smith still insisted that he go ahead.

Prescott spoke from the heart, untidily, sometimes awkwardly, warning the delegates that what mattered was how the outside world perceived this affair. This tangled paragraph was the essence of his appeal: 'This man, our leader, put his head on the block by saying basically: "I fervently believe" because that's what he believes of a relationship and a strong one with the trades unions and the Labour party. He's put his head there. Now's our time to vote. Give us a bit of trust and let us have this vote support,' he urged.

In the next day's papers, Prescott's words read as nothing very much. They don't read as much now. But, as my friend John McCririck says in another world: 'Come racing!' Sometimes television and newspaper reports are simply not enough to convey the sheer chemistry of a big occasion. There was no polished rhetoric, there were no ringing phrases. But in its raw emotion and gut instincts, Prescott's appeal gave those of us who were there to hear it a truly powerful conference performance. There is no doubt it swung the waverers.

It was a prime example of the importance of personality in politics. It wasn't what he said that mattered so much as who he was. Probably no other man in the Labour party could have pulled off the trick in that place and at that time. But John Prescott did, and the reforms squeaked through – even if the conference, typically, voted also for another motion which seemed to contradict them. John Smith's position, I reported, would be strengthened. Never again after such a gamble would he be accused of being a play-safe bank manager. But, I added, he had got the tactics wrong; he should never have allowed the issue to build up into the crisis it became.

Two days later I went in to do an end-of-conference interview with him and, as I sat down, he suddenly launched into a furious though unspecific assault both on the BBC and on me personally, saying that our reporting all week had been a travesty, that we had done everything possible to undermine him and that we were totally biased against him and his party. Somewhat shell-shocked, since we had not received an iota of criticism from any other Labour figure or from the party's media team, and I had never had a cross word with him before, I defended myself and the BBC against the diatribe, especially since the ITN team were still present.

Later I asked David Hill, Labour's director of communications, 'What the hell was that all about?'

'Search me,' was his reply.

I think it was perhaps a release of the incredible tension which must have built up over the previous days. I noted in my journal at the time that I had heard during the week that John Smith had been effing and blinding at people and very on edge. 'He cannot expect me to be a choirmaster conducting a chorus of praise. It is my job to put things into context,' I noted on the day of his outburst. A bit precious, perhaps, but it was, and it is.

Typically, the next time I went to see him in his room in the Commons he stuck his head round the door where I was waiting, grinned and asked: 'Friends again?' Smith was not one to bear grudges, and every one of us involved with politics felt a desperate sense of loss at his tragically premature death.

The row with John Smith came as a particular surprise to me because in mid-September I had taken him for a very jolly dinner at the RAC, a dinner at which he had told me that the Labour party 'can have John Smith and OMOV – or neither'. He had begun and ended the meal with a fizzing glass, joking about being a 'champagne socialist' and speaking quite candidly about some of his reshuffle intentions.

He did not mind demonstrating his calculating side, revealing that he had kept going the row over the fugitive Asil Nadir's contributions to the Tory party to deter other potential donors; and he was honest, too, about his own mistakes. He said he had pressed Neil Kinnock to send Bruce Millan to Brussels as a European commissioner and had pooh-poohed the idea that the resulting Govan by-election could be lost to the Scottish Nationalists. But it was; yet Kinnock, he said, had never reproved him afterwards.

I was intrigued to hear him argue, in contrast to Blair and Brown, that Bill Clinton hadn't broken new ground in the 1992 US election. Smith's view was that Clinton had merely rebuilt the old Democratic vote, and that he too would be able to rebuild the old Labour vote in Britain.

He also revealed his human side and demonstrated the wider camaraderie that sometimes binds even opposed politicians. Smith told me that immediately he heard that Michael Heseltine had suffered a heart attack in Italy he had faxed him a letter via the consul in Venice to reassure him, following his own earlier experience.

'The first day, with your wife and family round the bed, you feel exultant, a hero, you've survived,' he wrote. 'Then everybody goes, you're left with the nurses and nobody can tell you for days whether you will ever work again.' He wanted to spare Michael Heseltine that anxiety. What a hideous irony that after kindness like that in May 1994 he should himself fall victim to a further, fatal heart attack.

John Smith wore the mantle of leadership easily, combining a sharp wit with a safe pair of hands. He fought his battles hard but without malice. His rare combination of humour and solemnity made him a trusted figure, someone who did not alienate those who did not share his views. Tony Benn greeted Smith's death with the most eloquent comment: 'Inside him burned the flame of anger against injustice and the flame of hope that we could build a better world,' declared the man of the left.

The last words John Smith uttered in public, at a Labour dinner the night before he died, were even more appropriate. 'The opportunity to serve our country, that is all we ask,' he told his audience.

No death of any political figure in my time so devastated the Westminster community. Robin Cook and Dr Jack Cunningham simply fell into each other's arms when they met after the news, and others were as deeply affected. For a short while, Smith's death at the peak of his powers brought politicians of all parties together in a reminder of the better instincts they shared. For a moment it even looked as though the mood might last when John Major, another man of decent instincts, appealed to a Tory conference immediately afterwards for a cleaner, less frenzied and less combative politics.

'I care passionately for what I believe in but I don't care passionately for damning what other people believe in,' he said. 'If people who attack the policies of others could respect their motives, then politics would have a fresher feel than it does today.'

We had a glimpse of what might have been. The public, too, seemed briefly to suspend their cynicism about politics and politicians. But, inevitably, the mood did not last. Soon normal disservice was resumed.

The question is sometimes asked: Would Labour have done so well in 1997 if John Smith had still been leading the party? Certainly there were a good few in Labour's senior ranks who had their doubts. In conversations I had at the time with Mo Mowlam, Chris Smith, Peter Mandelson and indeed Tony Blair himself, there were constant mutters that Smith was not moving fast enough to change the Labour party. Tony Blair and Gordon Brown were impatient with the pace of reform under his leadership. Though admirers of Smith, they believed that he was a 'one more heave' man, convinced that electoral victory would fall into his lap without the need to do anything too drastic to his party. Blair thought Smith over-confident; he felt that Smith believed his leadership was in itself enough to clinch victory for Labour, which might have been won before had the country not been suspicious about the genuineness of Neil Kinnock's conversion to moderate policies. Chris Smith, who used to go hill-walking with his namesake, told me in January 1994 that Labour needed three things to win the election. 'We need a country as fed up as it is now with the Tories, no sense that Labour will be a threat to people and a genuine sense of excitement about what a Labour government would bring.' The implication was obvious when he added: 'We've got the first two.'

Blair in particular was keen to move things on. Around this time Mo Mowlam told me that he was unlikely to stay in politics if Labour didn't win the next election, and Blair himself, over lunch with me in March 1993, as good as confirmed it, moving his face but not uttering the words when I asked him if this was true. Peter Mandelson, although sharing Blair's impatience, liked Smith's confidence. In politics, he said, confidence is vital, and Neil Kinnock had always lacked it. He told me in September 1993 that Smith should have moved against Kinnock and replaced him before the 1992 election. He had had a chance in 1988–9 but missed it, partly because of his heart attack. Smith, he said, didn't like the way Kinnock dealt with him through intermediaries and resented not being invited like others to the Kinnocks' home in Ealing; and he worked constantly against Kinnock in private without letting it be seen in public.

Smith was, of course, surrounded by all the usual top-level intrigues. One senior figure told me that while Smith used to joke about Robin Cook's deviousness he relied upon him for tactical advice. He told me that the day Neil Kinnock resigned Robin Cook rang Smith and offered to manage his campaign. The next day Cook was in Smith's office along with Jack Cunningham, an old Smith ally, who had also hoped to run the campaign but who hardly managed to get a word in that day. 'By the time we got to the first press conference there wasn't even a chair for Jack,' I was told.

According to my informant, during this period Cook was manoeuvring for his own future in everything he did, planting stories against Gordon Brown in the hope of forcing him to the right so that Cook himself could run the leftish ticket in a future leadership election. In opposition, Cook used to tell friends that Labour's economic policies as outlined by Brown were 'fine, just so long as we don't do anything like that when we are in government'.

Cunningham, who did the foreign affairs job for Labour for some time in opposition, found himself, after a bad round of shadow Cabinet elections, reduced to the role of shadowing the national heritage department. It was, he said 'not exactly part of my career development plan'. His foreign affairs job, he said, had been 'carved up' and given to Robin Cook as a consolation prize, 'because Gordon Brown won't have him in any economic job'. The wily Cook, according to one fellow frontbencher, had asked both Neil Kinnock and John Smith for the shadow Chancellor's job after running their leadership campaigns. Frustrated by Gordon Brown's closure on him, Cook had carefully obtained the grinding role of chairing Labour's national policy forum so that he kept himself in the economic policy debate.

One of their shadow Cabinet colleagues once told John Smith in opposition: 'Look, all this enmity between Gordon Brown and Robin Cook has got to become ancient history. I'll start taking them out for meals together and we'll all get to sing from the same hymn sheet.' Smith told him, though he inserted a crude adjective, that he would be wasting his time. After three months the colleague came back. 'You're right,' he said. 'I have been wasting my f****** time. If Robin came up with a plan for doing down the Tories it would be derided by Gordon. If Gordon came up with a scheme it would be rubbished by Robin.' The dislike is visceral, instinctive and, it seems, ineradicable. New Labour's problems are not with policies but with personalities.

During his time as Foreign Secretary, Cook, a brilliant debater who used to be short of small talk and not very good at glad-handing, turned himself into a highly effective schmoozer. Continentals tell you that while the supposedly pro-European Gordon Brown cannot wait to get away from European Council meetings the moment he has read out his brief from his folder, Cook would stay on for dinner afterwards and chat with all and sundry. Robin told me once that politics in Europe seemed to be one long meal: 'I have munched my way through the colleagues,' he complained, patting his stomach.

I don't believe that Labour's margin of victory in 1997 would have been as big under John Smith. Blair brought to the party a momentum and excitement that it lacked under his predecessor, who came from a more traditional political mould. But there would have been plenty of reform if Smith had lived to make it to Downing Street. In a long talk with me in November 1992 he was passionate about improving education and told me he wanted to reform the whole British constitution. Labour's devolution programme and the party's commitment to a referendum on proportional representation for Westminster were, after all, legacies to Blair from Smith.

Smith wanted regional tiers of government to balance the powers being ceded to Europe. When I queried the demand for English regional government he was lofty, insisting that the demand would grow inevitably after people saw a Scottish Parliament in action. He wanted a reformed House of Lords, preferably replaced by some kind of regionally elected senate – a step too far, it seems, for his successor; and while Blair the modernizer has been supportive of the royal family, Smith left me with the clear impression that he planned action there too. He had been, he said, shaken by all the panoply of the Palace – by 'all this nonsense of people walking backwards holding wands' when he first went there.

Party reform, to him, was a different matter. He insisted that the unions didn't have much say in his Labour party and that public concern about the moguls' power was overdone: 'Gavin Laird and John Edmonds simply aren't menacing figures.' I commented that Labour had taken a pretty close look at Bill Clinton's campaign and that Clinton had deliberately cut himself off from organized labour to woo the middle classes. But Smith dismissed that as irrelevant. Two days before he died, John Smith told Murdo Maclean, a buddy and a key figure behind the parliamentary arras as private secretary to a series of chief whips, that he had made all the changes he intended to make to Labour's constitution.

Smith was certainly a realist. When I asked him about communication within his party, he said, 'I will work hard to be open and available to Labour MPs.' Then he grinned and added: 'But not too hard.'

Tony Blair's reshaping of Labour, starting with the highly symbolic removal of the nationalizing Clause Four from its constitution, has been a revolution. But he is an impatient, top-down politician, not a bottom-up, grass-roots man. He has done great things for his party, not least by winning a second successive majority big enough to see them through another full term. The rank and file, even in New Labour, respect him for his achievements rather than loving him for what he is; but he does have an inner core behind that soggy Third Way theorizing which allows him to communicate with Old Labour. Twice I have seen him nearly get the bird at a sullenly suspicious TUC conference, the jokes falling flat, the chummy allusions ignored. Each time he threw away the final few pages of his prepared speech and made an impassioned defence of what his kind of socialism was all about. But he is not instinctively part of the traditional, sentimental labour movement, and is often impatient with his own party. He is an undoubted control freak and, deeply influenced by American practices, he has taken the passion out of Labour politics.

In the old days at Labour conferences we used to have real drama at the seaside. The process would begin over the weekend before the conference proper opened. The national executive would huddle with union bosses and constituency activists in smoke-filled rooms to conduct the mysterious process of 'compositing'. This involved taking a variety of policy proposals submitted by constituencies and unions and agreeing the precise sentence construction of 800-word motions committing the party, say, to nationalizing the leading 300 companies in Britain or to abolishing nuclear weapons overnight. Union leaders would trade favours, one agreeing to drop a motion in favour of another's pet hobby-horse, or to switch a key sentence if the other grandee would guarantee his union's block vote for the right candidate in the national executive elections. Ministers would plead with figures like Jack Jones of the TGWU or Hugh Scanlon of the AEEU not to rubbish their policies from the conference floor.

The motions themselves – demanding, say, a basic pension of £200 per week or the disbandment of NATO – would be passed after ninety minutes' debate by notional majorities of four million to one million, with the unions wielding block votes allocated according to the number on which they had paid affiliation fees to the Labour party. It was all such nonsense. Everybody knew that a Labour Prime Minister, with his Chancellor looming at his shoulder, would ignore any such instruction from conference. But it was enjoyable nonsense. It provided great political theatre and huge backstage excitement, not to mention the occasional sight of political bloodstains seeping out under hotel room doors. And it drew public attention to political causes and debates.

Under Blair, building on a process begun under Neil Kinnock, Labour's conference has been refashioned to remove the capacity for self-destruction. There are no more compositing deals and virtually no crucial card votes on hot issues. Famous names no longer fight each other to win places on the national executive, now sidelined. In essence, the drama has been taken out of the policy-making function. At its 1997 conference Labour agreed to a series of procedural reforms; now, a rolling two-year process grinds on inexorably through local policy forums, the national conference, policy commissions, the national policy forum and then back to conference again – if anybody can remember the numbers they first thought of. This reform process has destroyed the ability of non-representative left-wing cliques to hijack the policy process, it has outlawed blood-sport politics and it has neutered Labour's conference. It has also downgraded the politicians who can move people's hearts and take politics to the people it might not otherwise reach. Mo Mowlam, Clare Short and John Prescott could do that; few of the others at the top of the party can. It says something about the nature of modern Labour politics that Mowlam has quit, Short has never been given a top line job and Prescott, for all his deputy leader's status, is somehow sidelined when the big decisions come along.

The Tories, of course, have never pretended that their conferences were policy-making occasions or had to bow to the power of the representatives gathered at the seaside. Balfour once declared that he would sooner take advice from his valet than from his party conference – and, provided that the valet was a genuine floating voter and not a paid-up party hack, he would probably have got much better advice that way.

Pre-Thatcher Tory conferences were largely social, not ideological. They rarely voted down the adulatory motions congratulating the party bigwigs on their efforts; indeed, they rarely voted at all. Conference audiences contained many more first-timers there to see the stars, to have a few good meals out – preferably at least one of them at the expense of their constituency MP – and to listen out for decent speakers in well-cut suits who might make a good replacement for him (and it usually was a him) when the time came.

The Tories used to specialize in conference management. At a post-1987 election seminar I was chilled to hear John Sharkey, a Saatchi and Saatchi executive, claim that the advertising agency had written most of the ministers' speeches for the key 1986 conference which set off the Tory revival with a series of 'active government' policy announcements. The Conservatives have somewhat lost the art of late, but now, like all the parties, they run their conferences as showcases for the national television audience, not for the participants, promising policies which the focus groups have told them are safe and popular.

Over the past decade, party conferences have changed significantly. Labour and Tory conferences especially have become American-style rallies, predictable advertising vehicles for parties dominated by spin doctors, focus group gurus and advertising men. The Tories have grown more political; Labour has grown more social and adulatory. (I have even seen Labour delegates brandishing autograph books.) Even the Liberal Democrats, changed by wielding power in so many local authorities, have 'got responsibility', with Liberal flair somewhat submerged now beneath SDP practicality.

Conferences are no longer raw exchanges of political instinct and party prejudice from which policy is extracted. They are now money-making events where the focus is on attracting the maximum number of trade stands in the adjoining halls. They provide animated advertisement hoardings for pre-set slogans and 'opportunity knocks' slots for candidates in forthcoming by-elections. They are no longer about grainy reality and grass-roots experience but about glossy illusion. Most of all, they are now about image rather than information.

I feel that patter is replacing political debate. Policy lines have been pre-tested by opinion polls. Backdrops are planned to induce a particular mood and the participants even joke openly about the sophisticated techniques now in use. Thus in 1999 John Prescott played about with the coloured backscreens, moving from blue to purple until he got what he wanted. 'Ah, red, now you're talking!' he exclaimed. His audience laughed, but with a bitter edge to their humour. The cynicism of the new non-tribal politics showed, too, when earlier that week Prescott used the all-but-banned word 'socialism'.

'All right, Tony?' he asked, grinning at his leader. Blair waved a deprecating hand, a bit like a Roman emperor consigning a Christian to an underfed lion, and they carried on.

Largely thanks to Labour, what we have seen is the Americanization of British politics. The very naming of New Labour followed Bill Clinton's 1992 introduction of the 'New Democrats' at a time when Philip Gould, Blair's focus-group and polling guru, was working with the Clinton campaign. Blair used to enjoy his policy-wonking sessions with Clinton in almost the way that Margaret Thatcher used to recharge her batteries with

Ronald Reagan. Gordon Brown, Blair's partner in The Project, holidays regularly in Cape Cod, and his working families tax credit was modelled on the American earned income tax credit. His pro-enterprise tax breaks have an American flavour, and all the Blair/Brown talk of matching rights with responsibilities harks back to US workfare schemes. Although they shied away from the precise term, Brown and Blair were happy to talk of their 'New Deal' policies, consciously adopting a title made familiar to Americans by Franklin D. Roosevelt. Upwardly mobile members of the Blair Cabinet like Jack Straw and David Blunkett came back from trips across the Atlantic with notions like 'three strikes and you're out' and 'employment action zones' for their departments. Even William Hague popped in to see Governor Bush in Texas to inhale a whiff of his 'compassionate Conservatism', while Tory ideas men like Danny Finkelstein and George Osborne took ringside seats at the Republican Convention in 2000.

Of course, there is no great harm in much of this. Parties should be aware of new ideas and policies the world over, and America's economic success made a strong argument for looking at the US way of doing things. But British politicians have made too much of a fetish of America's money-based politics, failing to note that the United States was increasingly becoming a kind of electronic chessboard for a fascinated minority class of apparatchiks, pollsters, lobbyists, machine men, academics and journalists, while the general public were feeling ever more alienated from politics. The big US TV networks noticed this some time ago, and cut back their live coverage of the conventions. They could see that the huge effort expended by politicians and their spin doctors on image-making as opposed to policy-making was breeding public cynicism about politics. They could see the disillusion spread by the vastly expensive game of political advertising, beyond the pockets of all but the rich lobbying groups which would be expecting a return on their money. No wonder that the turnout in American elections has dropped and that the turnout in Britain is following it down.

You can see people's reasoning. If the politicians are playing fancy games and the economy is doing OK, then why bother to watch them? If the line between politics and show business is being shaved wafer thin, why not go and watch some real show business? If all the parties are giving you not solutions they have devised to the country's problems but simply a regurgitation of what the focus groups have told them you want to hear, then why listen? Leave policy to the single-issue pressure groups. Let the pundits talk to themselves about politics like harmless old men muttering over their dominoes in a corner of the bar.

No longer are the party conferences about new ideas and channelling raw enthusiasms. They are about image-branding and keeping politicians from stepping into puddles. We need them still to provide a rhythm to the political year and as a social base for our politics. But with little ideology or commitment, they are no longer compelling political theatre.

I will continue to attend them because I always do. But it no longer takes wild horses to drag me away early. Any old donkey can do the job now.

9

LIFE ON THE BOX: TAKING YOUR FINALS EVERY DAY

SOON AFTER THE THATCHER YEARS HAD COME TO AN END, AND early on in John Major's time, I was offered my own chance of a dramatic career change – and I took it, switching from my much coveted job as political editor on *The Times* to try my hand in television and radio. Some friends thought me crazy. On TV your mistakes are made in front of millions. You are a constant target for the spin doctors. The working days are formidably long. And all the time you are potentially half a sentence away from the slide into chaos. As my long-time colleague John Sergeant once put it to me: 'It's a bit like taking your final exams, every day.'

The simplest answer to the question 'Why?' is: 'Because I was asked.' Having been invited to become political editor of the BBC, tolerated if not always welcomed in millions of homes up and down the land, I would have kicked myself for the rest of my life if I had said no. You become a journalist because you want to communicate. You don't turn down a potential daily audience of six million on the *Nine O'Clock News*. Being BBC political editor may have obliterated my social life for eight years, but television and radio are thrilling mediums in which to work. There is no substitute for ad-libbing chunks into live programmes when the story is still forming around you. The sheer immediacy of it all gives you a buzz. So does the size of the audience. And so does the potential for disaster. If I ever give up live television for good I will have to take to white-water rafting or something similar to replace the missing adrenalin rush.

When I was still political editor on *The Times* and speculation began about who was to succeed the inimitable John Cole in the same role at the BBC, Anthony Howard wrote a piece in which he declared: 'The best job in journalism used to be political editor of *The Times*. Nowadays it is to be political editor of the BBC.' At the time, not seeing myself as a candidate for the BBC post, I was mildly irritated. Having then, to my surprise, become the BBC's choice, I had to revise my opinion. I have often been asked since which job I preferred. But you cannot really compare the two.

As my friendly rival Michael Brunson, the long-time political editor of ITN, told me at the time: 'You will find working for TV is only 20 per cent journalism and 80 per cent logistics.' It was an exaggeration – Mike never knowingly undersold a story – but I soon learned what he meant. In newspaper journalism you can travel lightly, operating with no more than a sawn-off ballpoint, a notebook and a telephone. For television you need camera crews, lights, cables, feed-points, producers and studio staff. On newspapers the merest veiled hint over lunch with a minister or his shadow can form the basis of a story. On TV you generally need somebody willing to speak out on the record. On newspapers, your audience has time to think, to go back and reread a paragraph or two. On TV people have to take your product at the pace you offer it. In newspapers, if the story is complicated, say about devolution or the single currency, you may be able to spread yourself over nine hundred words. On TV there is always the problem of compression. A reporter colleague was once asked if he could manage to do a complicated European Union story in one minute forty-five seconds.

'No problem,' he replied. 'I can give you World War Two in one forty-five if you want it. But it might lose something in the detail.'

In terms of words, the entire contents of the *Nine O'Clock News* would not cover the front page of *The Times*.

Radio, in some ways my favourite medium, is a little easier. On radio you can combine the flavour of some writing craft with the immediacy of broadcasting. Greater knowledge can be assumed because radio news bulletins often have current affairs discussion programmes built around them, as with *Today*, *The World At One*, *PM* and *The World Tonight*. Television rarely has that luxury; but that is the challenge of the medium. The compliments I value as a TV broadcaster are not those from politicians who have recalled a colourful phrase but those from strangers in the street who stop to say, 'I'd never really understood about the single currency [or, say, the welfare benefits row or the Section 28 homosexualiyt controversy] until I saw your report last night.' Hopefully you become, as Jonathan Baker, the *Nine O'Clock News* editor, once called me, 'a trusted guide'. Although it made me feel a bit like an ageing Labrador, I knew what he meant.

From the outside, television looks pretty smooth. Part of the fun on the working side of the camera is watching the frantic paddling beneath the surface which provides that swan-like progress. So often you are only a single wrongly flicked switch away from disaster. Only a few weeks after starting with the BBC

I dashed across one day to Abingdon Green outside the Commons to do a live 'two-way' on the *Six O'Clock News* about some late-breaking story. As I got my breath the microphone was clipped to my lapel and the sound cable joined to my earpiece. I was just in time to hear Martyn Lewis, the presenter, introduce me and begin his question, 'Robin, what . . .' and then the sound died. I looked at the cameraman and said, 'No sound. No sound.' It was lucky that was all I said, because while my earpiece had parted from its cable, ensuring that I could hear nothing, my microphone was still live. *Six O'Clock News* listeners could hear every word I said. Those words might so easily have been, 'What the bloody hell [or worse] is going on?' Swiftly I learned that when troubles come, the less you say the better.

Even the elements intervene. At the TUC conference in September 1993 I was doing a live broadcast into the *Nine O'Clock News* about a crucial speech from the Labour leader John Smith. I had been told there would be time for three questions. Unfortunately, we were on an outside balcony and just before the interview began the heavens opened. With the rain pelting down and dripping off the end of my nose, I answered the first question and was then furious to hear the presenter, Michael Buerk, conclude with a 'Thank you, Robin.' Angrily I rang the studio and complained. But the editor explained that they had really had no option but to cut short the interview. The rain pouring down my face had been steadily soaking me. Even in the studio nobody had been listening to my reply. All eyes were on the wet stain spreading relentlessly down my shirt. They had realized quickly that viewers' reactions would have been exactly the same, and therefore cut me short.

Radio is less dependent on such factors. But it can have its glitches. From the next conference I was doing a live interview for the *Today* programme with Sue MacGregor when suddenly there was a terrible noise like a huge tent collapsing and all the studio lights went out. Through my headphones I heard Sue say, 'I'm afraid we have lost Robin Oakley in Brighton.'

'No, you haven't,' I chipped in. 'I've been plunged into pitch darkness but I'm still here.'

'Oh, fine,' said Sue, and we completed the interview with added intimacy. From the letters I received on that and other occasions I realized that there is nothing viewers and listeners like more than a bit of a cock-up, especially when problems are surmounted.

But you do not always surmount them. I have kept going despite a producer having to leap to catch a toppling light that was about to land on my head. From Dublin I once did a live into *Breakfast With Frost* with David and the viewers unaware that the whole way through my earpiece was blasting away at me with an untalented pop band from some local radio station. I have got through whole interviews when the sound link was so bad I had to guess each question that I answered. But once, in the worst moment of my broadcasting career, I dried completely during a live interview on the *Nine O'Clock News* – and I had no such excuse to offer.

It was at a Scottish Conservative party conference in Edinburgh. I was pretty dog-tired, having flown back and forth to London a couple of times that week on other stories and having done an early slot on *Breakfast News* that day. It was the end of the conference, and on the stage behind me men with hammers were knocking down the scenery. Normally, concentration would have seen me through but, for some reason, I began to be distracted by the noises off. Suddenly I came to a complete stop. I had completely forgotten what I was talking about.

I stared dumbly at the camera, hoping miserably that the earth would open up beneath my feet. But it did not. There was just silence, me and the camera. I do not know how long it lasted. I have never wanted to see a replay. Racing drivers don't play back their crashes. It may have been two, five or even ten seconds before presenter Michael Buerk, who had probably been talking to the studio director at the time, saw what had happened and rescued me with the next question. But it felt like an eternity. If the BBC had sacked me the next day I would not have been surprised. After that, I kept a small piece of paper or notebook with me with a couple of starter words in case it ever happened again.

The story goes that after that 'dry' my deputy John Sergeant, who had been John Cole's number two and who quite naturally had wanted my job when I was chosen, came up to me and remarked with one of his famous put-downs: 'Such bad luck, Robin. It's *nearly* happened to most of us.' Neither he nor I can recall his doing so, but I wouldn't have blamed him if he had – and I repeated the tale amid my tributes to John at his BBC leaving party.

The downside of the TV life comes with the public recognition. Greater publicity for your mistakes and the prying eyes of the gossip columns are the penalties you have to accept as a TV performer. When I was a newspaper journalist nobody ever spotted me from my minuscule byline photographs. On going to the BBC I never believed that I was going to be recognized on the street as John Cole had been – I didn't have a distinctive accent or an eye-catching overcoat – and indeed, for a year or two there were few approaches. But gradually people did start coming up to say hello, and by the time I left the BBC it happened regularly. It culminated for me in the moment when, as an enthusiastic bird-watcher, I had snatched a few hours off at a Commonwealth Conference in Auckland, New Zealand, to visit a nearby gannet colony. I was in scruffy clothes and, unusually for me, a hat. That far away from home I felt as comfortably anonymous as a man could be. But as I went to get back into my hired car a cheerful Essex voice called out: 'Hello, you're Robin Oakley, aren't you?'

People never come up to be rude, only to say pleasant things, a common phrase being, 'Keep up the good work.' Rudery is reserved, it seems, for letter-writers, some of whom used to accuse me of being an agent of the hard left, some of whom insisted I was in the pay of the Tory party. So long as such accusations of partiality kept roughly in balance I felt I was doing a reasonable job: everybody sees political reporting through the prism of their own beliefs. I had been told that when you become a 'face' on TV ravishing women write to you proposing secret trysts. Sadly, in my case this turned out to be a myth. The best I managed was Christmas cards in spindly handwriting from West Country nursing homes.

Almost everybody who comes up to say hello addresses you by your first name: it is the intimacy conferred by being on the little square box in the corner of people's living rooms. They feel they know you personally. Indeed, some complete strangers come up and are convinced they have met you at dinner, or that maybe you use the same gym. You are never quite sure, at first, that they aren't right, and you worry that you are failing to recognize, say, an old schoolfriend. It just sounds too big-headed to say, 'Well, you may think that because you have seen me on TV.'

Of course, people don't always get it right. There is a drunk who regularly comes up to me in Kennington, where I now live, to say how marvellous he thinks I am on TV. He then ruins it by calling me Michael Brunson, not only a rival but a retired rival. Since my boozy acquaintance normally goes on to request the loan of a fiver and then shuffles away muttering that I am a mean bastard when he doesn't get it, I have not bothered to correct his misapprehension. I fear Michael Brunson may have acquired a reputation for tight-fistedness around the Lambeth pubs.

The disadvantage of being recognizable is that you feel you have lost your privacy. Often, people don't know exactly who you are; but you see them looking at you in the baker's queue, half-recognizing you and obviously wondering: 'Is he on *EastEnders* or was he in that dreadful play last Sunday?' As a result you know you cannot be rude to an incompetent supermarket cashier or wind down your car window to have a go at another driver, just in case somebody has clocked you.

As for the diary and gossip columns, I never cease to be amazed at what they reckon to be a story. Nobody ever wrote anything about me when I was political editor on *The Times*. Once I did the same job for the BBC, it seemed I was fair game. The height of absurdity was reached when I was called by someone from the *Daily Express*.

'Are you on a diet?' he enquired. No, I said. I probably should be, but was he going to go on to say that I had been seen jogging on Epsom Downs?

'Well, yes, as it happens,' he replied. Could I confirm that?

Since I had been jogging spasmodically on the Downs for some twenty years to try to counter the effect of all those political lunches, but with very little effect on the waistlines of either me or our lovely Labrador Sorrel, I could.

'Let me give you the line I used when the *Mail* diary rang me a few weeks ago with the same query, that I am very careful as a result not to back any Epsom-trained horses which jog even more slowly than I do,' I told him.

Undeterred, they used the 'story'. And some enterprising morning retriever-walker no doubt collected his second tip-off fee. But who the hell cared or was remotely interested whether or not an overweight Oakley had been seen out jogging?

It is not just the publicity you attract which makes TV journalism different from print. Although I had some exclusives at the BBC (especially in terms of accurately forecasting reshuffle moves, once by standing under the window of Number Twelve Downing Street talking to the chief whip), I had more obvious 'scoops' as a newspaper journalist. That was partly because most such exclusives involve leaked documents, and the leakers like to see the results in hard copy. Another factor was that leaks often go to the partisan who can be trusted to present them in a particular light to suit the leaker. The BBC can never be in that position. Certainly leaks, although much boasted about by newspapers, are rarely the result of some special individual piece of journalistic initiative or cunning. Much more often they are the result of having good contacts and being chosen as the recipient of the information by somebody who wants it out in the public domain.

That is how I secured an exclusive just after Christmas 1995 when Tory MP Emma Nicholson defected to the Liberal Democrats. She was not a particular contact of mine, but Paddy Ashdown and the Lib Dem guru Lord Holme appreciated the way I attended all their conferences, including the spring conferences, when many other political editors did not bother. They knew they could trust me with a confidence. Richard Holme made the arrangements and Paddy rang to let me in on the story. I was given an exclusive interview with Emma, and the other broadcasters and papers were left scrambling. Michael Brunson was back at his Norfolk home for the holiday period and had to drive twenty miles to Ipswich along icy roads, making catch-up calls along the way, to do his report for ITN. He had hoped his whereabouts wouldn't be revealed, but they flashed him up with an Ipswich caption. I know how he felt; there were times when he did it to me.

Incidentally, although I like Emma Nicholson I don't in general have much respect for politicians like her who cross the floor and join another party. There is nearly always a considerable degree of personal pique or frustrated ambition involved, however well it is camouflaged under the guise of principled conviction. On the night I broke the Nicholson story I was frantically busy doing follow-up interviews for various radio programmes and the World Service. It wasn't until later that I caught up with a message from Michael Heseltine claiming that Emma had twice approached him in the previous few months about the prospect of getting a government job. She denied it, and Hezza can play it rough. But I was left with at least the germ of suspicion.

The more politicians like Shaun Woodward suddenly switch sides, spouting the slogans of the next party as vociferously as they did the clichés of the one they have left, the more they undermine public belief in principled politics. In my book, you merit one go in politics. If you fail to advance in the party you have first chosen to represent and don't like it, then slope off and try something else, like ostrich-farming or charity work. If you reckon the party you joined has gone wrong and changed its character, then stay in it and fight to wrest it back onto the right path. The only real exception I would make is for those who joined the SDP, because that was an attempt at a new style of politics and an altogether new party, not a long-time opponent which those who joined it had been ridiculing for years from the other side. And yes, I do know about Churchill.

While I am giving vent to my prejudices, there is one other phenomenon which always irritates me: the way in which sacked ex-ministers suddenly discover that there was so much wrong about the government they have been happy to serve and start joining in backbench rebellions. I have little respect for late conversions of that kind. Bryan Gould, a highly talented academic who left British politics for New Zealand soon after failing in his bid for the Labour leadership, proffered an interesting slant on this issue when he said there was no point in his sticking around in the shadow Cabinet. 'I know that, far from providing a sounding board and a position of influence, the shadow Cabinet in those circumstances merely acts as a gag and a straitjacket which suppresses real debate.' He didn't want, he said, to be one of those 'who waits until his voice no longer counts before expressing his true opinions'. Many of the dispossessed do precisely that.

Returning to the subject of scoops, one brown envelope job did bring me a brief notoriety, and a mention at Prime Minister's Questions. In July 1998 the entire fifty-seven-page defence review was leaked to a few newspaper reporters twenty-four hours before the report was due to be published. Following tip-offs, copies had been left for collection at strategic points around the Commons – one of them, to add insult to injury, outside the government whips' office. As the biggest breach of security since the 1996 Budget leak, it was whipped up into a huge row by the opposition.

Having been primed by a source on some of what was in the report and done stories about it, I confirmed in one live interview that I had actually seen a leaked copy in Tory hands. So I had: the Conservative frontbench defence spokesman Robert Key, who had been sent one anonymously, had pulled the full report out of his briefcase in front of me. Respecting the confidence, I was careful not to name him in my two-way broadcasts, referring only to 'a Conservative frontbencher'. But a frantic mole search was going on, and the government was looking for ways of diverting the blame. At Prime Minister's Questions Tony Blair picked up on my report. He told MPs: 'The BBC correspondent Robin Oakley said he was shown a document by a Conservative frontbencher, a copy of this review, at six p.m. yesterday ... If I find anybody at the Ministry of Defence or any other ministry that has leaked this document I will dismiss them.'

Some of the next day's papers reported that I had 'revealed' Robert Key as the person who had shown me a copy of the report. The *Independent* even declared erroneously that the Prime Minister had told MPs in the Commons that it was Key who had handed me the report. I was much embarrassed, especially since I had refused to name anybody when pressed by other reporters, and I rang Robert Key to apologize and explain that I had not named him. In fact, since he was a Tory defence spokesman, since he and I had been strolling across Millbank in broad daylight when he showed me the defence review, and since I doubt that I was the only correspondent to whom he had mentioned it, it did not take a great feat of detective journalism to identify him as my source.

Some good stories, however, get away. When John Sergeant left the BBC to succeed Michael Brunson at ITN, the potted biographies at the time made much of his 'scoop' in securing the first interview with Ron Davies after his resignation following an incident on Clapham Common. John did the interview brilliantly and deserved the break, but Downing Street told me later that Ron Davies had asked for me; John only got his scoop because

I had left my mobile phone behind when I went to lunch that day with the chief whip, Ann Taylor. She had received an urgent pager message over lunch from Downing Street, but would not tell me what it was about. Number Ten had paged me on my way back later, but they were in a frantic hurry to get the interview done, and by the time I had got off the bus and found a working phone box to call back they had John set up for it.

John and I, incidentally, had a far better working relationship than the gossip columns ever wanted to believe. We enjoyed entertaining politicians together and our news judgements almost always coincided. I can't say we never had a spat. That would have been absurd in such an adrenalin-charged business, and he was perfectly honest about how he had felt about my arrival at the BBC, having wanted, quite naturally, to succeed John Cole himself. 'Sergy', as we knew him, admitted his feelings to one interviewer on his departure for ITN. 'Was I disappointed when the BBC brought Oakley in? Of course I was. He was an outsider, from print journalism.'

That was why I took pains to see he had a satisfying role; indeed, I was sometimes a little envious of his lifestyle. John, who had somehow managed to get it across that he was not available for *Breakfast News* slots, concentrated on Radio Four's *The World At One* (known in the BBC as *WATO*, pronounced What-O) and on the television *Six O'Clock News*. We would sometimes meet on the traffic island in Millbank at about 6.45 p.m. John would be on his way home to Ealing; I was facing another three hours working for the *Nine*.

One story I broke was that of the separation of the Prince and Princess of Wales. On Wednesday 9 December, 1992 I did a live spot from Downing Street on the latest development in the Maastricht Treaty story for the one o'clock TV news. As I switched my mobile phone back on afterwards, I received a call from a good contact with half a tip-off that an announcement on the royal couple's future might be coming soon. I rang in to Number Ten to check, and we had three minutes of conversational thrust and parry. The key thing was that they did not knock the story down. So I went back live on the *One* with the news that a statement on the future of Charles and Diana could be expected from the Prime Minister that afternoon.

In those days there was a weird BBC rule about not taking calls into live programmes from mobile phones. So to do a live spot into *The World At One* radio programme, which at that time went on for longer than the lunchtime television news, I dashed round to a phone box in Whitehall. There was no time to reverse charges. I made my report and finished the last answer with the final 10p of credit on the call just running out. Such are the resources of a mighty newsgathering corporation.

Mobile phones have transformed reporters' lives. At the Edinburgh EU summit in December that year I had another lucky break. With frantic negotiations going on, the newspapers had gone to bed with their first editions running 'stalemate' stories. Just as I finished my report around 10.15 p.m. I saw Gus O'Donnell, the Prime Minister's press secretary, a hundred yards away, talking on his mobile. I grabbed him and he confirmed the details of a settlement. I went back on air to tell that story too. To my frustration, with all of Europe's media assembled in the press centre, the monitor TVs had just before that switched to ITN, who did not have the story.

The mobile phone has transformed politicians' lives, too; and sometimes this helps us journalists. At the Florence EU summit in June 1996 Britain was refusing to co-operate in European Union business until there was a timetable for the ending of the ban on British beef introduced in response to BSE. Furious wrangling was going on. Kenneth Clarke, the Chancellor, was talking on his mobile phone while waiting to do a lunchtime interview. I urged the camera crew to film him for a set-up shot. As they did so, we heard him say: 'So we've got a deal then? That's great.'

Ken Clarke is one of those politicians with an instinctive feeling for the broadcast media. I remember once as I was about to interview him he asked if it was to be pre-recorded or live. I told him it was a pre-record.

'What a pity,' he replied. 'I always prefer the lives. It is that extra frisson you get from the feeling that in half a sentence you can destroy your whole career.' We who earn our living before the cameras know that feeling only too well.

But you did need Ken without the distractions. I once interviewed him at a G7 summit in Tokyo. Unfortunately the interview took place in the ambassador's garden, where the Chancellor, like me a keen bird-watcher, had been told that he had a good chance of seeing an azure-winged magpie. It has to be said that he did not on that occasion lavish his full attention either upon the interviewer or, afterwards, upon Prime Minister John Major, who strolled up nonchalantly but was clearly nervy about whether his Chancellor had said anything out of turn about the euro, on which they did not see eye to eye.

You don't get lucky every day, and sometimes I was beaten to the draw. But part of the satisfaction of working for radio and television is that you are constantly recording mini-scoops, breaking information for the first time to update a running story. Another satisfaction is noting phrases and expressions which you have originated pass into the vocabulary of politics. I claim paternity, for example, of the term 'the Ministry of Fun' for what later became the more prosaically titled DCMS or Department of Culture, Media and Sport. My expression PRT for Pre-Reshuffle Tension came into vogue for a while. And after the 1993 local elections I noticed in several places in print my reflection, uttered on the results programme, that the usual cycle in politics was honeymoon, depression and recovery but that the Major government had scarcely reached the bedroom door before depression took hold.

The biggest problem with working in broadcasting is the hours. Being the BBC's political editor is a way of life rather than just a job. Our household was selected once for one of those government occupational surveys. When the researcher asked me what hours I worked and we totted them up, he was astonished.

'We don't have any category that covers that,' he declared in disbelief. 'You're off the top of my scale.'

In truth, stamina was the chief qualification for the job. You could be asked to do a live interview or 'two-way' at any time from 6.30 a.m. for the *Today* programme or Five Live, although admittedly in my last few years that was not quite so daunting. The advent of ISDN lines, giving you studio-quality sound from a home phone line, meant that you could do those interviews in your pyjamas, although I always preferred to wake myself up first with a shave. In earlier days, the programme would sometimes send down a radio car which would park outside our house and extend a telescopic forty-foot aerial. You sat in the back with your headphones on and a microphone on the tiny table. There were little curtains round the cubicle. I pulled them back one day, and there was the milkman with his face pressed up against the glass. Nobody else would have been around at that hour. But if you were wanted for a two-way in the White City studios on

Breakfast News at 7.00 a.m. that meant a pretty early start for me from Epsom, and a pretty long day with the *Nine O'Clock News* at the other end.

'So why do it?' friends used to ask me. 'Is it worth it?'

Certainly Carolyn, Annabel and Alex paid a price. Friends dropped away after you had missed three supper parties in a row. Commitments to the *Nine* and the constant travel meant that too often I was not there for the carol service, the school play or the graduation ceremony. Carolyn brought up our children. Perhaps if I could have been there more often she would not have been banned from the touchline on one occasion for cheering on Alex rather too enthusiastically during his appearances in the Bedales soccer team. But, having worked on *The Times* herself, she has always understood my compulsion as a news junkie. She understood that neither at *The Times* nor with the BBC could my job be done on a standard hours basis. She knew the excitement I always felt, flying into some foreign city to cover a prime ministerial visit or a summit, being met by a local fixer and some crazy driver who had seen too many films of men with green eyeshades and armbands and would hurtle you through the traffic with total disregard for life and limb. She understood the buzz I felt on those sleeve-tugging days when the air in the Members' Lobby was crackling with expectation at the crisis point in a minister's career, a backbench conspiracy was being hatched or the whips were arm-twisting MPs for a crucial vote. You had to be there for the breaking stories and, once they had broken, you had to see them through to the end. My job was to provide as near to a continuous service as the human frame could manage. And if I ever looked like weakening, sounding doubtful about doing a 7.00 a.m. two-way with *Good Morning Scotland* or Radio Belfast, it was Carolyn who would be urging me on in the background, whispering: 'You can't say no to *them*.'

Days varied enormously according to the pace and intensity of the news. On a reasonably busy day I would arrive in my office in the press gallery in the House of Commons between 8.00 and 9.00 a.m. to finish reading the papers, do some correspondence and make some check calls. On Mondays in recent years I also had to add the final touches to the Turf column I write for the *Spectator*, to the weekly look-ahead I wrote for BBC Online, and to monthly pieces for the parliamentary publications *The House Magazine* and *Parliamentary Monitor*.

At 11.00 a.m. I would attend the morning lobby briefing in Downing Street. From there I would walk back to Number Four Millbank and brief the rest of the BBC political team. There would be calls then to the *Nine O'Clock News* desk about the likely shape of that night's story and perhaps to the *One O'Clock News* too if they wanted me on for a two-way or needed briefing on the background of a story. If they did, there would be further calls to Downing Street, to the other parties, and to MPs and groups with a particular interest to seek more information. After any appearance on the *One O'Clock*, two or three days a week there would then be lunch with a minister, MP or contact.

Early in the afternoon my *Nine O'Clock News* producer and I would discuss the potential ingredients for our story, decide on whom we needed to interview as its component elements and consider what outside filming might be required. I would monitor statements and questions in the House of Commons, attend press conferences and make calls in pursuit of our story. At 4.00 p.m. I would attend the second lobby briefing of the day, this time in a garret room high up among the Palace of Westminster rooftops. These activities might be punctuated by two-ways on the afternoon *Westminster Live* programme or on *PM* at five, or by a WIDIAM for the 6.00 p.m. radio news. You don't know what a WIDIAM is? Nor did I until some time after I had been recording them, when a kindly radio producer explained. It stands for 'What Does It All Mean?' and is a think-piece on the political importance of the day's events.

The *Nine O'Clock News* package, lasting anything between two and, on a really good day, four minutes would take from around 7.15 to 9.00 p.m. to assemble with the aid of my producer and a picture editor. Usually it was a 'live inject' into the programme; that is, it would be cued in and fed directly into the programme output at the White City studios from our smaller operation in Millbank. We rarely finished cutting the piece more than two or three minutes before it was due on air, and sometimes there were only seconds in it, with the picture editor sprinting round from the edit suite to the transmission room. An American crew came to film us in action one day and were amazed how closely we ran things. If reports had been run as close to the wire as that at home, they said, there would have been nervous breakdowns and prostrate bodies all over the floor.

I normally stayed until my package had gone out. I was then free to leave, unless it was a hectic day and I was wanted for *The World Tonight* at 10.00 or to do a piece for the midnight radio news.

Out of interest, through the year of 1997 I kept a list in my diary of my daily work. I probably missed a few items, but this is how it worked out:

TV	RADIO
Nine O'Clock News packages 129	Radio bulletin reports 93
Breakfast News two-ways 46	Five Live two-ways 72
Live Nine O'Clock News	
two-ways 41	*Today* two-ways 38

One O'Clock News two-ways 36

PM two-ways 18

Weekend packages 27

World Service two-ways 8

Westminster Live two-ways 22

GM Scotland two-ways 8

Six O'Clock News two-ways 12

Radio Belfast two-ways 8

News 24 two-ways 11

WATO/WTW two-ways 7

World TV two-ways 10

Radio bulletin packages 5

Results programmes and Budget
  specials 8

Miscellaneous two-ways 5

Rolling programme two-ways 7

World Tonight two-ways 5

Weekend two-ways 6

Rolling programme two-ways 4

Breakfast News packages 6

Today packages 3

Conference programme two-ways 6

Radio features 2

Six O'Clock News packages 4

PM commentaries 1

BBC2 packages 2

Special programmes 1

One O'Clock News packages 2

Five Live packages 1

TV summaries two-ways 2

Five Live commentaries 1

World TV packages 1

World Tonight packages 1

TV summaries packages 1

PM packages 1

That made a grand total of 379 television items and 268 on radio. You earn your corn as a BBC political editor. I only ever missed my slot on the *Nine O'Clock News* twice, on both occasions because we were waiting for animated graphics which had to be prepared in White City and fed down to us.

Sometimes things go horribly wrong. Each night during the 1997 election campaign I would prepare a long package of around five minutes at Millbank. This would then be sent across to White City for transmission while I would leap into a waiting car and watch the news on a small portable TV as I was driven over in time for a live round-up in the studio with Michael Buerk or Peter Sissons at the end of the extended programme. One night after I had completed my piece and jumped in the car, the tape of my report jammed in the machine in the edit suite where I had been working. I could not understand, as I sped to White City, why a Northern Ireland story had run at the top of the news. Michael Buerk then began a live two-way with our marvellous Ireland correspondent Denis Murray. The questions went on, and on, and on. By the last one, said Michael afterwards, the pupils of Denis's eyes were visibly swelling as a one-question interview had developed into four. They had been keeping him on while they struggled with the technology and finally had my report ready. We all owed Denis a large drink for that one.

One great advantage of such a system, I found – and, as an ex-newspaperman, very much appreciated – was the degree of control it gave you over your own material. You would discuss the piece in outline with the *Nine* editor; but the first time he or she saw the completed story was the same time the viewers did, live on the programme. In newspapers you were always much more at other people's mercy. You would press a button on your keyboard and send your story over to the newsdesk and sub-editors, and then back in the office a chief sub or backbench executive might decide that the story you had written at seven hundred words had to be squeezed into a space which only permitted four hundred. The sub-editor or any of the executives above him might decide that they preferred an angle developed by one of the news agencies and choose to wrap that in. Or they might decide to combine your story with that of another specialist correspondent who had produced something similar, under a joint byline. The result could be that, without malice on any-body's part, you found your name on a story you scarcely recognized and did not approve. At least in television you are left to make your own mistakes.

Mind you, those mistakes could come in various shapes and forms. On one occasion my producer Julian Joyce and I were preparing a package about the National Health Service. As so often, there was no time to arrange special filming and we needed some archive footage of nurses and hospitals to overlay one or two points we were making. Having a quick run through some library shots, we selected some a few months old which included the Prime Minister talking to an old chap in his hospital bed. It was only on our final run-through that the keen-eyed Julian noticed that the grinning old boy in the shots had actually pulled back the blanket at the end and exposed himself! We had the shot changed, editing out the embarrassing portion, and congratulated ourselves on a fortunate escape. People with large screens would have been ringing in for hours filling the duty log with complaints. Unfortunately, it was only the next day that we discovered that, in between those hospital shots being recorded and our composing our news item, the old chap in the pictures had died. Sometimes you just cannot win.

As well as watching out for any such basic mistakes, I found that my duties as political editor for the BBC involved hosing down programme editors as often as geeing them up. Perhaps I can illustrate the sheer cannibalism and the occasional absurdity of political journalism by giving a typical example from the mid-1990s. I might, say, have been phoned by the editor or a producer on the *PM* programme:

'Look, Robin, there's this story on PA [the Press Association tapes] with two Tory MPs saying Major should go. What do you think?'

Having checked that the two were regular backbench rebels, I might ring back to say, 'No story. It's Gorlowe and Marmon.

They've done it before.' The *PM* programme, hopefully, would then ignore it.

But it might be a quiet day. Young men from the tabloids with loose ties, empty notebooks and names to make would see the PA story too. They would go on the prowl in the Members' Lobby for other MPs of like mind to Gorlowe and Marmon. They would inveigle them into providing some lively quotes or indulge in some vigorous paraphrase so as to win space in their papers with 'New Blow for Major' stories.

Political correspondents on the heavier newspapers, working in the same congested rooms in the press gallery as the tabloid reporters, amid desks piled high with news cuttings, dog-eared white papers and half-used notebooks, would be aware of the calls being made by their colleagues. Not rating the story any more highly than I had, they would still want a defence ready so as not to be badgered into making late night follow-up calls by their night desks when the first editions of the tabloids dropped around 11.00 p.m. So they would cover themselves by adding a paragraph or two at the end of a story about something else. 'Meanwhile at Westminster last night there were renewed rumblings among a few discontented backbenchers about the party leadership,' they might write.

Overnight researchers for the *Today* programme would note the story in their briefs for the next morning's editor and presenters, pointing out: 'It's not just in the tabloids. The heavies are running it too.' *Today* would then do its own ring-round, more than likely inducing a couple of gabby backbenchers, better known for their fondness for making it on air than for their political judgement, to 'freshen' the story with new quotes. The *Evening Standard* political team, first into the newspaper fray the next morning, would seize on those and hit the streets with a first edition story. That might talk perhaps of 'deep unrest becoming steadily more vocal on the Tory back benches'.

At the 11.00 a.m. lobby meeting with journalists to run through the programme of the day, the Downing Street spokesman would be asked for comment. On a hiding to nothing, he might then offer a stout denial that there was any crisis of confidence in the leadership. But the moment he had commented, he would have 'legitimized' the story. With Fleet Street up and running, the BBC and other broadcasters would then feel bound to offer coverage in their lunchtime bulletins so as not to look like government lickspittles. They would report, accurately: 'The government this morning denied that there was a crisis of confidence within the Tory party in Mr Major's leadership.' Tony Blair would then take it up and taunt John Major at Prime Minister's Questions.

Shortly afterwards, a reproachful *PM* programme editor or producer would say to me: 'Hey, I thought you told me yesterday that this was a non-story.' And next time I would probably be more reluctant to insist that was so.

No new facts would have emerged. Nothing would really have changed. Nobody, save perhaps those who had invented a quote or two the night before, would have done anything wrong. The BBC would – just about – have lived up to its insistence that it does not kow-tow to the tabloid agenda. But in a febrile political atmosphere boosted by a circulation war, there would be the appearance of movement. Momentum in itself becomes a story. Denial merely increases coverage. Once again, it's a case of strong media, weak politicians. The media, aided by the desire of a few politicians for self-advertisement, would have created a 'story' out of nothing.

10

CHARTING JOHN MAJOR'S
BATTLE FOR SURVIVAL

IF LIFE HAD BEEN ON THE UP FOR ME SINCE JOINING THE BBC IN 1992, it had all begun going downhill that year for John Major, virtually from the moment he had won his unexpected election victory. Many Tories have wondered since if they might have done better to lose that election. The Conservatives had out-stayed their welcome and the country was yearning for change. Uncertain, however, about a Labour government led by Neil Kinnock, many had decided that a change in the leadership of the Tory party was enough to be going on with.

Major's problem was that he was back in power with a party that was bitterly divided on Europe and with a small majority of twenty-one, which was going to make it difficult to last a full term.

'We cannot always grandly sail ahead oblivious to all,' he conceded. 'We may have to tack a little here, manoeuvre a little there. That's politics. We can't ignore the parliamentary arithmetic.'

The difficulty was that such manoeuvring was never going to

look heroic, and Major was leading a party which never came to terms with not being able to sail grandly ahead in the Thatcher style. He wanted 'a country at ease with itself'; but this was always going to prove an impossible attainment for someone leading a party that was far from at ease with itself. And yet Major's occupancy of Number Ten proved to be, in its way, a remarkable story of survival: time after time the doomsters would predict the end; time and again the smoke would clear from the battlefield and John Major, his face further blackened, a few more dents in his armour, would still be there, limping back from the fray.

For five of my years as political editor of the BBC, and as a journalist who knew Major better than most, I observed close at hand the collapse into incoherence of the Tory party he tried to lead. He wanted, as Tony Blair has attempted to do since, to make Britain more relaxed and confident about its relationship with Europe. But he was leading a party of zealots, and the task proved impossible. He was a natural pragmatist leading a party which had grown used to the ideological certainties of Thatcherism; and, with his lack of colour and style, not to mention of 'the vision thing', he was a disappointment to a Fleet Street which had grown accustomed to his predecessor's hand-bagging certainties. Once the papers sensed, after 'Black Wednesday' in September 1992, that the Tories had lost their reputation for economic competence and that the country was ready for a change, Major was pretty well doomed: in an age of media-dominated politics he did not have the allies in Fleet Street on which most Tory Prime Ministers had been able to rely.

No Conservative leader has sat comfortably at the pinnacle of the party since Thatcher's departure. Egged on by Fleet Street and encouraged by the lady's habit of finding her successors insufficiently attentive to keeping burning the pure flame of Thatcherism, there has usually been a bunch of conspirators behind the arras with an alternative candidate in mind. Usually that candidate has been Michael Portillo. Add to that the normal round of tensions between Prime Minister and Chancellor – a tension even more visible under New Labour – and it was not surprising that Major's premiership was such a tortured one.

Sometimes I gained a particular insight into the difficulties he faced as a leader, as I did at the Bournemouth party conference in 1994 when he was having to tackle the new threat posed by Tony Blair's arrival as opposition leader. Major's natural instincts were those of the moderate, leftish Tory. Many in his party – among them Portillo, who published a pamphlet under the title – wanted to establish more 'Clear Blue Water' between them and a moderate-led Labour party by moving to the right.

I went round to the annexe of the Highcliffe Hotel where the Prime Minister's support staff were quartered. I had arranged to do an interview about speech-writing for Prime Ministers with the amiable Sir Ronnie Millar, one of Lady Thatcher's key word-smiths who had stayed on in John Major's team. Bumping into Major himself, I seized the opportunity for a background chat on his strategy. He said that he was a One Nation Tory and that he was sticking to the centre ground. There would be no lurch to the right, and he would not let the Tories become an anti-Europe party. There was quite enough difference between the parties, he argued, where they already stood.

Using the 'friends of the Prime Minister are saying' formula, I relayed all of this live on the *One O'Clock News* an hour or so later. I was hardly off air before I received a phone call from Sarah Hogg, head of Major's policy unit. They were quite happy with my interpretation, she said, but in one answer I had given the impression that Mr Major was trying to fight the right. The real message was that he was not backing either the left or the right, but felt that there was plenty in the present programme to keep the right happy. Clearly somebody weighty from that end of the party had been complaining already.

My tape recorder had developed a glitch and I had to go back two days later to re-interview the patient Ronnie Millar. This time I bumped into Major's political secretary Jonathan Hill. I asked him for the leadership's verdict on Michael Portillo's conference performance, and was told that they were 'relaxed and happy' to have both him and Michael Heseltine – the balance thing again – bringing the conference to life.

'But perhaps Portillo might be wise to stop listening so much to his fan club and to take his foot off the accelerator,' added Jonathan. I had my line for lunchtime again, and blessed my faulty tape recorder. It was ironic that William Hague, despite having dispensed with the balancing factor – and with Ken Clarke and Michael Heseltine – by staging a party ballot to win backing for his sceptical line on the single European currency, suffered just as badly in his time from the machinations of the Portillistas, as the fan club became known.

Portillo was at it again the next year with a furiously Eurosceptic speech to the party conference, insisting that if Europe were to develop its own army the European Commission would spend its time standardizing cap badges and sending half the forces on paternity leave. This time, however, Major's people told me it was 'harmless ribbing' and Portillo was considered 'very much back in the team'! But once one minister got away with that kind of thing, others were bound to try. Peter Lilley won himself some conference cheers by listing three things on which John Major had opposed the Brussels line.

'I like a Prime Minister who says no, no, no,' declared Lilley, subtly harking back to the 'No, no, no' speech on Europe that had helped to bring down Lady Thatcher and signalling where he was pitching himself in the internal party debate.

I noted after a drink with the ever-courteous Portillo as far back as February 1995 that underlying his conversation there was a rather chilling certainty that his arrival in the party leadership was only a matter of time. He imparted an air of having been clapped on the shoulder from on high and charged with a mission. Cocking his head slightly on one side in that way he has, smiling his full-lipped smile without fully engaging the eyes, he confessed as we talked that the previous May he had quite deliberately tested the Cabinet deal on the single currency (the idea that they were not to have a line on it at all) by making clear his opposition to the euro. He reckoned that as Ken Clarke was making no secret of his belief in the euro, he was entitled to put a counter-case. 'Number Ten came down on me like a ton of bricks,' he complained, clearly feeling that the same had not applied to Clarke.

In those days, of course, Portillo was still Thatcher's anointed, confident of her support for the succession, and he was content then to bide his time. 'Younger men', said Portillo, were not in a hurry to rush to lead the party in its present parlous state, whereas 'older men [like Heseltine and Clarke] might be'. He could see, as we all could, that the essential contract between the Tory leadership and its MPs was breaking down. When the government lost a key vote on fuel VAT in December 1994, suffering a huge blow to its authority, MPs began despairing of the party's fortunes and doing things off their own bat. The more they did so, the weaker the party looked. As party leader in such circumstances you could placate, trying to pull the factions together; or you could offer firm leadership and defy the critics to bring you down. Major oscillated between the two courses, trying too often to be all things to all men, and Portillo, later to become an advocate of a more inclusive Conservatism, was then critical of his leader's style. 'You can't solve problems by bisecting the angle,' he told me at that time.

Portillo had a point. Nowhere was Major's precarious balancing act more apparent than over Europe. He tried to reason with his party, telling a Tory conference in 1993 that 'Britain's hard economic interest depends upon having influence in Europe, on winning arguments in Europe, on building alliances in a Europe we can live with and be comfortable with. You cannot build such a Europe if you denounce it daily, misrepresent it hourly and poke suspiciously at it by the minute.' But, egged on by much of Fleet Street and accustomed over a long period to Lady Thatcher's strident tones, that was exactly what the majority of his party wanted to do.

Curiously, as Michael Portillo once pointed out to me, John Major was in some ways bolder than Lady Thatcher, who never felt obliged to be consistent in applying her ideology. She was, for example, loath to let the market rule so far as to tamper with the mortgage interest tax relief so beloved of the Tory-voting middle classes. For the Portillo of those days, before his own mid-life political crisis moderated some of his views, Major's problem was that he did not have a coherent ideology or the capacity to express things in ideological terms. But Major was not afraid to tackle mortgage tax relief; and he was prepared, too, to take on the denationalization of British Rail, which had proved a privatization too far for Thatcher. I suspect he may now regret his declaration to a Downing Street press conference in January 1995.

'Frankly, I'm not content with the service we've had over many years from British Rail,' he insisted. 'I want to remove British Rail for good from the stand-up comedian's jokebook and to turn them into the envy of the world.' Sadly, the piecemeal privatization that was pushed through in such a hurry in the latter days of the Conservative government left Britain with a shambolic and seemingly dangerous railway system which is today a national badge of shame.

Rail privatization, I suspect, had its psychological roots in John Major's desire to outdo his carping predecessor. He was always looking, consciously or unconsciously, for some 'Big Idea' to measure against Thatcher's pioneering of popular capitalism, with council house sales and privatizations. This goad affected his policies and his tactical decisions. From the notes I made of private and public conversations at the time, I have a clear picture of how much her behaviour affected him.

On 7 October 1992 I wrote: 'At a late night Jeffrey Archer party, as Norman Tebbit and Ken Clarke were almost coming to blows over Europe in the room next door, I asked the PM about Thatcher's intervention. Looking edgy and beleaguered he said: "It isn't just this week. I've had it every week for two years." He insisted with great force that he would get the Maastricht Bill through "and so defeat *her*".'

On another occasion in his study in Downing Street he told me angrily that what he really resented was being accused by her and her acolytes of lacking political courage when in fact his life would have been so much easier if he had relented a little in the battle against inflation and, as he put it, 'donned a Union Jack vest on Europe'.

Thatcher was never a great believer in the correct behaviour for an ex-party leader, once defined by the ex-naval man Jim

Callaghan as 'Never enter the wheel-house and don't spit on the deck.' Given her dominance in British politics for so long, it was not surprising that she should have resented the way in which her party had ejected her. Once freed from the constraints of office, constraints which tied her rather less than some even when she was there, she could rarely resist expressing her opinion on how things ought to be done. And even when she tries to help Tory leaders, she does not always have the desired effect.

She marched into the 2001 election campaign to support William Hague, of whose Euroscepticism she heartily approves. But when she strode on stage in Portsmouth in that trademark electric blue suit, I had a feeling that the party hierarchy ought to heed the instructions they used to put on fireworks in my childhood: 'Light blue touch paper and retire swiftly.' Sure enough, Lady Thatcher went off script and right over the top: instead of backing the Hague line of keeping the pound for the lifetime of the next parliament, she insisted: 'I would *never* enter a single currency.' This single pronouncement shattered party unity and encouraged rebel Tory candidates to make the same insistence in their election material.

She rarely even tried to be as helpful to John Major, whom she rapidly came to regard as soft on Europe. But there were occasions when she did. On 14 June 1993 I was in the Members' Lobby talking to a government whip when Jeffrey Archer dashed in and told me that Lady Thatcher had just declared in front of two witnesses in the Lords that John Major was the Tory party's best hope for the next election and that the party must rally behind him. Chopping and changing leaders, she had said, would achieve nothing. She wanted Number Ten to know that she was taking that line, she had told Jeffrey, and he had duly rung Major's private secretary Alex Allan in his Downing Street office to pass on the glad tidings.

This was obviously a good story, but if I was going to go hard with it on the *Nine O'Clock News* I needed a second source. In a quick ring round I managed to get hold of Sir Tim Bell, Thatcher's favourite PR guru. He confirmed that he had heard Lady Thatcher say exactly the same thing in his company over dinner. He added that she was highly alarmed at the virulence of Fleet Street attacks on John Major, which she regarded as an interference with democracy and which she was determined to frustrate. Even the 'great news editor', as she was sometimes called, had had enough of Fleet Street for a while.

That was enough for me to go with the story. But as I probed the Thatcherites further that night and afterwards, it turned out that her intervention was less of a selfless action than first depicted. What Lady Thatcher really wanted to ensure, said some of her trusties, was that Major was not so weakened that he was pushed out of the leadership, because she was worried at that time that the party might choose as his successor the pro-European Kenneth Clarke, one of those who had insisted she had to go. In those days the Thatcherites did not want a contest before they could be sure that Michael Portillo could win it.

The break between Thatcher and Major had all the predictability and inevitability of Greek tragedy. She thought she had moulded him in her image, but he had never been quite what she thought him. He was a genuine Conservative, but at core he was always too much of a One Nation man for her.

One key relationship which fractured publicly was that between John Major and his first Chancellor Norman Lamont, the man who had in 1990 proposed Major for the Tory leadership and run his campaign but who later derided him as a weak leader, famously declaring in his resignation speech after being dumped from the Treasury that under Major the Tories were 'in office but not in power'. Seeing both men regularly, I had a privileged front-row seat as the relationship cracked, split and finally sundered. With both of them now out of full-time front-line politics, I feel free to record the process: it gives a picture not only of the demise of a close political relationship but also of the kind of insights which make the job of a political editor so intriguing.

Lamont, a sociable man but somehow never a true political heavyweight, was the Chancellor who was forced to send interest rates soaring during the crisis of Britain's being forced out of the exchange rate mechanism of the European Monetary System in September 1992. Many in his party felt he should have left the Treasury sooner than he did; Lamont felt bitter that he was removed at all, even though it was nearly a year later.

On 8 October 1992 I noted in my journal that the pasty-faced Chancellor would be heading for a bad press in the morning after his lacklustre party conference speech. After a late-night party in the conference hotel I wrote:

> Norman, who had had a glass or two of Krug too many, says vehemently that he and John Major are closer than they have ever been.
>
> 'All differences of approach, any minor policy disagreements, are forgotten,' he declared. 'I will never be another David Mellor to him but I will be ringing him up long after all this is over. We are going to come through and prove them all wrong.'

Brave words, which were to develop a hollow ring.

On 24 November I noted after a lunch with Norman that he had been very self-centred and that our conversation had been 'the usual bland fencing'. My notes went on, 'He says he believes John Major wants him to carry on and that they have been "forged together in adversity". Norman says he told the Prime Minister after the election that he shouldn't feel under any obligation to keep him in post and to let him go when it felt right.'

In fact, some senior Tories had been surprised that Major had kept Lamont as Chancellor for as long as he had. One insider told me that it was only a sense of insecurity about their mobile phones (the Tory high command believed that the *News of the World* had been intercepting calls from their leader's battle-bus as he campaigned around the country) which had averted a furious row between Lamont and Major during the 1992 election. At one point Major pledged to cut taxes year by year, carefully framing the pledge so that it could be done by tax allowances, enabling the government in a bad year to maintain the promise without losing as much revenue as it would by a 1 per cent cut in the standard rate of income tax. At a different venue, Lamont, told about this, publicly threw cold water on the idea.

'When he heard about this, Major was incandescent with rage,' my source told me. 'He was all for ringing Norman and threatening to sack him on the spot if he did not fall into line. Jonathan Hill, his political secretary, had to physically restrain him from lifting the phone.'

Through the winter the demands for Lamont to go grew, both on the Tory back benches and in the media. MPs complained that Major was being too loyal to him, and the Chancellor himself grew jumpy. I noted on 2 February 1993 that when I had rung the Treasury spokesman with a query about interest rates and monetary policy, the response had come not from the press office but in the form of a personal call from the Chancellor, anxious to set out the background.

On 5 March I had a talk with a clearly frustrated Major, who complained to me of what he called one great problem. 'No-one, not the City, not the CBI, not the media, will publicly call an end to recession for fear of it being another false dawn.'

This had to be a reference to Lamont's premature declaration, two years before, that he could see the 'green shoots of recovery'.

'Somebody is going to have to stick their neck out and say it,' Major continued. 'Unless we build confidence in the economy we won't come out of the recession.'

It was hardly a ringing vote of confidence in his Chancellor, and at lunch three days later Kenneth Clarke, who was then Home Secretary and later to become Lamont's successor at the Treasury, argued that Lamont should be moved, although he felt Norman should stay on in the Cabinet. 'He's been taking the flak for us all,' he said.

On 10 May I was invited into Number Ten for an off-the-record talk with a weary-looking, somewhat dispirited Major. It was the first time I had been in his private flat, where I noted a nice Sisley painting and commemorative cricket plates on the mantelpiece. Pride of place was given to one depicting the achievements of the New Zealander Sir Richard Hadlee.

Major inveighed against Margaret Thatcher and her 'court in exile' for all the trouble they were causing him, even appearing on rebel platforms the night before local government elections. He would not be drawn on the question of a reshuffle but, significantly, agreed that Norman Lamont was unwise to have made his 'Je ne regrette rien' remark at the Newbury by-election. Nor, when I trailed the subject deliberately, did he say that all the hoo-ha about Lamont was unfair. After this conversation I had no doubt, though the Prime Minister had said nothing directly, that Norman would be leaving the Treasury, and this certainty coloured my reporting from then on.

Major invited me to stay on for supper that night. In the confessional mood he was in, I would dearly have loved to have done so; but, with commitments to the *Nine O'Clock News*, *The World Tonight* and the next morning's *Today* programme, I could not. Before I left, though, I enquired if there would be any post-Maastricht peace offering in terms of a job in the reshuffle for a prominent Eurosceptic. The response was emphatic – a tightening of the lips, a sucking in of those pale cheeks and a clear declaration.

'I'm not giving any jobs to people who've been voting consistently against the government.' Major was not one to forgive or to forget.

At times, I believe, he became dangerously isolated. Norma often preferred to stay in the country; and, although he bred loyalty in many who served him, he could be bad-tempered and was not always good at keeping relationships going. Few could have served him more faithfully than his press secretary Gus O'Donnell. But after Gus went back to the Treasury, Major failed to contact him for months. He fell out, too, with Richard Ryder, the chief whip who saw him through many a parliamentary trauma. On occasion John Major's prickliness even upset the equable Douglas Hurd, who muttered about his selfishness.

In the summer reshuffle in 1993 Lamont was told he was leaving the Treasury, but was offered the chance to become Secretary of State for the Environment. He turned it down and quit the Cabinet, taking his sacking bitterly. He felt that Major had allowed himself to be hounded by the media into getting rid of him; I was more inclined to take the view, held by Norman Fowler and others, that Major had kept Lamont too long at the

Treasury for the good of his own and the Cabinet's reputation. Fleet Street had long been determined to get their man, and the constant sniping at Lamont harmed the rest of the team. Major's loyalty may not have lasted indefinitely, but he paid a price for letting it last as long as he did. The Prime Minister had, however, made one silly tactical mistake: Lamont was especially bitter because he was the only person to leave the Cabinet in the re-shuffle. Ex-Chancellor and Prime Minister did not exchange the usual letters on his departure; Lamont replied with a curt fax. As I told viewers at the time, the only surprise was that he didn't wrap his missive round a brick and hurl it through next door's window.

For me, Lamont's departure and the bitterness he displayed subsequently epitomized the problem of all those Tory years in office. There were too many discontented, discarded ministers who had nothing to lose by breaking ranks. Early in 1993 I counted fifty-nine ex-ministers sitting on the Tory back benches. A long time in office is not an aid to party management. There are too few left before whom you can dangle the carrot of prefer-ment as an inducement to good behaviour.

At another Lamont lunch in November, just before Ken Clarke's first Budget, it became clear that any pretence of linger-ing affection for the Prime Minister had gone.

'How could he act like that in panic when we'd been two and a half years in the bunker together?' Lamont complained. He told me that he had refused to go to a Number Ten dinner for the retiring governor of the Bank of England 'because I want absolutely nothing to do with Major'.

I noted after this lunch that Lamont was still obsessed by his sacking – a condition with which I was later to have rather more personal sympathy.

*

Thatcher was strong enough to defy Fleet Street when she wanted to, although she did not make the attempt too often. When John Major tried to cling on to ministers like Lamont whom Fleet Street had determined had either passed their sell-by dates or offended middle-class morality, he had neither Thatcher's personal authority nor her solid parliamentary majorities to sustain him; and he tried too often to be her, instead of himself. It was, I believe, his complex about Thatcher and his eagerness to please Fleet Street in the way she had done that led Major into the crucial error of his 'Back to Basics' campaign.

The increasingly powerful media were demanding that he, like Margaret Thatcher, should have a 'Big Idea'; and so, at his party conference in 1993, he gave them 'Back to Basics'. Major regarded this as a call for a return to old standards, such as the traditional teaching of reading and writing in schools. He did make a small obeisance to the hanging and flogging sector of his party too, saying that punishment was an idea which 'remained in his dictionary'. But to him, the campaign was all about education, community values and courteous behaviour to the old. It was the moral majoritarians in his party who turned his appeal into something else altogether. Tory spin doctors like the spokesman Tim Collins, later to become an MP and one of William Hague's key opinion-formers, briefed journalists that it was a call for a 'get tough' moralism, a strike-back against the permissive society which would become a cornerstone of Tory policies.

The result was inevitable. Back to Basics became a kind of hunting licence for newspapers to probe the private lives and business conduct of Tory MPs, some of whom were inevitably found wanting. Sleaze was added to division to make the Tories unelectable. From then on, sin scored doubly against the

Tories. Every Tory parliamentarian who was caught with his trousers down or his fingers on a cheque caused not just the usual amount of embarrassment to his party; he was held up to public gaze as an example of the hypocrisy of a party which was preaching old-fashioned moral virtues.

'We're not in preaching mode. We do want to see high values, but I am not in the business of individual witch-hunts for individual transgressions,' Major insisted. But it was too late: this was not how Fleet Street wanted to see it. And John Smith had great fun with the whole idea. Tory MPs' interpretation of Back to Basics, he suggested, was 'Back to my place.'

By January 1994 frontbencher Tim Yeo was in trouble over an affair and his fathering of a child outside his marriage; the eccentric Tory MP David Ashby confessed to having shared a bed with a male friend; the Tory peer Lord Caithness, who had been conducting an affair, later resigned his frontbench position after his wife shot herself. A month later there was the tragic case of Stephen Milligan, who accidentally killed himself in the course of an erotic experiment. There was probably no more immorality around overall than there had been in the previous twenty years, but Major's Back to Basics programme had given Fleet Street a theme song to link all such episodes together and confer on them an added political importance. It all added to the frenetic atmosphere in the Conservative party and to a sense of decaying standards in a party which had been in office too long.

The wisest words I heard at the time were those of Tory chief whip Richard Ryder. 'Never have an affair with anyone who has less to lose by its disclosure than you do,' he advised MPs. And I warmed to Lena Jeger, who told the Labour whips in the Lords: 'Don't worry, dears, all the people I have slept with are dead.'

Far, far worse to my mind than the sexual peccadilloes of

various politicians which came to light during the Back to Basics period were the revelations around the same period about Tory MPs who had taken cash for asking parliamentary questions. These exposed the murky and increasingly sordid area of parliamentary lobbying and of MPs' 'consultancy' relationships with commercial interests outside the Commons. As someone who had boasted for years when abroad that we had the cleanest politics in the world, it made me sick to my stomach that a few money-grubbing bad apples succeeded in tainting the whole box. MPs were too slow to discipline themselves, and I do not believe that we should any longer leave the task of doing so to pretentiously titled parliamentary committees. It was during this period that politicians sank to a new low in the eyes of the public; and it is no coincidence, I feel, that since then we have seen such pitifully low turnouts in a whole series of elections.

Coping with sleaze, especially the kind involving MPs' private lives, used to send shudders through the BBC hierarchy. Poor Stephen Milligan, for example, had worked for the BBC before becoming an MP, and his death in a sexual experiment involving women's tights, partial strangulation and an orange caused an especial fluttering of fans and inhalation of smelling salts along the managerial corridors. I remember the details only too well, because a minute before going on air to discuss his demise on the *Today* programme I was still locked in a conference call with two BBC executives urgently debating whether we could mention the tights or the orange in our broadcasts. I said we would look ridiculous if we did not. People would have all the lurid details spread out in the newspapers on their breakfast tables; we could hardly pretend in our discussions that nothing had happened. I listened to the advice from on high, ignored the detail and advised my fellow correspondents to use their common sense

On the *Sunday Express*: checking every word before John Junor did. *Sunday Express*

The *Daily Mail* newsroom during the 1983 election: you could beat hell out of those old typewriters.

RIGHT: Carolyn, my beautiful bride, after our wedding in 1966. I tried to tell her what she was letting herself in for, but luckily she didn't believe me . . .

BELOW: The team on *Now!* magazine. It didn't last long but it boosted low Fleet Street salaries.

LEFT: With Margaret Thatcher in Christmas party mood on her RAF VC-10 in December 1984, and my note of thanks from the lady herself for the cabaret laid on by the media.

A marvellous return journey – especially from Washington when we were all able to relax – thanks to the Press "concert-party"

Margaret Thatcher
5/1/85

BELOW: Interviewing Thatcher as Prime Minister in Downing Street. You always had to be careful which button to press.

© Times Newspapers Ltd/Graham Wood

LEFT AND BELOW: Before and after the war against Saddam Hussein. With John Major in Saudi Arabia before the war and in Kuwait afterwards.

BELOW: A front row seat for John Major's extraordinary gamble in the Downing Street garden, resigning his party leadership and inviting all-comers to challenge him for it.

News International

ABOVE: Out in the open: interviewing John Major in South Africa in 1996.

At the Khyber Pass in 1992 with my friendly rivals Michael Brunson of ITN and Judith Dawson of Sky News.

RIGHT: With Czech President Vaclav Havel in Prague in 1990. Politicians, he said, should remember to look out of the aeroplane windows to remind themselves how others lived.

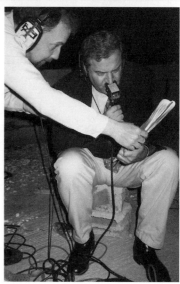

ABOVE: With Chris Patten in Government House in Hong Kong, shortly before the Chinese takeover in 1997.

RIGHT: The rougher end of the trade: late-night reporting by torchlight for BBC Radio in 1997. We were on the roof of an unfinished building in the Gaza Strip.

The free show on College Green opposite the Palace of Westminster as the Tory leadership contest was fought out in 1995. I am awaiting my turn with presenter Edward Stourton after John Redwood has been interviewed. © *The Independent/David Rose*

ABOVE LEFT: With John Cole, my predecessor as BBC political editor. The BBC chose not to do any joint publicity shots of me with my successor, Andrew Marr.
Atlantic Syndication Partners

ABOVE RIGHT: A scoop for the BBC. Emma Nicholson tells me she is to defect from the Tory party to the Liberal Democrats. *BBC Worldwide Ltd*

RIGHT: In action at an election press conference in 1997 with Peter Mandelson, prince of spin doctors, in the background. © *The Independent/David Rose*

Out with the horses on Lambourn Downs – the other side of my journalistic life. *George Selwyn*

Forty winks in the Kremlin, Moscow, 1992. As a travelling reporter you snatch your sleep where you can. I always remembered Harold Wilson's advice that ten minutes during the day is worth an hour at night.

With my wife Carolyn, my daughter Annabel and son Alex. They haven't seen too much of me over the years . . .

and basic good taste, promising that I would take any flak that came. None did.

The BBC in my time was blessed with some brilliant programme editors, particularly on the *Nine O'Clock News*. Most of them were clear, decisive and yet open-minded when you had suggestions to make in a changing situation. The problems came only when you had to deal with further layers: executive calls in moments of crisis were the bane of my life at the BBC, usually coming just when you needed to concentrate on what you were going to say in a live broadcast or what questions you were going to ask a politician who had just resigned. You could tell by the tone as soon as a managerial figure came on the line: it was a call to cover himself for the post-mortem the next day. He was preparing his get-out: 'Well, I took this up with the political editor and his advice was . . .' Giving the advice I did not mind; that was part of what they paid me for, after all. But the waste of time I did resent.

The most dramatic episode of the Major years was of course his 'put up or shut up' challenge to his party when, in an attempt to stop the in-fighting, he resigned his party leadership and invited all-comers to take him on in the ensuing contest to win it back. It was an episode over which, unwittingly, I came close to the biggest scoop of my life. On 16 June 1995 I was interviewing the Prime Minister at a G7 economic summit in Halifax, Nova Scotia, for Radio Four's *Today* programme. After taking him through a range of G7 issues like reform of world financial institutions, Bosnia and AIDS, I turned to the state of the Tory party to see what I could rouse him to say about the rebels who were making his life such a misery.

Was there now, I asked him, a greater threat to his leadership than there had ever been? He deflected this by saying that he had lived with such stories for five years and was not going to deviate from his long-term aims. What about Lady Thatcher's criticisms that he was not a proper Conservative? He wouldn't be drawn. What about the humiliating criticisms to his face from the Eurosceptics, the attempts by his 1922 Committee backbenchers to tell him what his policies should be? Didn't he want to tell them all to go to hell? With an obvious effort, he remained dead-pan, saying that he had come into politics to do things he believed in, not for an easy life.

By now, similar questions would have had many a politician telling *me* to go to hell; but John Major remained polite. I tried a few more in the same vein, to no avail. The final exchange went like this:

OAKLEY: *With all the speculation that is going on, all the stories that run, hasn't it got to the stage where you would actually welcome a challenge to your leadership of the Tory party and be willing to take on your critics and beat them off?*

MAJOR: *Well, there is a procedure there. If anybody wishes to challenge the leader of the Conservative Party there is a constitutional procedure for doing so and if anyone chooses to do so that is their constitutional right. We will wait and see whether they do.*

OAKLEY: *Would you like them to?*

MAJOR: *We will wait and see.*

I noticed that on the first of those questions he appeared to be picking his words with particular care, and before he responded to the follow-up there was a significant pause and a rather direct look.

On the flight back from Canada, I learned later, John Major

told Douglas Hurd, the Foreign Secretary, and Kenneth Clarke, the Chancellor, that the situation was untenable and that he faced three choices. He could resign and go; he could tough it out until a probable leadership challenge in the autumn; or he could spring a surprise by resigning and contesting the ensuing election. The third option, he told them, was the one that he favoured.

We arrived back at RAF Alconbury at 2.00 a.m. on 18 June. That afternoon, walking in his garden, John Major finally decided to go for it. He held up the announcement until Thursday afternoon, after the second Prime Minister's Questions of the week, when the lobby were summoned, most unusually, to Downing Street; and not just to the press secretary's room, where the lobby briefings were held in those days, but to the rose garden. Again unusually, our mobile phones were confiscated from us as we entered.

We were deliberately kept waiting for around half an hour by the shrewd press secretary Chris Meyer, later the British ambassador in Washington, to build up the suspense. But at one point the surprise was nearly ruined. Gordon Greig, the *Daily Mail* political editor, who was always ready for a laugh, decided typically to liven up the tedium of waiting and strolled over to the wooden lectern that had been placed on the lawn. I think he was planning a mock announcement of his own. But before officials dashed up to stop him seeing any more, he read aloud the first sentence of the prepared text which he found lying there: 'Let me just make a brief statement to you. I have been deeply involved in politics since I was sixteen . . .'

Such a broad brush opening offered a clue as to what might be coming, and immediately a buzz of frantic speculation began: Had Major had enough? Was he quitting to hand over his job to somebody else? Was he ill? Had there been another scandal? We did not have to wait much longer before the Prime Minister put us out of our misery by walking down the steps to the trilling of a blackbird and making what must have been quite the most remarkable announcement ever made to the media in the Downing Street garden.

John Major confirmed that he had submitted his resignation – but not as Prime Minister. He was quitting as Tory leader to stage an election for the post in which he would be a candidate, so putting both his positions on the line.

So the honest answer to both my questions in Halifax would have been yes; he would welcome a challenge and he was ready to take it up. Later, after the leadership contest was over, I asked him if he had been tempted to answer me then.

'For a moment, yes,' he replied. 'Though only for a moment.' But since he had been spurred on to reveal his thinking to Douglas Hurd and Kenneth Clarke, I had at least accelerated the process.

John Major could be very tense, especially before an interview began. But on the day of his resignation, when I questioned him about his extraordinary statement and challenge, he was cheerful and almost serene, as relaxed as I ever found him on camera. He had taken a huge gamble; but what made him so calm, I think, was the feeling that his future would be resolved one way or the other.

The contest itself, a leadership election involving a sitting Prime Minister, was an extraordinary event. On that day, when he'd invited his critics, in effect, to 'put up or shut up', I reported that the Prime Minister had been destabilized by three things: Lady Thatcher's criticism that he was not a proper Conservative (i.e. not Thatcherite enough for her liking); the bruising criticism he had faced from Eurosceptics at a meeting with the right-wing

Fresh Start group; and the opinion polls showing the party at record lows, which had sown panic among his backbenchers. Some Tory MPs were calling his move a brave one which had given him momentum and the likelihood of victory; but if too many of their colleagues voted against Major or abstained, then his authority would be destroyed and he would have to stand down and open up the second round of the contest to the Cabinet.

'Lack of support from fifty long-term critics would surprise no-one. If it climbs from that to close on a hundred he's in trouble,' I told viewers, making the then common assumption that Major would be faced only by a stalking-horse candidate. After a few days of speculation that former Chancellor Norman Lamont might take him on, a challenger did emerge in the shape of the right-wing Welsh secretary John Redwood, former head of Margaret Thatcher's Policy Unit. Having a former member of his Cabinet pitched against him obviously increased the likely total of anti-Major votes. Early on, the Major team used me to pass the message to the Redwood camp via my broadcasts that the challenger hadn't burned his boats in terms of his Cabinet place if he pulled back, but there was no wavering.

Redwood scored a first in resigning his post by carphone, but his campaign was nearly wrecked at the outset when the opening press conference was invaded by a motley band of self-invited Eurosceptics, including Teresa Gorman in a vivid green dress and Tony Marlow wearing a hideous, garishly striped cricket blazer. I was probably the only other person in the room who recognized it for what it was – an Old Wellingtonian blazer from the school at which Marlow and I had been contemporaries.

A good-tempered Redwood proceeded, to many people's surprise, to run an effective campaign on the theme of 'No

Change – No Chance', a slogan which was enthusiastically taken up by Fleet Street. It gave John a new political status and wrong-footed Michael Portillo as a hero of the right. Michael wrongly predicted to me at the time that John Major had made a misjudgement. He believed the Prime Minister would be fatally damaged and would be out within months, whatever the result of the contest. But it was Portillo himself who was badly damaged when it emerged amid his protestations of loyalty to the Prime Minister that over-eager Portillistas had installed a phone bank ready for his candidacy in the second-round contest they were expecting.

The Tory leadership contest became London's most intriguing free street theatre show. There was a permanent cluster of cameras on College Green opposite the Commons, with teams of correspondents in constant debate with every Tory who had ever wanted to get his or her face in front of a camera. Crowds gathered around as we interviewed MPs or were quizzed by presenters for the latest news. Oddball publicity seekers and pressure groups saw the possibilities and started parading with placards, insinuating themselves into the background of the shots. I suggested to BBC bosses that perhaps we had better have some security on hand before there was a major incident with somebody interrupting a live broadcast.

The next day I dashed out late from a press conference to do a live on the *One O'Clock News* following appearances by John Redwood and Jonathan Aitken. I was heading for the set when my way was barred by a rope barrier and a man with a shiny peaked cap pulled down over his nose.

'Where do you think you're going, sunshine?' he enquired.

'I'm going on the set to talk to the presenter.'

'Oh, no, you're not, sir, there is live television going on here.'

So much for the recognition factor! I only just made my slot on the news.

The challenge of the contest brought out the fighter in Major, who produced his best ever performance at Prime Minister's Questions in the Commons. John Redwood probably didn't do himself much good by responding that it was three years in government which mattered, not fifteen minutes in the Commons. One day during the contest Douglas Hurd, his legs dangling over the side of an armchair in his vast, imposing office in the Foreign Office, told me that the Prime Minister was normally one for taking briefs which he deployed effectively, but that sometimes he had a breakthrough in his own mind, suddenly perceiving a clear course of action ahead. He believed that Major had now had such a breakthrough on Europe and was arguing from conviction. 'When he was just accepting the arguments of others you felt he might change – but not now,' Hurd concluded.

His fellow Cabinet member David Hunt told me that Hurd had even drawn a laugh from the Cabinet at the start of the leadership contest. He greeted news of the Redwood challenge by reminding them that in Nigeria the President had just announced that he was faced by some Cabinet rebels, and they were to be executed.

As the battle wore on, I was told by one source close to the Prime Minister that John Major had set himself a target of between 210 and 220 votes as the number required for him to continue in the leadership. (In his memoirs he says he was aiming for 215, so my source wasn't bad.) Many Tory MPs I talked to would not specify when I asked what vote he needed to remain credible. 'We'll know it when we see it,' said some. But the consensus seemed to be that he would need at least 200 votes, and preferably something a bit above that, to be sure of being able to remain Prime Minister.

Much of Fleet Street, which wanted a stronger and more colourful personality in Number Ten, reckoned that Major would go down. However, having talked to many Tory MPs of the kind who do not push their faces into television, I found a greater reservoir of support for John Major than I had first expected, and I predicted over several days that he would secure enough votes to survive. In the event the voting was 218 for John Major, 89 for John Redwood, 8 abstentions and 12 spoiled ballots. With 109 MPs denying the Prime Minister their support it was hardly a glorious victory. He was, as I put it when quizzed on camera for an instant reaction, 'just about in the comfort zone'. There may even have been a moment of doubt in his own mind as to whether he had reached that.

Brian Mawhinney, one-time party chairman and a good friend of Major's, told me later of the scene as the Prime Minister heard the results. Also in the room were Norma Major, the trade secretary Ian Lang, Major's PPS John Ward and the Northern Ireland secretary Paddy Mayhew. John Ward took the results by phone, wrote them down in silence and passed the paper to Major. 'He stood looking at them for fully ten to fifteen seconds, then he handed the paper to Norma. "I think that's all right," he said.' Displays of emotion were not John Major's thing.

But while the election contest discharged some of the tension in the party, it did not resolve any policy questions. It also built up a further danger for Major. A Fleet Street which had seen its advice to the Tories to get rid of the leader ignored was not going to forgive either him or his party for taking such a liberty. In the modern world of intermingled media and politics, that was a pretty insuperable handicap.

Ironically, the reshuffle which followed the contest, and in which there was no job for John Redwood, brought into the

Cabinet to replace him as Welsh secretary one William Hague, before long to inherit the poisoned chalice of the Tory leadership. As soon as Michael Portillo was back in the Commons, Hague too was on the look-out for the installation of Portillo phone banks.

Back in February 1997 I asked John Major in the course of a chat in Downing Street what he would do about the leadership if the Tories lost the election as expected. He gave me what he called an 'academic' reply, setting out three choices. One, he could try to 'hang around' and 'not let the bastards have their way, towing the party off to ideological extremes'. Two, he could put himself at the service of the party and go at the moment which best suited Tory interests. He knew that some wanted him to stay for a clearly defined period so the Conservative party could see who performed well in opposition before choosing his successor. Or three, he could take the view that until the leadership question was determined there would be 'mayhem' and that therefore he should resign speedily, either standing again as a candidate himself or 'taking the view that he had had six and a half years in the job and there were other things to do in life'. I knew he had already told others that he favoured option three and, without saying so directly, he left me in little doubt that was his choice.

My relations with John Major, though subject to the usual story stresses, were on the whole amicable. I liked him – though, come to think of it, I liked most of those with whom I had dealings in politics, which probably makes me a bit of a sad case. He was one of the straightest politicians I dealt with over the years, and on occasion he could be truly charming. Once when we met at a party he picked up my wife Carolyn bodily and swung her round in a circle before the bemused gaze of a Fleet Street editor. Even Michael Portillo, with whom he had a pretty see-saw relationship, told me one day: 'He can really make the sun come out and send you out wanting to do anything for him.' Once, when we were about to start an interview in Number Twelve Downing Street, the chief whip's abode, John Major seized the microphone and began interviewing me as if he were the correspondent. I played ball, talking about the 'splits in the BBC' and the leaks we suffered from. It was pretty childish stuff on both sides, but we could both hardly keep our faces straight when the real interview began. You do need a bit of light relief sometimes.

Major could be a touch unworldly, as he showed Jeffrey Archer one day. Still in government at the time, he was resisting Archer's urgings that he should write his memoirs when he left Downing Street.

'But I can get you a contract for six hundred thousand and two researchers to help,' said Jeffrey.

'No,' said Major. 'It's not me.'

Jeffrey got the same reaction after the election. Then Norma was sent out house-hunting in London. She came back and reported that the house she wanted would cost £600,000.

'I don't want a great big house, only a little one,' said the ex-Prime Minister.

'But it's the small ones which cost six hundred thousand,' said Norma.

'OK, I'll do the book,' said Major. It was a good thing he did. Few prime ministerial memoirs have been so readable.

Major could also be pretty pithy and direct on occasion. After his election defeat I several times invited him to lunch or dinner, but although he once described me to Norma as 'that rare thing, a civilized journalist', he never came. In July

1997, however, after we met at a memorial service, I had a long talk with him in his Commons room – at that time a surprisingly sparse and amazingly impersonal place, with not a personal memento or a prime ministerly knick-knack in sight. What sticks in my mind is the vivid phrase he used when telling me he planned to make only a brief appearance on the first morning of the Tory conference that autumn.

'I am not', he told me, 'going to be a pain in the arse like my predecessor.'

The problem with William Hague's first shadow Cabinet, he felt then, was that there was nobody who inspired affection in the public, or whom people would be inclined to forgive for their mistakes – no Willie Whitelaw figure. Ken Clarke, he agreed, could have filled that role.

Major is the only Prime Minister to have threatened my life – and in front of witnesses. During the 1997 general election there was a series of stories about Tory figures who refused to toe the 'wait and see' party line on the single currency and who came out against it on principle. On 16 April John Major tried vainly to get the journalists at the daily Conservative press conference to concentrate on the party's chosen subject of the day, employment, chiding us for our lack of interest in the subject. The official transcript which follows gives an idea of the cut and thrust on these occasions:

OAKLEY: *I'm interested in the employment prospects of John Horam and Jim Paice [two Tory ministers] because we have been told that while backbenchers have the freedom to speak out, ministers who defied government policy would face the sack. These two ministers have now defied government policy on the single currency.*

MAJOR: *Two ministers, Robin, have issued statements indicating what they should have indicated, that they supported the 'negotiate and decide' policy, that they were foolish in not doing so, that they do now and that they accept collective responsibility. I think they were extremely unwise and said so earlier. I've nothing to add.*

OAKLEY: *But Prime Minister, is that not an act of cynicism? Are you not leading your party into this election on the basis of a policy of options open on a single currency, while being perfectly happy to have the large bulk of your party now representing itself as a party against a single currency . . .*

MAJOR: *. . . Well, I have to say . . .*

OAKLEY: *. . . and this explanation that ministers are allowed to give – they are allowed to say anything they like so long as at the end of it they say 'I believe in government policy'. If a candidate comes out and says that he's all for the slaughter of the first-born that's all right so long as he adds, 'I believe in government policy on post-natal care'?*

MAJOR: *Are you perhaps the first-born, Robin? [I nodded assent.] I mean, if you are, I'm prepared to give the policy serious consideration. And just to prove I really mean it, I'll write it out in my own handwriting . . .*

All good clean fun, and of course it enabled him to dodge the question. It reminded me of the moment during another interview, in the Cabinet Room in Downing Street, when he had taken down from the wall a splendid sword given to him by King Fahd of Saudi Arabia after the Gulf War and waved it reflectively above my head.

At the same press conference as the 'First-Born Question' (as my BBC colleagues kept referring to it), John Major made his extraordinary appeal to his party not to tie him down on the question of the single currency but to settle for the wait-and-see policy he called 'negotiate and decide'. (History does repeat itself. Labour, with much the same policy in office, insisted it was not 'wait and see' but 'prepare and decide'.) Going for entry immediately would be a wild gamble, said Major, and so would ruling it out for ever; Britain could be badly damaged by staying out of a single currency which worked. Then came that nakedly heartfelt appeal to his fractious party:

'Whether you agree with me or disagree with me, like me or loathe me – don't bind my hands when I am negotiating on behalf of the British nation.' It was the one truly electric moment of the whole campaign.

John Major, who has a fighter buried somewhere behind that bank manager's exterior, was probably better at elections than anything else he did.

11

UP CLOSE AND PERSONAL: TRAVELLING WITH PRIME MINISTERS

IF SOMEBODY HAD TOLD ME WHEN I WAS WORKING THOSE LONG hours at the *Liverpool Daily Post*, driving back late at night to the draughty flat Carolyn and I had on the Wirral, that my career would take me to more than fifty countries, I would probably have laughed at the idea. In those days a day trip to Manchester was an excitement. But through the BBC years I certainly clocked up the air miles in the media's inner circle which travelled with the Prime Minister.

Such travels are the exotic element in a political editor's job, but they are also very important. You have more close contact with a Prime Minister over a few days on these trips than you have in several months at home, and it is virtually the only time you have contact with some of the senior officials; so it gives you the chance to develop relationships of some sort. But you have to guard against letting your objectivity slip, to be wary of that tendency to identify with the travelling Prime Minister, as sometimes happens with the 'boys on the bus' in election campaigns. It is too easy to fall into the 'Didn't our man do well?' frame of mind.

Mind you, the intimacy does not always help political leaders. It was on one such trip abroad that my one-time *Daily Mail* colleague Gordon Greig – not Alastair Campbell, who has sometimes been credited with the discovery – noticed that the casually dressed John Major had his shirt tucked into his underpants, which were showing just above his trousers. He wrote about it, the cartoonist Steve Bell took up the theme and a generation of cartoons was born.

John Major, who regarded foreign travel as more of a duty than Margaret Thatcher, who had taken great pleasure in grandstanding her way around the world, developed her practice of taking cohorts of businessmen with him to help them with contract-sweetening contacts in foreign parts. The growing numbers suited the press corps: we found ourselves on chartered BA jumbos with room to stretch out, instead of being cooped up, knees under chin, in the back of the fun but cramped RAF VC-10s. There was more room, too, to chat when the Prime Minister and his advisers risked a foray into the press quarters.

My most vivid memory of travel with John Major is of the time we flew out to Saudi Arabia before the Gulf War to see the troops in the desert. It was early in his premiership, and shortly before we arrived he slipped into the seat next to mine for a brief chat. He looked pale, tense and strained, and I asked him quietly how he felt. Very daunted, he replied, at having to go out and tell young men why they must lay their lives on the line for his policies. There was no more daunting duty, he said, for a Prime Minister.

Later, as he walked out into the first group of squaddies and clambered aboard a Challenger tank to deliver his message, you could see the tension in his tight shoulders and awkward walk. But he addressed them with an unscripted, un-varnished sincerity. It was simple and straightforward, more headmaster's study than Henry the Fifth, but they responded warmly. You could actually watch the tensions, his and theirs, evaporate into the desert air. Soon the body language was altogether different, and by the third homily of the day he was confident and in control.

I flew back with him into Kuwait after the Gulf War, and was lucky to be one of the few reporters chosen to go in on the escort helicopter. With the oil rigs still burning from Saddam's sabo-tage, the sea was full of heavy black slicks and the air was dense with acrid, oily smoke. Peering over the pilot's shoulder, I could only marvel that he was taking us anywhere: the cockpit window was covered with a dark, greasy film that made it look as though we were flying through the night. In Kuwait City heavily armed troops in chequered headcloths still manned the foxholes, keep-ing a wary eye out for snipers. It was in some ways John Major's finest hour. Briefly the walk was almost a strut, and for a few weeks the opinion polls had him down as one of the most popular leaders in British history.

Major was the most courteous senior figure in politics with whom I had dealings, a genuinely nice man who always tried to answer your questions if he could. And he was a shrewder operator than he looked. On that first trip to the Gulf in January 1991, his initial overseas foray as Prime Minister, I remember his first stroll to the back of the aircraft to talk to those of us in the media party. He hesitated as to where to stop first. Three or four of us, including me, Elinor Goodman of Channel Four and George Jones of the *Telegraph*, caught each other's eyes. Each of us had imagined that we knew the new Prime Minister rather better than any other journalist, that we had something of a special line in Majors. At that moment we realized that an ambitious and able politician had made quite sure that he had cultivated a range of media contacts on the way up and knew us all equally well. Courteous, yes; but careful too.

I often interviewed John Major in the air on the way back from one foreign trip or another. His reaction was nearly always the same, almost a ritual. He would have a mutter as I arrived, recorder and microphone in hand, back in his quarters. He would tell me how tired he was and what a headache he had got, and ask if we really had to do it. When I quietly insisted, he would say: 'All right, give me a moment.' He would put his head in his hands for thirty seconds to concentrate, and then signal his readiness. Sometimes when I finished he would complain, 'You were very aggressive with me today,' but when I was, I was doing him a favour. He always responded best when you pepped him up. With John Major, soft questions produced soft replies.

What always intrigued me was how much more passionate he was when he began talking about Northern Ireland. If we were sitting on the bed in his quarters on the plane, he would thump it so hard in his responses that I had to pick up the recorder. And once his passion on the subject brought me something of a coup.

It was a curious sequence of events. In February 1996 we were in Bangkok, Thailand, at a Europe–Asia summit, and for the official dinner Major and the other leaders had all politely donned the silk shirts they had been given by their Thai host. Major looked a wally in his black silk shirt and knew it, but he looked a great deal better than German Chancellor Helmut Kohl, who resembled a walking magenta tent in his – and one could see why: I had manoeuvred my way to sit at a terrace table close by to the two of them as they waited for their bilateral talks with Chinese premier Li Peng, and as I watched the waiter brought a beer for John Major and a huge plate of cream, cake and ice-cream for Kohl. And that was after the official dinner.

Eventually, after the Li Peng meeting, John Major came to do a press briefing for the British media, who had been smuggled in via the kitchen because the authorities were restricting access. He talked on the record for the newspapers but, self-conscious in his shirt, refused to do anything in front of a camera. This left us badly disadvantaged. Michael Brunson of ITN and I argued that it was unfair but, sensibly for him, he was adamant. On the way out of the hotel later, though, Major was ambushed by the Hong Kong media and did speak to them on camera. I had a furious row about this with the new press secretary Jonathan Haslam, and he promised to keep trying to get me an interview if I came along to the embassy. Everybody else had given up, but I hung around for an hour or two. In that time John Major was faxed a copy of a very negative letter from the IRA appearing to wreck the hopes of a peace deal in Northern Ireland. Blazing with anger in a way I had never seen him, a dog-tired Major agreed to be interviewed by a dog-tired correspondent in what was now the early hours of the morning local time.

Even now, with much water having flowed since under Northern Ireland bridges, his words have the raw edge that struck so many so forcibly at the time, coming as they did from a normally passionless and reasoned Prime Minister. When I asked him what he thought of the IRA's response to the latest call for a ceasefire, blaming the government for the breakdown in the peace process, this is what he said:

> It seems, frankly, like a rather sick joke. For the last twenty-five years the IRA have murdered people, they have bombed people, they have knee-capped people. They have dealt with people in a quite disgusting

and disgraceful way. For them to claim that anybody is responsible for what has happened over the last twenty-five years except them will be received with incredulity by anyone who knows anything about Northern Ireland. People will be fed up to the back teeth with these comments of the sort we get so repeatedly from the IRA. It's time for them to realize that for twenty-five years they have behaved in an appalling fashion. Nobody is going to give way to them. Not now. Not in the future. Not ever. They either decide to behave properly and get into democracy or democracy will go on without them. The sort of nonsense we had from them this evening is a pathetic response to the hopes and dreams of the people of Northern Ireland.

I had agreed that if I got an interview with Major I would talk to him on a 'pool' basis, that is, I would make the text available to other broadcasters too; and back at the conference centre I duly gave a copy to the ITN office. But at that hour Michael Brunson could not be roused from his slumbers. My anger and perseverance, and the Prime Minister's fury at the IRA, combined to give the *Nine O'Clock News* and a range of other BBC programmes a significant scoop. It was, I think, the longest soundbite we ever used from him in a news clip.

What I never confessed to John Major is why he never got the drink he had ordered while in his meeting with Li Peng that night. A bemused-looking waiter appeared with one beer on a silver salver. He stopped amid the waiting press in the room outside and asked who it was for. It was a long and sticky night. I was nearest, and there was only one possible answer. Sorry, John.

One time I did feel guilty towards John Major was when we visited Soweto in South Africa in September 1994. The cricket-loving Prime Minister donated some sports aid to local youngsters and was encouraged to have a go in the nets. In a photo-opportunity no-one could have contrived he had just bowled the South African sports minister first ball, middle stump, and was clearly flushed with success when I appeared and thrust a camera into his face. I asked him what he thought of people who criticized efforts by governments to push commercial organizations to invest in countries like South Africa. He responded sharply. What I had not told him was that it was a certain Margaret Thatcher who had made the initial criticism.

I found it particularly intriguing how much more candid politicians at that level can be when they are away from home. We were chatting in the ambassador's garden in Tokyo at a G8 summit when I asked John Major if he could not have made life much easier for himself if he had chosen to sack David Mellor from his Cabinet much earlier than he did.

'I couldn't have sacked him just for sleeping with somebody who wasn't his wife,' he confessed. 'On that basis, half my Cabinet would have had to go.'

I travelled with John Major to Kennebunkport, where he visited George Bush Senior and was greeted by Barbara Bush wearing non-matching sneakers. I travelled with him to Bosnia, where I had to sprint across the tarmac from his helicopter to another to persuade a four-star general to act as the BBC's courier and take an interview tape back to base. And I went with him to the Commonwealth Conference in Auckland, New Zealand, where he was given a hard time over his refusal to condemn French nuclear testing in the South Pacific.

I went with him, too, on one trip which took us first to Washington, then to Cartagena in Colombia, then on to the Earth Summit in Rio de Janeiro. In Cartagena the Major team and attendant media went for a walk with President Gaviria round the old town. As it began to rain, a truly beautiful woman came up to me and asked if I would like to share her umbrella. She proved a fascinating and informative guide, taking me down a sidestreet to see an ancient monastery bell and other local features. Suddenly, as we approached the building where the more ceremonial aspects of the visit were to begin, she declared: 'I had better rejoin my husband now.' And she left me to link arms with the President. You simply don't expect to meet that kind of informality, not to mention the lack of security, in a South American country.

The last trip on which I accompanied John Major took us to India, Bangladesh and Pakistan in January 1997. With an election defeat looming, it probably did his morale a power of good. In Calcutta he was lionized. At the Tollygunge Club his entourage had to link hands to protect him from businessmen eager for his autograph, mobbing him like teenagers round a pop star. Women queued to press a kiss on the prime ministerial cheek, and local papers ran headlines like 'Major takes city by storm' and 'He came, he saw, he conquered'. In Pakistan we went up into the mountains to the famed Khyber Pass, passing en route hill towns where drugs were openly displayed on backstreet counters, next door to gun shops which would arrange to sell you anything from a dozen Kalashnikov rifles to a SAM missile to help you protect your drugs consignment on the way to its destination. Major took pains not to be seen in those surroundings, but when we got to the pass he visited one mountain village where he was presented with an ornate piece of headgear, like a yellow bowler on which some mountain milliner had been allowed to indulge her wildest fantasies with swathes of bathroom curtain material. Refusal to accept it would have caused offence to a tribe where insults are not forgiven for seven generations. Even as he donned it with a weak smile in front of gloating cameramen, Major must have been saying to himself, 'Oh God, if this doesn't make the cover of *Private Eye* then I'm an Afghan.' For television, the pictures were far too good to resist.

Of course, both as political editor of *The Times* and on the *Daily Mail* I had travelled in the prime ministerial entourages for some time. How else would I have got to be harangued by Prince Sihanouk on the Cambodian border, visited Armenia in the aftermath of an earthquake or strolled through the Gdansk shipyards in Poland with Lech Walesa? How else would I have got to see Lenin's private apartments in the Kremlin, with his cracked war maps still rolled up on the wall and a gift from Armand Hammer still on his desk? But in January 1988 I very nearly became the first journalist to be lost abroad on a prime ministerial trip – and it was all my own fault.

I tended always to take a fairly bulky camera with me on such visits, for two reasons. One was simply that I was unlikely ever to be in many of these places again and it was nice to have a memento or two. The other was that I discovered that if you hung a hefty camera and flash equipment round your neck, officials tended to assume you were a cameraman. You were therefore permitted closer to the action than the writing journalists, who were often held back in a separate pen. Thus advanced, I could pick up extra phrases and greater detail for my colour pieces. There might, too, be the chance of exchanging a few words with officials travelling with the Prime Minister as they hovered on the fringes of the action or waited to get into their cars to leave a welcoming ceremony.

This time, though, my habits landed me in real trouble. We had travelled up from Margaret Thatcher's talks with President Babangida in Lagos to Kano in northern Nigeria, where the

Prime Minister was to attend an amazing event, the Durbar held by Alhaji Ado Barbero, the Emir of Kano. In less than perfect visibility, it took more than one attempt to land. The problem, it was explained, was that we were already in the season of the harmattan sandstorms which often meant Kano airport having to be closed for two or three weeks. When we did land successfully, we were greeted by a highly colourful welcoming party, including a costumed musician on a camel's back blowing a trumpet-like instrument seven feet long. To get a shot of this I fumbled in my camera bag to change to a wide-angle lens. I got my shot – but alas, when I looked up it was to hear a shout from a helpful colleague in the press bus as it sped away at the end of the prime ministerial motorcade.

I was marooned, and it posed a problem. This was before the era of commonly available mobile phones. I had no means of contact with the official party. We were only due to be in Kano for a few hours. Should I, with no map and no idea of how far away the Emir's palace was or how long it would take to get there, set out by some means after Mrs T and my colleagues? What if I tried and failed to meet up with them and they came back to the airport and left, as they would have to, without me? I could then, thanks to the harmattan season, be marooned in northern Nigeria for weeks with very little cash on me and my passport in the hands of Number Ten officials. Should I therefore accept the ignominy of being unable to report on a colourful occasion and stay at the airport in the comforting presence of the RAF VC-10? There was the added risk that even if I did get close to the Emir's palace I would be unable to gain entry without the accreditation that was presumably being handed out on the press bus.

For a journalist, today's story always instinctively takes

precedence. Tomorrow, I decided, would have to sort itself out. Seeing the bandsmen who had played at the welcoming ceremony loading themselves and their equipment onto a truck, I decided to go for it. On the assumption that their barracks would be somewhere near the palace, I used sign language to beg for a lift. But unlike the official party, we did not have outriders and a police escort. We had not got very far before the truck slowed to a crawl. The roads were choked with hundreds of thousands of cheerful people who had turned out to see the Thatcher entourage go by and who appeared to be making a day of it.

As the only foreigner among a throng of friendly but unfamiliar faces, I began to fear the worst. And then suddenly I saw a police jeep parked up a side road. In the middle of heaven knows where, I jumped off the bandsmen's truck, dashed to the police vehicle and, armed with nothing more than a House of Commons press pass, did my best to impress on them that it was a matter of life or death that I was delivered to Margaret Thatcher's side – where she would certainly have been surprised to see me – at the Emir's palace.

We hooted our way through the milling crowds and eventually I arrived at the palace, dusty, dishevelled and highly relieved. I was just in time, as I made my way to our viewing position, to see Bernard Ingham, Mrs Thatcher's long-serving press secretary, getting a rifle butt in the stomach. An unseemly fracas had developed involving under-briefed and over-excited security men and local officials as he and some young ladies in the entourage made their way as invited to the Emir's box to be with the Prime Minister. It was a story which made *The Times*'s front-page splash and it required eye-witness input. It would have been a disaster if I had not been there.

The Durbar itself was a wonderful show (and, I would imagine, a security man's worst nightmare). Tribesmen wheeled and charged across the huge parade ground in a heady amalgam of the Arabian Nights and the Royal Tattoo. The participants, and their horses and camels, were richly bedecked with sumptuously embroidered costumes, gold and jewels. Some of the horsemen flashed swords and scimitars. Others randomly discharged what appeared to be ancient flintlock muskets with a hefty kick, the smoke from their weapons drifting across the sandy arena. On this occasion I had plenty of time to make use of my camera. But it had been too close a call for comfort. I resolved from then on not to seek to combine tourism with my journalism. In future, most of the fancy equipment stayed at home.

Every Prime Minister has his or her style, and some like to get abroad more than others. Margaret Thatcher was the great traveller, relishing the glamour of her world trips and much in demand by foreign leaders keen to see if a bit of her gloss would rub off on them. She would time her overseas expeditions shame-lessly to advertise her status as a world leader compared with her opposition challengers in the run-up to an election. One such occasion was the visit to the Soviet Union shortly before the 1987 election, when she 'lit a candle for peace' at the Zagorsk monastery near Moscow. Foreign Secretary Geoffrey Howe, who, like me, used to take a camera with him on such occasions, was nearly barred from the church by security men who thought he was a press photographer.

Sometimes a Thatcher visit seemed more like a royal progress – or something even loftier. On that particular Moscow trip she went shopping in a supermarket, to the delight of the doughty babushkas in their firmly knotted headscarves. Incongruously, she bought breads and pilchards. Looking at the huge crowds outside, one official mused, a touch sacrilegiously, in my presence: 'Loaves and little fishes . . . surely not?' Since Mrs Thatcher was carrying no money with her, her aides had to pay.

Travelling with her also meant we sometimes got a touch of the glamour treatment: never more so than when we flew once from Moscow to Tbilisi in Georgia. For some reason we were forced to use two Aeroflot planes rather than the RAF VC-10. It was a cold morning, with frost and a light dusting of snow crunching under our boots. We were to be well fortified, however. Breakfast on board came on not just one but two elegant wooden trays, and included fruit, eggs, smoked sturgeon and caviar. There was also a large tumbler of amber-coloured liquid. Assuming this to be apple juice, I took a hefty swig and nearly spluttered all over my tray. It was neat brandy – at 7.30 a.m.! We were getting a glimpse of how the old party bosses used to travel. It made you wonder how anybody in the upper echelons of the old Soviet Union ever managed to make a decision.

There was no doubt about Thatcher's remarkable relationship with Soviet President Mikhail Gorbachev, the man she declared famously that she could do business with. Their talks during the interval at the Bolshoi Ballet one night became so intense that the second act was delayed for nearly a quarter of an hour. In another session, conducted with her foreign affairs private secretary Charles Powell sitting in, Powell's fountain pen literally exploded as he raced to keep up with the pace and intensity of their conversation. 'Every molecule was engaged,' she told me on the plane back. It was not a love affair, but with their 'flashes of passion', as one official described the relationship, it was certainly more than diplomacy.

Nor was there any doubt that Thatcher used her charm where it helped, even flirting with French President François

Mitterrand, a notorious womanizer. John Major once asked him if he had said of Mrs Thatcher, as one French official had claimed, that she had 'les yeux de Caligula et la bouche de Marilyn Monroe'; Mitterrand denied it, but the phrase had the ring of authenticity about it.

On occasion Mrs Thatcher would also use her charm on the media; but she and Bernard Ingham did find means of getting their own back when they were displeased with what you had written. Once when she was visiting the Armilla patrol in the Gulf, the main press party was taken out to the vessel with Mrs Thatcher in a comfortable, sedate launch. Three of us were told that room was limited and that we would be coming by helicopter. That was fine until we got there and discovered that, in a buffeting wind, we had to be winched down to the bucking deck by rope, much to the amusement of the party watching from the launch.

There were ventures abroad with opposition leaders, too, and a trip with Neil Kinnock showed me how sensitive they can sometimes be. Seeking to build his international stature, Kinnock bravely ventured to America in December 1986 to try to sell his party's defence policy to US politicians. It was not going to be an easy task, since Labour was at that stage committed to scrap Polaris, cancel the Trident missile system and close down US bases in Britain. Nor were the omens good: on a previous US visit Neil had clashed with the US Secretary of State George Shultz over Central America and told reporters that Shultz had 'got out of his pram', a remark later interpreted by a spokesman as: 'the Secretary of State had departed from his normal diplomatic calm.' The US Defense Secretary Caspar Weinberger had attacked Labour's defence policy as one which would wreck

NATO and lead to US forces withdrawing into a Fortress America.

The trip began in Atlanta, where Kinnock made an appearance with the charismatic mayor Andrew Young after saying that America should not overreact to Labour's message on defence. As the rain bucketed down only fifty people, including the British Council contingent, turned up for Kinnock's speech at the Martin Luther King Center. He and his team were angered by my front-page sketch piece in the next day's *Times*, in which I pointed out that his trouble was not any overreaction but getting a reaction at all in a country where the only three Britons known were the Queen, the Princess of Wales and Mrs Thatcher, and where with him it was a question of 'Neil Who?' I wrote of the occasionally over-loquacious Labour leader:

> Mr Kinnock, who had spent most of the Atlantic crossing toiling on a rousing and effective anti-apartheid speech clearly designed for delivery to an emotional packed hall, was left to go through the motions on adjectival auto-pilot while his host, Mayor Andrew Young, quietly nodded off on the platform behind him. You see more passion over the bridge table in Budleigh Salterton.
>
> Labour's leader, who remarked ruefully, 'I'm better at pulling the rain than pulling the crowds,' did, however, have his revenge. After a quick sighting shot with a 2 minute 10 second reply to the first question his answers to the next three lasted respectively 14 minutes 10 seconds, 13 minutes 17 seconds and 6 minutes 8 seconds. Maybe word about him had reached Atlanta after all. I doubt if many in his stupefied audience would have rushed to hear another British politician on tour after that.

In the *Times* piece I had also remarked upon the number of

leading Americans whom Kinnock would not be meeting, including Senator Daniel Patrick Moynihan, who, I wrote, had 'opted out, pleading pressure of alternative business, turning knives in President Reagan's wounds'. This was based on information from one of Kinnock's official party. But the Moynihan meeting was rescheduled, and when the pair emerged from their talk for a TV photocall Moynihan opened the proceedings, on camera and beside a grinning Kinnock, with a direct enquiry.

'Which one of you lying bastards is Robin Oakley?' he asked.

I stepped forward to say that I answered to the name but not the description, and Moynihan argued, with some justification, that their joint presence showed how inaccurate my story was. Neil, with whom I have had a happy relationship over many years since, then left and Moynihan invited us in for a beer from his fridge.

'Sorry about that, fella,' he said to me, smiling broadly and shaking my hand. 'But Neil wanted me to do it.'

I am sure it had made the Kinnock entourage feel better, but I am not sure it was the best use he could have made of television time.

The more image-conscious Tony Blair has proved rather less of a traveller, not wanting to be accused at sensitive times of neglecting domestic problems and swanning off around the world. Although he enjoys trading ideas with like-minded leaders at 'Third Way' seminars from time to time and fulfils his summit quotas with Europe, the G8 countries and the Commonwealth, he does fewer bilateral visits than either Major or Thatcher.

Blair has looked bored by the Commonwealth. Admittedly when Britain hosted the Commonwealth Conference in Edinburgh in 1997 he was preoccupied by a weekend-long row with Gordon Brown over the single European currency. But his premature departure from that event, after a skimpy final press conference held before journalists had seen the economic document which was allegedly the conference's centrepiece, was just plain rude. I won a round of applause from Commonwealth journalists for taxing him with it.

At the 1999 Commonwealth Conference in Durban he was right to draw attention, while in Africa, to the problems of AIDS, even if the specific package of help he announced was a bit of recycling. But his call for 'modernization' of the Commonwealth was a sign that he could not think of anything else to do. Whenever Blair is in doubt about a course of action he urges modernization of the nearest institution. Modernization is his mantra. Nevertheless, while he does not give the impression of being particularly enamoured of the Commonwealth, Tony Blair does seem to have a genuine interest in Africa. He and Cherie privately help an AIDS children's charity in South Africa, and he has helped to chivvy other world leaders into doing more to counter the disease which has become the African continent's scourge.

The African experiences of my childhood have remained a vivid and cherished memory, and for me one of the greatest pleasures of my journalistic travels with Tony Blair and others has been the chance to get back to the African continent at regular intervals. But the near-stranding in northern Nigeria was not the only adventure such expeditions have provided.

Even on prime ministerial trips, of course, there are moments of leisure. With three hours to spare at the Commonwealth Conference in Zimbabwe in 1991 and the heads of state and government 'in retreat' at Victoria Falls, four of us journalists decided to go into the local safari park. Since all the proper safari jeeps had been commandeered for the VIPs, the only vehicle we could find was a beat-up hire car from a local garage. As we drove into the park we were warned that we must at all costs be out by nightfall.

All went well at first. We saw plenty of game and then, just after we had encountered several lions, we noticed that dusk had crept up on us. As the driver, I was virtually rallying us out of the park along the sandy tracks, but it was already pretty dark when I clipped a rock and burst a tyre. My wife Carolyn and daughter Annabel will confirm that I am the world's worst handyman and mechanic. But in that park two of us changed a tyre in the dark a great deal faster than I have ever managed it before or since. We did so to the mournful accompaniment of a distinguished tabloid newspaper diplomatic correspondent whose generous proportions would have made him the first choice of any hungry beast for tourist tartare.

'We're all going to die. I know it. We're all going to die,' he wailed, jumping up and down and urging us to hurry.

We were not harmed, there and then. But ironically, we were in greater danger once we emerged from the park onto a short stretch of tarmacadam road back to our hotel. We were doing about sixty when a large buck, a kudu I think, crashed through the bush and jumped gracefully right over our bonnet. The car, of course, had no seat belts. Had the kudu made even the finest misjudgement in his leap there would have been a sudden cluster of vacancies in the upper reaches of Fleet Street.

In 1997 I visited Mozambique with producer Simon Smith to make a film on why the former Portuguese colony had chosen, intriguingly, to become a member of the Commonwealth. The Portuguese years having been followed by those of the revolution, Mozambique must surely be the only Commonwealth country where addresses for the British high commission in the capital include one on the Avenue Mao Tse-Tung and another on the Avenue Vladimir Lenin. Outside the Hotel Polana, the elegantly refurbished stately pile which is the architectural showpiece of the capital, Maputo, the weaver birds wove and chattered in the jacarandas. Inside I met Hernando – a local Portuguese bank manager, a fund of knowledge and a fount of speculation on the local political scene as the one-time Marxist government pressed ahead rapidly with a Thatcherite privatization programme.

As we shared a few beers, I enquired about Hernando's crutches. A tendon pulled on the tennis court, perhaps? An ankle sprained on the dance floor at the then fashionable Mini Golfe nightclub? Not quite. Hernando had woken in the night a few weeks before to the sound of someone cutting through his telephone wires. Leaping out of bed and seizing a panga, a Mozambican machete, he found himself faced by four bandits armed with AK-47s. He had taken out the first three with his panga before the fourth one felled him with shots to his hip and stomach from a Russian Makarov revolver. Not quite bank managerly behaviour, I suggested. But it turned out that Hernando was not quite your average bank manager. He was a veteran of the 'dirty war' in Angola and knew some very interesting people.

Hernando dismissed his injuries as just one of those things. But his experience did make me pay heed to local advice not to walk far in Maputo after dark, though in truth my producer, cameraman and I felt more at risk of shakedown from the predatory policemen with their endless paper checks and prominent palms than we did from muggers. Putting people in positions of authority then paying them peanuts, irregularly, is a classic encouragement to corruption far from unique to emergent African economies. We soon learned that it was wise when leaving our car to entrust it to the largest of the street urchins who surrounded us offering their security services, paying him off on return with soggy notes in the local *meticais* which were then running at something like 18,000 to the pound.

Travel in general was hazardous. Crossing Maputo Bay on the battered, rusting ferry the *Bagamoyo*, I noticed a wall plate which stated that it was allowed to carry 60 people in bad weather, 120 in good. I lost count at something over 220 passengers as they piled aboard, huge wicker baskets of oranges or coconuts or vast yellow plastic cans of kerosene perched on their shoulders. Finally, just before we set off, the deckhand beckoned on a wheezing twenty-year-old Russian pick-up and a lorry loaded with ballast rubble, its position secured by what the locals called a 'Navambo handbrake' – a brick behind the back wheels.

It was a touch worrying to see a bed in the captain's wheel-house; even more so to watch a man with the only lifejacket in sight step off as we left, clutching a large piece of engine. But we made it over to the Gatembe shore, where skinned octopus dangled from the handrails and fishermen stood in the shallows chewing sugarcane as they pulled in their nets. And we were back in time for an appointment arranged through a freedom fighter to whom Hernando had introduced us.

We were to meet the Renamo leader Alfonso Dhlakana at his villa. As we were ushered in with all the curtains drawn I could just make out the figure of the opposition leader, surrounded by three large men, at least one of them in shades. My team suggested with what seemed to me rather indecent haste that they would go and set up in the garden while we talked. Before long, we too emerged from the oppressive gloom for the interview beside his swimming pool, with mousebirds trailing their long tails in the trees above.

The questions over, we were somewhat surprised when, at three in the afternoon in the blazing heat, a white-gloved servant appeared with a silver tray bearing a bottle of Johnnie Walker black label and three enormous glasses of neat whisky. It would have been churlish, not to say unwise, to refuse, and I toasted the health of the man who had spent sixteen years fighting a guerrilla war in the bush. Somewhat to our surprise, this created consternation. Casting rapid glances at each other, a huge, soft-spoken general, the hospitable Mr Dhlakana, and his other aide rapidly summoned three more glasses and toasted our health in return, with much clinking of glasses and fruity cries of 'Cheers!'

We had, I learned later from a local diplomat, behaved unexpectedly. The form for local journalists was to down the glass gratefully and return to the office to write a glowing report. Used to treating politicians as equals, we had, with our more confident behaviour, caused a problem of etiquette. But natural Mozambican courtesy had seen them through. I have never again drunk whisky at 3.00 p.m., but it is a memory I treasure.

My other enduring image from Mozambique is of a classroom of civil servants studying English, mostly at their own expense, listening earnestly to a Jonathon Porritt interview on ecology. Their land, they pointed out, was surrounded by English-speaking Commonwealth countries and English was the worldwide language of computers. If you wanted to get on, you had to speak English. It was not the love of William Shakespeare which drove them on, but the worship of Bill Gates. And if some feel that ex-Portuguese Mozambique is not yet the perfect fit with the Commonwealth, it was clearly on its way. The videos available in my hotel were *Dad's Army* and *Fawlty Towers*.

Travelling with Tony Blair, in Africa and closer to home, I

have been struck by his confidence in the foreign arena. In June 1998, during Britain's occupation of the revolving chair presidency of the European Union, I arranged to do a special feature on the Prime Minister's day during his round of preparations for the Cardiff EU summit. We started in Brussels before 8.00 a.m., visiting the Belgian Prime Minister Jean-Luc Dehaene before flying on to Luxembourg, Bonn and Paris for him to see in turn the Luxembourg Prime Minister Jean-Claude Juncker (a conservative who finds Mr Blair too right-wing for his taste), German Chancellor Helmut Kohl and French President Jacques Chirac. During the leg from Luxembourg to Bonn I conducted an in-flight interview on the tiny plane, imagining that I would be dismissed soon afterwards to my seat while he prepared the business for the next stage of his trip. But no. The thick file of briefing papers was on the table in front of him, little coloured marker tabs sticking out to highlight key areas for discussion, but Blair never even reached for it. He stayed happily chatting about domestic politics until we taxied down the runway on arrival.

The Blair glamour factor was particularly evident on a trip to Egypt, Saudi Arabia, Israel, Jordan and Palestinian Gaza in April 1998, where on several occasions he was mobbed by crowds shouting 'Tony, Tony'. In Egypt his good temper was tried by a non-functioning microphone and in Riyadh his patience was stretched by a welcoming ceremony at which he had to shake the hand of every member of the Saudi Cabinet and most of the military top brass too. But his smile never faltered on either occasion. Nor did it when he had to improvise rapidly to cope with Benjamin Netanyahu, the then Israeli Prime Minister who was his own spin doctor too.

Media smiles were not quite so wide, however, when the Israeli police escort taking Blair and the media to the Gaza border lost the press bus at the first set of traffic lights in Jerusalem. Late at the border checkpoint, we were off-loaded into three minibuses led by a jeep full of gun-brandishing soldiers determined we would make up ten minutes on a twenty-minute journey. Hands on hooters, enveloped in clouds of dust, we screamed around corners on two wheels, probably doubled the local incidence of heart failure and arrived just in time to set up and film a welcoming ceremony notable for the all-pervading smell of burning rubber.

At a local school, girls in blue denim dresses and white head-scarves gave Mr Blair a pop star's welcome. On the wall was a sign in English saying 'Try, try and try again – never stop trying.' But the difficulties of doing so in that part of the world were clear when the children outside were carrying placards proclaiming 'Jerusalem is ours – we concede not an inch' and when Yasser Arafat at his press conference called Netanyahu a liar.

Mr Blair did his best to use his celebrity value to push on the peace process, but relaying his words to BBC listeners in Gaza late that night was not easy. My last three radio reports came from the long-unfinished twelfth floor of an office building, read from my notebook by shaky torchlight. There then remained the little problem of how to get back at 1.30 a.m. across one of the tightest security borders in the world, between Gaza and Israel, without the passport which the Downing Street party had carried with them when they left for dinner some hours before. I had just about talked my way through with two stubble-headed squaddies when another one found my passport. Thoughtfully, somebody in the Downing Street party had done a head count earlier and left it there for me. We were out in ten minutes.

It made an interesting contrast with our experience later the same day after arriving back at Heathrow. Transferring us from

Mr Blair's VIP suite to Terminal Four for customs, the press bus went 150 yards down the wrong road and it took jobsworth security officials fifty minutes to acquire the authority to allow us to turn round and resume our journey. Sometimes it isn't so nice to be home.

12

'BEWARE! LOBBY JOURNALISTS ARE STAYING IN YOUR HOTEL': SUMMITS

I RARELY MISSED A MAJOR SUMMIT WHILE I WAS WITH THE BBC. A congregation of world leaders is irresistible to journalists, whether the participants look like having anything new to say or not. There is always the hope of friction, fuss or even flop to provide a story.

Nowadays there is quite a selection open to us. Most countries holding the European Union presidency for their allotted six months like to stage a couple of gatherings, making four summits a year, plus such annual gatherings as the Europe–Asia summit or the EU–US get-together. The G8 summits happen once a year, and the Commonwealth leaders convene every second year.

Summits are good therapy for world leaders. They find it comforting to learn that the other chaps have problems too, specially when the opinion polls show that many of the participants are politically 'dead on arrival' at the chosen venue. But in truth, these days they are a cosy, costly conspiracy between world leaders and the media. Summits were originally conceived as 'fireside chats' among a handful of leaders, enabling them to pool their experience informally to help them solve common problems.

In the world of the all-powerful media they have been inflated into formalized monsters.

The G8 world economic summits began in the shape of the 'Library Group' founded in the early 1970s by the US Treasury secretary George Shultz. He got together with the British, French and German finance ministers to discuss how they might stabilize currency turbulence. Soon the Japanese finance minister was co-opted, and before long two of the original members, Germany's Helmut Schmidt and France's Valéry Giscard d'Estaing, had become Chancellor and President respectively. They decided to expand the finance ministers' meetings into an annual gathering of heads of state and government, holding the first at Rambouillet in 1975. A little later Canada and Italy joined up, and the group was christened the Group of Seven or G7. Russia was admitted later, as an encouragement to Boris Yeltsin to adopt economic reforms and not to make too much fuss about the eastwards expansion of NATO, and the group accordingly became the G8.

The original idea, in a world of fragile economics, was to boost international co-operation in fiscal, monetary and commercial matters. Through the 1980s, however, the agenda became more political. The likes of Kohl, Reagan, Thatcher and Mitterrand were happy to co-ordinate thinking on strategic political matters and to look as though they were doing something about drugs and terrorism. The Japanese, often under pressure at the G7 finance ministers' meetings to do things they did not want to do to their economy, and without a permanent seat at other top political tables like the UN Security Council, were equally happy to support a switch of emphasis. Suddenly, instead of an economic think-tank or currency stabilizing mechanism, these heads of state and government had created a kind of

Seven-Think-About-How-To-Run-The-World Club, a sort of capitalists-only version of the UN Security Council. Attracted by such a powerful assembly and with countries vying with each other to provide ever more exotic backgrounds for the event, hundreds of journalists began to turn up; and the showbiz–politics conspiracy was born.

Now thousands of journalists descend on the summit city on the assumption that the public back home want to know what their leaders are doing there. The media need a 'story' to go with their pictures, so for months beforehand summit 'sherpas' pre-cook the summit's final communiqué to ensure that it will look as though all the travelling and expense – for politicians and journalists – are justified. But for all the column inches occupied and all the TV news packages put out, it is often the case that little new has happened at the summit venue at all, bar the getting together. Mostly, these occasions are triumphs of recycling.

A concentration of world leaders almost inevitably brings protests and demonstrations these days, and protesters know that there is scope for them, too, in the concentration of the media present. After the street battles at the World Trade Organization meeting in Seattle in December 1999, there were follow-up protests at the IMF session in Prague the next summer, at the EU summit in Nice in December, at the Davos World Economic Forum in January 2001 and in particularly nasty form at the EU Summit in Gothenburg this June. Cameramen, producers and correspondents cannot resist the 'live action' pictures of a bunch of protesters trashing the local McDonalds, or of jumpy police forces overreacting and being brutally heavy-handed with the demonstrators. They are 'good shots'. Innocent bystanders choking on tear-gas fumes or police drenching demonstrators with water cannon provide much more eye-catching images than another bunch of suits walking into a meeting. But compared with the decisions formalized inside the meeting room, is another street protest 'news' to the extent that it is allowed to take over so many bulletins?

The security aspect at summits adds in a curious way to the spurious grandeur of the occasion. No police force wants to lose a world leader on their watch; so huge areas of cities are sealed off, causing great disruption to the lives of local people and ridiculous expense for the host country's taxpayers. Two journalists at the Okinawa G8 summit in 2000 asked their hotel excursion desk if they could take a sailing trip on the day their paper was not being published.

'Sorry,' they were told. 'The sea is closed.' And so it was – for a mile offshore, with warships patrolling. On the island, there was little traffic for the 22,000 police drafted in to control: locals had been told to keep their cars at home unless their journey was strictly necessary.

Nowadays the G8 summits, with Russia enjoying membership under President Putin despite its economic dependency, represent the game of PR politics played out at the ultimate level. Their organizers, with their protocol-on-wheels choreographed motorcades, 'family photos' and cultural banquets, are the Cecil B. De Milles of the photo-opportunity. And yet the G8 remains a bizarrely self-selected affair, neither a decision-making body nor a representative one. The eight members are not the top eight military powers in the world, nor the top eight economic powers; nor do they comprise the eight fastest-growing economies in the world. Since the original seven set up shop there have been huge changes in the world. We have seen the collapse of communism, the emergence of the Asian tigers and the growth of global finance. But the G8 group remains heavily Eurocentric. It leaves

Asia under-represented and Africa and South America ignored. If Italy, Britain and Canada are members then why not India, China or Brazil?

In Okinawa I asked President Bill Clinton, at his last summit, if his G8 years had prompted any thoughts about reform of such events. He welcomed efforts to reintroduce a greater informality but justified the meetings on simple grounds.

'These people need to know each other,' he told me. 'There are a lot of decisions they have to make, a lot of conflicts they can avoid if they know each other and trust each other. So I'm not troubled by the format.' So there we are. Not much desire there for changing either the cast list or the procedure.

I have never met a media operation, incidentally, quite as ruthless as that run by the Clinton White House. Its treatment of the foreign media was ill-mannered in the extreme and bordered on xenophobia. When we visited the White House with British Prime Ministers, the staff made no effort to see that visiting journalists got a question or two in joint press conferences between the President and his guest, which is bad enough. But at the Cologne G8 summit in 1999 I encountered the worst example yet of the administration's arrogance.

Tony Blair and Bill Clinton had promised to emerge for questions after a bilateral meeting at Clinton's hotel, and several British film crews and news agencies went along for the 'doorstep'. Ninety minutes in advance we were searched and swept for security purposes. Eventually the leaders appeared. Clinton took three questions on US domestic issues from White House reporters and then an American voice shouted 'That's it, fellas!' and the lights were turned off. In the darkness I yelled that this was a joint press conference in a third country and that the British media had the right to a question too. After some muttering in the dark we heard Blair ask for the right of reply and Clinton told his people they had better turn the lights back on. Grudgingly they did so and I got my question. Afterwards I approached the American organizers and said their behaviour had amounted to gross discourtesy. They did not even deign to reply, but merely eyeballed me with maximum aggression. At White House level, the most powerful nation on earth still has something to learn about basic politeness and what we British like to call 'fair play'.

The best summits for access, on the whole, are the Commonwealth Heads of Government Meetings, known as CHOGMs (pronounced Chog-Ums). Partly because they find it harder to get their proceedings reported and are keen to stimulate any interest they can, Commonwealth leaders tend to make themselves more accessible. Usually there is at least one big party where all the journalists and leaders present can mingle. And story security is looser too. At the Commonwealth Conference in Auckland in November 1995 I had a good contact in the secretariat, and as the leaders on their 'retreat' discussed what should happen to Nigeria following the execution of Ken Saro-Wiwa and other human rights protesters I was able via mobile phone to do three live 'hits' into the *Today* programme from the garden outside the meeting, first setting the scene, then saying the meeting was likely to suspend Nigeria from the Commonwealth, and finally confirming it had done so.

At the party that day I took my hat off to Simon Walters, my intrepid colleague from the *Sun*. As the hefty Nigerian foreign minister Tom Ikimi walked around the seafood buffet heaping his plate, Simon dogged his every step, enquiring persistently, 'How can you stand here stuffing your face when your government has put a noose round Ken Saro-Wiwa's neck at home?' Answer came there none, but from the looks Simon received I'm sure he has crossed Lagos off his holiday list for a few decades.

The Commonwealth is an institution that is being neglected by too many of Britain's leaders. John Major made the effort, but Margaret Thatcher set most Commonwealth leaders' teeth on edge and they hers. Tony Blair has been patently bored by his CHOGMs so far, simply going through the motions. He left the Edinburgh CHOGM – his first, at which he was host – before it was over; at his second in Durban, he arrived just in time for the opening ceremony and again left before the proceedings were over. But the Commonwealth does offer real opportunities. Few other organizations represent a quarter of the world's population, some 1.7 billion people, crossing such a wide range of races, cultures and languages. Its fifty-four members comprise a unique blend of developed and developing countries with informal networks reaching into other bodies like the Organization of African Unity. It may have little economic muscle and no military clout; it does not seek a security role. But its networking style and 'family' contacts bring with them the ability to cut across regional blocs. It gives smaller states a better deal than they get with the United Nations, and it has learned to work effectively with non-governmental organizations. It can even be justified in the UK on the 'What's in it for us?' principle. The Commonwealth brings more invisible earnings to Britain than does the European Union.

Britain is in the Commonwealth, to some extent, to provide a post-colonial after-sales service. But the Commonwealth is bound together by choice, not by sentiment or obligation or geography. Countries as diverse as Rwanda and Yemen are still queuing to join, and Ireland is beginning to debate re-entry. Operating by consensus rather than control, it has a unique role to play in combating poverty, promoting human rights and good governance, and preventing or resolving conflicts. But year after year in Britain it is a neglected parliamentary Cinderella, rarely debated at Westminster and largely ignored by media and MPs alike.

One of the problems is that people only seem to notice the Commonwealth at those biennial CHOGMs. Rightly, the public is sceptical about the flummery and pre-prepared communiqués which feed the image of such gatherings as shopping jollies and international wine-tasting festivals for the pampered prime ministers of undernourished states. The proceedings are too long-winded, and few can recall the leaden prose of their leaders' declarations even three weeks later. CHOGMs remind us, too, that the Commonwealth is too ready to search for a lowest common denominator rather than to take a decision. Although member countries must be true democracies, its leaders are far too slow to act against the backsliders who run their states as personal mafia fiefdoms, like Zimbabwe's Robert Mugabe, a grotesque caricature of the political leader he once sought to be.

But what matters about the Commonwealth is the day-to-day practical work it does, the common business culture and the shared expertise which enable it to perform tasks such as helping member countries to run elections, build ports, reform their courts, develop forest programmes or provide health education. Those, sadly, are functions which excite neither political nor media interest.

The Commonwealth is in danger of becoming an attractive listed building which is crumbling into disrepair. What it needs is the political leadership to start living up to its own ideals and the professional skills to sell what it has on offer. It needs more definition; it needs to become less of a talking shop and to develop a more practical edge; and it needs to sort out what it does best that cannot be duplicated by various branches of the UN. Perhaps, too, it should become a more effective voice for the world's underclass. 'Human rights', its distinguished former secretary-general, Nigeria's Chief Emeka Anyaoku, has declared, 'cannot thrive on empty stomachs and an intolerable quality of life.' In Durban, Tony Blair said that the Commonwealth should modernize itself and seek a new sense of purpose, and called for a commission to be set up to speed the process. I have already said that the word 'modernization' shows the Blair vocabulary in default mode; I hope he will prove in his second term in office that this appeal was something more than the usual politician's search for a quick headline.

Although most of us would find it hard to kick the habit of attendance, some summits can be truly frustrating for journalists. Loitering with intent in the precincts of your own parliament, you have ready access to ministers and to information. Not so at summits. In the press centre, usually a hideous modern complex ten miles out of town more used to hosting the biennial gathering of the World Plastics Federation, you may be miles away from the schloss or chateau where the leaders are having their pow-wow. Small groups cluster round fast-talking spokespersons whom the French rather more elegantly call *porte-paroles*. Photocopiers hum incessantly, churning out vast mounds of documents about some summit subcommittee's efforts in Upper Volta; monitor screens flash up messages about the latest briefing by Luxembourg officials, or instructions on where Pool Group F should meet to be bussed off to a hotel entrance to record the third handshake of the day between the summit host and the Danish foreign secretary. The Danes dash, others stay put. Rumours drift through the building like barbecue smoke. The announcement of a briefing by a key player sets off an undignified stampede. And many false hares are run.

On these occasions journalists are far too heavily dependent on spin doctors and briefers, most of whom are themselves operating on secondhand information, having been debriefed rapidly by diplomats who did not have the demands of the media much in mind when they sat in the fringes of the relevant meeting. Sometimes the process feels like the journalistic equivalent of those whispering team games we used to play as children. You know the kind of thing: the message which started as 'She has missed all her history lessons and wasted the whole term' became 'She has hissed all her mystery lessons and tasted the whole worm.' At an all-night session at the EU summit in Nice in December 2000 there was suddenly a frantic scramble at around 2.00 a.m. 'It's finished!' people were shouting. But it wasn't. One of the Scandinavian teams had arrived to give an update briefing to their national media team: Finnish, yes; finish, no.

Sometimes spokesmen are candid enough. At the Lisbon EU summit in 2000, Alastair Campbell was asked about the British government's attitude to a European stock exchange regulator. He mumbled a non-reply.

'Why are you ducking the question ?' asked one of the Brussels correspondents.

'Because the guy from the Treasury isn't here and I can't remember what the line is,' Alastair admitted.

It is, I discovered, an advantage at a summit to work for television, as this improves your access to the politicians. It is not that they like the sight of our familiar faces, just that they appreciate the size of our audience. We are the means by which they can seek to reassure those audiences back home that they are in whichever exotic spot it is for a purpose which really matters. At a European or G8 summit, for example, newspaper journalists might not see the Prime Minister, Chancellor, Foreign Secretary or any of their senior officials until the final press conference, and they are entirely dependent on briefings by press spokesmen. But TV journalists will be invited into the leaders' conference hotel, through the security cordons, for brief 'doorsteps' and sometimes more extensive interviews, because the politicians want their doings reported on the TV news. This gives us a precious few minutes' conversation with them or with the officials we know in the entourage while cameras are set up.

Even diplomatic entourages, though, are watchful. We journalists were amused to discover that a special warning had been issued to officials staying in the same hotel as us during the December 1999 European summit in Helsinki. 'Be on your guard,' their briefing packs told them. 'Lobby journalists are staying in your hotel.'

Sometimes, however, there can actually be too much access. At an EU summit in Pörtschach, Austria, in 1998 I had arranged to have a brief interview with Tony Blair. When I arrived, he was having a chat on the balcony with Bertie Ahern, the Irish Prime Minister, and Alastair Campbell suggested I could have two for the price of one. Although I was not seeking a chat on Anglo-Irish affairs, I knew BBC Belfast would want it. So I had to find a way after a few questions of politely dismissing the Taioseach and getting down to business with Tony Blair. Catching on quickly, they said their farewells on camera in mid-interview.

At the same summit I was watching on the TV monitor the progress of the pleasure boat chugging across the lake with assorted premiers on board as I called Alastair Campbell to check the Prime Minister's view on a particular point. 'Ask him your-self,' said Alastair, handing his mobile phone to Blair, whom I was still watching on screen.

Mind you, the granted access does not always bring the results the politicians want. At the so-called 'dot.com summit' at Lisbon in March 2000 – where, ironically, the ever-helpful BBC technical experts could not get my laptop to work at all – I had a snatched interview with Tony Blair. I asked him about the economic reform issues and about relations with Austria, then being snubbed by the EU for including the right-wing Freedom Party in its coalition government. I also tossed in a few quick questions about whether he planned to take paternity leave when he became a parent again shortly, knowing that the *Six O'Clock News* was interested in the subject.

Unfortunately, that was all the *Six O'Clock News* was interested in. They ran the paternity leave exchanges and made no other reference to the admittedly rather bland summit. The *Nine O'Clock News* ignored Lisbon altogether. The result was a furious letter from Alastair Campbell to Tony Hall, the chief executive of BBC News, which Downing Street made public. 'If anyone needed further evidence of the dumbing down of TV news they should look no further than your six o'clock bulletin earlier this evening,' the letter declared.

The Prime Minister and other ministers are attending a summit addressing issues of economic reform which the UK has been trying to get taken seriously in Europe for some time. They are making decisions that have a real impact on the jobs, education and future prosperity of Europe's citizens. Yet the only coverage of the Prime Minister, or of Lisbon, was a couple of clips of him answering questions on whether he intends to take paternity leave, which the

BBC has been interested in since the subject formed a small part of the Prime Minister's interview on the *Today* programme which was broadcast this morning.

On that occasion I felt that Alastair Campbell had a point, and I later made that plain to Tony Hall. It probably did not help me with Tony that Alastair's letter went on to add: 'I attach no blame for the undoubted dumbing down, of which this is but the latest example, to Robin or several other members of your political team who often appear to be as exasperated as we are at how difficult it is to get serious coverage for serious issues.' But who knows? As the BBC's political editor, leading many news bulletins with my reports, I met somebody called the head of news about once a year on average.

The Downing Street team were pretty angry with Fleet Street, too, about Lisbon, because many papers made much of the fact that the Prime Minister, the Foreign Secretary and the Chancellor arrived within a few hours of each other in three separate planes. But they knew the first-day story, however worthy, was not an eye-catching one. One friend in the Blair entourage revealed to me that he had proposed staging a row on one particular issue to ensure that they got some coverage, but he had been overruled.

At summits, it has been intriguing to observe Tony Blair on exactly the same learning curve as John Major. Both began by saying they were going to obtain better results from the EU by putting Britain at the heart of Europe, and both became steadily more irritated with Europe's way of doing business. Both told the media at their first G8 summit that there was far too much flummery, and urged cutting down on the motorcades, the show-piece dinners and the family photos and getting back to proper fireside chats; and both forgot that with thousands of the world's media on hand that would be impossible, and that each of the other leaders too has an electorate to satisfy at home.

Of course, one must not be entirely cynical about summits. They can do some good. Like political fund-raising dinners, their banquets carry a price per plate. Without the focus provided by the G8 summit at Okinawa in 2000, it is doubtful if the Japanese hosts would have provided their $15 billion programme to help the developing world by narrowing the 'digital divide'. We might not have seen President Clinton's $300 million 'food for education' programme for the poorer nations, or Tony Blair's doubling of Britain's contribution to spending on the prevention of malaria, TB and AIDS from £50 million to £100 million. And, at their most basic, summits can make a contribution to peace. Robin Cook puts it well: 'It is better to send middle-aged men to bore each other than to send young men to kill each other.' It was at Okinawa that Tony Blair won backing from Russia's President Putin, who has quickly picked up the summit game, for a conference on 'conflict diamonds', the gems which finance some of Africa's dirtiest wars.

But it was in Okinawa, too, that Blair announced a conference in Britain the following February on curbing international crime and drug traders' profits. That would have sounded pretty impressive if I had not felt a stirring of memory and looked up my notes on the G8 summit in Denver in July 1997. (That had been Tony Blair's first G8, at which he found himself embarrassingly without a chair as the leaders went to sit down. He recovered with aplomb by telling us he had given up his seat to an older person: 'Not difficult to find.') And what had Mr Blair then done in Denver? He had promised to double Britain's health spending in Africa, just as he did at Okinawa. And he had been asked by his fellow leaders then to produce a report on international drug crime for the Birmingham G8 which he hosted the next year. For that the G8 justice and interior ministers duly produced – yes, a ten-point action plan. At least it was a shorter document than the G8 leaders' list of forty recommendations for tackling crime concocted for the Lyon summit in 1996. We certainly can't accuse them of failing to recycle their resources.

The problem is that once the summits are safely over, the space has been secured on the TV bulletins for the rehashed 'initiative' or 'task force' and sufficient headlines have been garnered, the reports are mostly filed and forgotten. It is only when some powerful pressure group like Jubilee 2000 compares performance with promise – highlighting, for example, the vast discrepancy between the $15 billion of developing-country debt which was on the way to being forgiven by Okinawa and the $100 million promised at the Cologne G8 in 1999 – that the world leaders are held to account. As I noted in a *New Statesman* piece at the time, it is not that the leaders are lacking in sincerity when they sign up to their pledges. They mean to be good. But the G8 has no permanent secretariat, and when the meetings are over the participants move back into the all-consuming concerns of domestic politics. Somehow it seemed symbolic, at a summit allegedly preoccupied with Third World health and communication, that when I went to talk with Médecins sans Frontières in the backstreet building allotted to the non-governmental organizations in Okinawa they had just had their telephones cut off.

It was on returning from that Okinawa summit, the last one I covered for the BBC, that I figured in a story covered in almost every national paper diary or gossip column. There is nothing Fleet Street likes better than a falling-out among TV men. Anxious on my last trip to get a radio interview with the Prime

Minister, I was keen to see as much of him as possible. It is useful in preparation for such an interview to have the wider off-the-record talk you get when he comes back to the press seats on the plane for a general chat with reporters. I was somewhat taken aback, therefore, to be told that Mr Blair had offered to come and talk to us but that his offer had been refused on the say-so of John Sergeant, my former number two and now the political editor of ITN.

According to the Number Ten staff, it seemed that John, settling in after we'd all enjoyed a good dinner, had suggested that if the Prime Minister did want to come and see us he should do so after those who wished to had finished watching the in-flight movie *Erin Brockovich*. Officials had clearly taken the hump at such a response, and I feared that Blair might too, in which case we might not get to see him at all. I was even more worried that I might therefore lose the in-flight interview with the Prime Minister which I had been promised for the *Today* programme. Knowing that others were equally put out, I went forward to first class and told the Downing Street team that John should not be taken as speaking for the rest of us, even if he were the current year's chairman of the lobby. Many of us would like to see the Prime Minister at a time of his choosing and preferably as soon as possible. Back in our quarters, I went over to John's seat and protested at what he had done, saying he had no right to make the decision for the rest of us. John denied having refused the offer of a briefing from the Prime Minister, and we had what an official briefer might afterwards have called a 'forceful exchange'.

The upshot was that a grinning Blair and Campbell soon appeared in our cabin and we had a useful background session during which, probably for the first time in his life, John did not ask a single question. More importantly for me, I then got my *Today* interview and scored a reasonable coup. I drew from the Prime Minister the pledge that if he were re-elected in the 2001 general election he would serve as Prime Minister throughout the next parliament, a significant story which was followed up across the next day's media.

Unfortunately – but inevitably, with so many journalistic witnesses to the earlier episode – the little fracas over the briefing session also figured strongly in the next day's papers, appearing in virtually all the diary columns, characterized in some as a case of air rage among the hacks. I was sorry about that, because it fed the gossip column stereotype that John and I were bitter enemies. We were not, and are not. He is normally the most amiable and witty of companions, and we agree about much of modern politics. Our spat was soon forgotten. But it was nice for once, I must admit, to be the hero of the gossip columns, with the *Guardian*'s Matthew Norman, frequently a scourge, opening his column by declaring, 'Nothing so became Robin Oakley, legend will record, as the manner of his leaving . . .' I never have asked John if he had to go to the cinema to see the end of *Erin Brockovich*.

13

EUROPE AT THE HEART OF
BRITISH POLITICS

THROUGH MY YEARS AT THE BBC, ESPECIALLY AS I WATCHED JOHN Major stretched on the European rack by his divided party, I found myself becoming more and more fascinated by the effect Europe has on the British political scene. Periodically it rouses the British populace to a degree of fervour shown on almost no other political issue. We are, no doubt about it, a quirky, awkward island people, suspicious of grand alliances and jealous of our sovereignty. As a consequence, managing the relationship with our continental neighbours has been the biggest test facing British governments and would-be governing parties since the 1950s. Most of them have failed it at some time. Since the 1960s I have seen Europe split, break and refashion British parties. It has made and unmade party leaders. It has changed the British constitution. And of all the major political controversies, it has been the one on which the politicians have been most pushed around by the media.

Governments of both complexions have been convinced, when in office, that Britain is better off in the European Community or

Union than outside it; but, nervous of media reactions, few of them have been entirely honest with the people about European issues. All of them have found their political fortunes profoundly affected by what they have done or failed to do in Europe. When Edward Heath took Britain into the Common Market in the 1970s he alienated a section of the Tory party which has remained dissident ever since. Harold Wilson, in an attempt to cover over the divisions in the Labour party in the days when many of its members and supporters looked upon Europe as a capitalist conspiracy, gave the country a referendum on Common Market membership – a stratagem which succeeded only in emphasizing Labour's divisions on the subject. That referendum also led the electorate and Fleet Street to expect a direct hand in more of the decisions which had previously been left to governments and Parliament to decide. Now virtually every major development in European affairs leads to demands for further referendums.

There was a further spin-off from Europe: Labour's period of Euroscepticism meant that Roy Jenkins, a man eminently qualified to lead the party, lost the chance of doing so. He went off instead to head the European Commission, and, when he returned, to help found the SDP. As I have recounted in an earlier chapter, I was an eager spectator as the whole shape of British politics changed during this episode. Few of us imagined at the time what impact it would have, but the SDP's splitting of the Labour party and the division of the anti-Conservative vote between Labour and the various forms of Liberal–Social Democrat alliance helped to keep the Tories in office and Labour out of it for eighteen years.

After she came to power in 1979 Margaret Thatcher won huge popularity by swinging her handbag in pursuit of what she insisted on calling 'our money', clawing back some of Britain's contribution to the EU budget. But over a period her Euroscepticism and her resistance to British involvement in the European Monetary System alienated several of her senior ministers, notably Foreign Secretary Geoffrey Howe and Chancellor Nigel Lawson. Her increasing antagonism to most things European began to alarm what was then a much more Europhile Tory party. She gloried in isolation and in 'fighting Britain's corner'. But people weren't convinced that they always wanted to be in the corner. Her shrill 'No, no, no' retort to the Rome European summit in 1990, shattering the line the Conservative Cabinet had agreed, triggered Sir Geoffrey Howe's resignation and his speech in the Commons which precipitated her downfall. In all my time at Westminster I never remember such electricity in the air as when he accused her of being a cricket captain who sent her team out to face the opposition with bats she had broken in the pavilion. From that moment on, a challenge to her leadership of the Conservatives was inevitable.

Because Europe (with a little help from the poll tax) brought down Thatcher, John Major, a pragmatic but not a romantic European, inherited an all but unleadable party composed largely of Thatcherites who regretted her passing, other Tories who felt guilty about her abrupt dismissal, and a further group who took their tone from vociferous sections of Fleet Street who identified with both categories. Consciously or subconsciously, those categories adopted Euroscepticism as their creed. Quite apart from any personal convictions on the European issues themselves, for many Tories Euroscepticism became a sort of political cap badge worn by those who wanted to signal their regret at Thatcher's passing. Many of the newer MPs had been chosen in the days of Thatcher's dominance and still wanted to march to the beat of her drum. Major never had a hope of fulfilling his expressed aim of putting Britain at the heart of Europe.

It was made all the harder for him because so much of Fleet Street lamented Thatcher's political demise and sought revenge on those whom Thatcherite proprietors and columnists believed responsible. Newspapers need hate figures to maintain sales. The menace of the Soviet Union was no more, union chiefs had lost their clout, and so 'the bureaucrats of Brussels' – who are rather fewer in number than those employed by the British Ministry of Agriculture – became the new hate figures, especially as the North American hold on the British newspaper industry, in the shape of Rupert Murdoch and Conrad Black, became ever stronger. They did not want a Britain looking to Europe rather than across the Atlantic.

Much of EU politics is long-winded, tangled and wearisome. Most of the British media have preferred to treat the subject with the subtlety of a football crowd chanting slogans reflecting on the paternity of the away side. The demonizing of EU figures like Jacques Delors and Romano Prodi has been a prime example of the media's tendency to play the man rather than the ball. They were comfortable with Thatcher's Euro-bashing rhetoric and they have never had much time for attempts by Major or Blair to play a more subtle game in Europe.

Major fought for, and won, concessions for Britain at Maastricht, notably on the opt-out from the Social Chapter and on the single currency. But he never brought back enough for the Tory Eurosceptics, egged on from the sidelines by a vengeful Margaret Thatcher. He pleaded with continental leaders like Germany's Chancellor Helmut Kohl for time to bring his country round to greater European enthusiasm, and was accorded some.

At one of Jeffrey Archer's Christmas parties Major told me how a red-faced Jacques Delors, then President of the European Commission and an eager integrationist, had accused him of trying to frustrate every move he made, so ruining the 'European architecture'.

'You're trying to put all the furniture up in the attic,' complained a visibly angry Delors.

Kohl, at that stage trying to turn Major into an ally, leaned across. 'Oh, no, Jacques,' he said. 'We're merely rearranging a few vases.'

But when Britain found life unsustainable within the exchange rate mechanism of the European Monetary System in September 1992, no help from Kohl was forthcoming. Major felt betrayed, and on Black Wednesday he and Norman Lamont had to pull Britain out of the EMS in humiliating circumstances.

'It was at that moment we lost the 1997 election,' Major told me later. ' There was never any real hope after that.' He acknowledged that at that point the Conservatives' reputation for economic competence had been destroyed, and they never again recovered their position in the opinion polls. It was Europe at the heart of British politics once again: the period of currency instability which brought about the run on the pound that summer was set off by fears that the French might reject the Maastricht Treaty in their 1992 referendum, as they came close to doing. Meanwhile, the bitterness of the battle on Europe within the Tory ranks, and Major's weakness as his tiny majority of twenty-one was whittled away by defections and by-election defeats, turned the party into what a then undisgraced Lord Archer memorably described at a later party conference as a 'circular firing squad'. No party could have hoped to survive the triple whammy of Black Wednesday, sleaze and total dissension in the ranks; and Europe was the key element in two of those factors.

John Major came to office determined that he could make Europe work for Britain and keen to get Europe to concentrate on practicalities like employment instead of constitutional navel-gazing. But he became disillusioned with his European counterparts. He was never a supporter of the single currency, and he insisted on keeping open the question of British entry only because he feared that Kenneth Clarke would resign from the Cabinet if he didn't.

Although they were friends and allies, when Clarke knew I had been talking to Major he used to quiz me as to how resolute the Prime Minister had been on the euro issue. He knew the strength of the media and was always nervous that the Prime Minister might buckle under the pressure and make more concessions to the Eurosceptics, both in Fleet Street and in the Commons. Major, too, was jumpy when he knew Ken had been talking to journalists. If they were both on the same plane with the media on a foreign trip, the Prime Minister would come back for a chat after his Chancellor had been putting himself about, cloaking nervous inquisitiveness with excessive joviality.

'So, what has the Chancellor been leaking to you this time?' he would enquire, clearly anxious to check whether the carefully negotiated policy line had been held.

There was a genuine respect between the two, but even though they were instinctive 'One Nation' allies on the government's general stance, the bond of trust did not hold on Europe. With his party as bitterly divided as it was on this issue, Major was always anxious to rein in Clarke's Euro-enthusiasm. Clarke, for his part, was always worried that his friend – and he once memorably told the Tory party conference, 'Any enemy of John Major's is an enemy of mine' – was too inclined to concede ground to the Eurosceptics which could never be regained.

In my regular conversations with them both I could see the tensions ebb and flow. Clarke behaved as he did at the famous Chez Nico lunch in December 1996, uttering threats to resign, largely because the *Daily Telegraph* had reported that week that Major was about to switch from the 'wait and see' policy and come out with a declaration against the euro – exactly what Clarke constantly worried he might do. Major, as he told me on a number of occasions, was no enthusiast for the single currency, but he did not want to lose his Chancellor. This made life particularly difficult for Major, because once Labour had promised they would stage a referendum before taking Britain into the single currency, many in the Tory party were desperate that they should either match Labour's move or, preferably, have something to demonstrate what was avowedly the case, that theirs was a much more Eurosceptic party and much less likely to take Britain into the euro. Clarke, however, was determined to block any commitment to a referendum.

His colleagues told me that in Cabinet Michael Howard, among others, pressed for a compromise, a declaration from Clarke that there was so much fudging of the convergence terms for euro entry going on in other member states that it would be right for Britain to rule out entry in the first wave, but Clarke fought against this too because he feared a ratchet effect. Once this compromise was conceded, there would be pressure to rule out the euro in principle.

'Peter Lilley is worried about the wait and see policy,' one senior figure told me at the time. 'Michael Forsyth doesn't like it but doesn't think it is worth a fight. Michael Portillo runs away, and Michael Howard goes through the motions, telling people like you more than he tells the Prime Minister.'

Outside the Cabinet, John Redwood told me that if the government gave the people a lead in that direction he was sure the country would vote to come out of the EU. When a few of us lunched a few days later at the Foreign Office, Malcolm Rifkind was asked if he could ever remember the Tory party so divided. 'Yes – at the time of the Corn Laws,' he replied sardonically. Divided parties, he emphasized, did not win elections. Perhaps that was one reason why Malcolm had himself tacked firmly in a Eurosceptic direction. It was no accident when somebody with his command of language got himself in trouble for declaring that the majority of the Cabinet 'opposed' the single currency.

At various times Major confused his party and infuriated the media with his European policy lurches. Sometimes he chose to be Eurosceptic macho man, as when in June 1994 he vetoed the appointment of the federalist-minded Belgian Prime Minister Jean-Luc Dehaene as the next President of the European Commission. At other times he tried to have it both ways. He initiated a period of non-cooperation with the rest of the EU in protest over the ban on British beef in 1996, and then called it off without securing a precise timetable for the re-acceptance of beef exports on the continent. Earlier, in March 1994, he and Douglas Hurd talked big talk about how they were going to fight a furious battle for British voting rights in European Councils; but when it came to decision time, they failed to walk the walk. Such manoeuvrings left neither the Eurosceptics nor the Euro-enthusiasts in his party satisfied. Nor did he please other European leaders. Yet he had started off taking a strong pro-European stance, insisting on staging what many saw as an entirely unnecessary Commons vote to prepare the way for debating the Maastricht Treaty Bill, the so-called 'paving vote'. He was permanently scarred, I believe, by that vote, which nearly finished him within months of his 1992 general election victory.

During this period, in my early days at the BBC, the government was in trouble on every front, beset by grave concerns about the economy, rising unemployment and the de-industrialization of Britain which came to be symbolized by the normally sound Michael Heseltine's insensitive handling of the massive programme of pit closures. Norman Lamont told me that the Treasury was surprised that Heseltine had not sought funds for a gentler phasing-out scheme. He thought that Heseltine had taken a hard line because he wanted to convince the party that he too was a believer in markets and a Thatcherite toughie: once again, her shadow was falling over her former colleagues. Government defeat on a pit closures vote was averted only by a string of climbdowns and pledges to the Ulster Unionists on a power pipeline.

As the Maastricht Treaty paving vote came near, the atmosphere grew ever more tense. With the Eurosceptics growing more confident every day, Michael Heseltine and Kenneth Clarke were taking a very high profile in making their counter-arguments. It was, Heseltine told me, a deliberate tactic. The idea was to remind the Eurosceptics that if they helped Labour win the vote, and if Major then felt he had to go, they could finish up with a new, more pro-European party leader whom they disliked even more. It was desperate stuff, but it needed to be.

At a European summit in Birmingham in the middle of October that year, I went to interview John Major for the *Nine O'Clock News*. As we chatted off the record before the start he told me that he had not slept for three nights. It was an unwise thing to admit when he might have been overheard by any of the production team or piped through to an edit vehicle, and it showed how rattled he was.

The night before the paving vote I, along with many British politicians, was at Winfield House, the American ambassador's grand residence in Regent's Park, for dinner and then at the US embassy in Grosvenor Square, where we were further sustained by hamburgers, Cokes and pecan pie, for a late-night party to mark the US elections. Amid the hubbub, Tristan Garel-Jones, the Europe minister and a close ally of Major's, told me quietly that the Prime Minister was planning to quit if he lost the vote. As a group of us chatted later with Michael Heseltine, it was suggested the Tories might need to 'buy' the votes of the Ulster Unionists with a toothsome concession.

'Give them Donegal,' someone suggested.

'Ours is not a fastidious trade,' acknowledged Heseltine with a grin, clearly hinting that desperate deals might have to be done.

At the embassy I had a tortured conversation with Richard Ryder, the Tory chief whip. White-faced and tense, too honest a man to tell me lies, he responded to my every probe about whether they had the votes to win, and whether Major would quit if they didn't, with no more than grimaces. I then saw Sydney Chapman, another whip and an old chum, who confessed, 'The arithmetic isn't there yet.'

When the debate opened the next day Major was firm and combative, addressing the arguments of the Tory rebels. John Smith scored some stinging courtroom debating points, but didn't really tackle the question of why the Maastricht Bill should be delayed. After I had done a two-way on the *Six O'Clock News* saying just this, Gus O'Donnell, the Prime Minister's press secretary, phoned me to argue that Major had come out of the Commons exchanges well on top and that I had not reflected that sufficiently. He didn't often do that sort of thing, picking up on my reports, and it was another sign of how frayed the government's nerves were.

I had also said in my interview that the Tory whips were still worried that they did not have enough votes to win. I asked Gus whether he queried my arithmetic, and he did not. Was that, I wondered, because it was the truth or because it might help the task of the government whips if some of the Tory waverers believed the vote was still on a knife-edge? We always had to be alive to such considerations. The interaction of the media and the Commons was so close that it would not have been above Number Ten or the whips to try to plant a line with the six o'clock bulletins in the hope that it would push things one way or another in a ten o'clock vote.

Gus, though, was not an instinctive spinner or public relations man. A south Londoner like the Prime Minister who shared his boss's sporting pleasures, he was a career economist who had followed Major to Number Ten after working for him at the Treasury. I always had a bit of a soft spot for a press secretary who once confessed amid the gilded splendour of the Locarno Room at the Foreign Office that the only previous Locarno with which he had been associated was a cinema in Streatham.

In the end, the government scraped through that Maastricht paving vote by just three votes – but not before they had dismayed pro-Europeans in the Tory ranks by conceding to wavering sceptics that the bill would not go through its final stages before a second Danish referendum on Maastricht. Skipton MP David Curry, a keen Tory pro-European, told me that several of them had stormed into the chief whip's office to show, as he put it, that 'we too can throw the furniture around'. They were assured that the bill could not have reached its third reading much sooner than the Danish referendum anyway, but they were asked not to demand a public explanation: the whips did not want the doubtful worth of this concession to become apparent to those whose votes it had bought. Threats, deals, arm-twisting, phoney concessions – all the elements of drama are there on these occasions, and I enjoy every minute backstage while the political actors are strutting their stuff.

One key factor in that Maastricht vote was that the Liberal Democrats, to the scorn of Labour MPs, voted with the Tory government. When I was waiting with Paddy Ashdown the next morning to do a live on *Breakfast News*, he told me that Major had invited him to go and join the champagne drinking in the Tory whips' office after the vote. Not surprisingly, the Lib Dem leader had declined. Conservative ministers who approached him with congratulations and thanks were told to get away fast, although I had the impression that the language Paddy used was a little more vigorous than that.

The climax of the Major government's travails over Europe came, of course, with the withdrawal of the whip from eight Tory Eurosceptic MPs, seven of whom had defied the government in a key vote on Britain's contributions to the European budget in November 1994 – a defiance carried through despite the Prime Minister's threat to call a general election if he lost the vote. At a stroke, the government's majority was wiped out and ministers became dependent on the votes of the Ulster Unionists to get their business through. But the Eurosceptics, instead of being cowed by such a move, became an ever more cohesive force, a party within a party, with the eight 'whipless ones' enjoying their minor celebrity and mini-martyrdom. Fleet Street gave them copious attention, and the whole exercise gave visible shape in the public mind to the idea of a bitterly divided Tory party.

Buoyed up by postbags full of letters from people who saw them as heroes – little men and, not forgetting Teresa Gorman, little women against the machine – the rebels grew in confidence.

They were as exhilarated as teenagers who have just discovered sex. Before long they were producing their own manifesto, demanding a clawback of powers from Brussels, the scrapping of the Common Agricultural Policy and the abandonment of economic and monetary union. Soon the problem for the government, having withdrawn the whip from the rebels, was how to give it back without upsetting the loyalists who had toed the party line. Eventually the eight regained the whip without giving any assurances of future good behaviour.

John Major himself moved steadily in a Eurosceptic direction, first with his pitch in the European Parliament elections of 1994, then in a speech in Leiden in the Netherlands in September 1994 opposing any strengthening of the powers of the European Parliament, and then by promising to veto any constitutional changes proposed in Europe which might impact on the British Parliament. It was at that point that Kohl despaired of him.

Major's speech in Leiden was probably in response to Kohl's declaration that 'We do not in any circumstances want the slowest ship in the convoy to stop developments in Europe.' Frustrated by British intransigence on their project, Kohl and Mitterrand had begun to talk of developing an inner core of truly European nations, a two-tier Europe.

'I see a real danger', Major warned in response, 'in talk of a hard core, inner and outer circles, a two-tier Europe. I recoil from ideas for a union in which some would be more equal than others. There is not and there never should be an exclusive hard core, either of countries or of policies.'

At Nice in December 2000 Tony Blair, a more enthusiastic European than Major, formally endorsed the idea that groups of EU countries that wanted to go ahead with projects of closer integration should be able to do so, but only provided that they did not become an exclusive hard core and that others were free to join in later.

By early 1996 Major was issuing a white paper insisting that Britain would make no concessions in Europe's next round of constitution-mongering and describing the Social Chapter in a speech to the Institute of Directors as 'immoral'. He was caught between a rock and a hard place. As they sensed him being pushed by the Eurosceptics, the pro-Europeans began to exert their own pressures to hold the line, notably on the single currency, although they found themselves handicapped by the sheer unpopularity of much of what 'Europe' was doing – the ban on British beef, European Court decisions, the operation of the Common Fisheries Policy.

By April the Tory MP David Evans, who had been John Redwood's campaign manager for the Conservative leadership contest the year before, was declaring that it was now 'every man for himself'. MPs even began to blackmail ministers, as when John Gorst and Hugh Dykes threatened to desert if the government did not do what they wanted over a local hospital. The more the splits showed, the weaker the Tories' chances of re-election became; and all the while the Thatcher factor too was in play. When the Eurosceptic Bill Cash was berated by the Tory chief whip for taking cash for his European Foundation from the Referendum Party leader Sir James Goldsmith, Lady Thatcher let it be known that she too had given the Foundation money. *Agents provocateurs*, fifth columnists, anarchy: the Tory party had the lot.

Conservative divisions became ever more glaring when Kenneth Clarke argued that a single currency would not necessarily lead to political union across Europe and John Major refused publicly to endorse that view. Clarke fought a long rearguard action against committing the party to a referendum on the single currency question, but eventually Foreign Secretary Malcolm Rifkind produced an 'options' paper for the Cabinet to discuss edging the government further in a Eurosceptic direction, and Clarke stayed aboard despite reports in various quarters that he would resign. I was relieved he did. Good contacts had assured me that he would stay, but my rivals were reporting that he would go. Sometimes journalists are sweating on these stories as much as the politicians are.

It was his pro-European views which denied the succession to Ken Clarke, the man best qualified to provide an antidote to Tony Blair when Major stepped down. As the public tired of Blair's head prefect style and New Labour's media obsession, the cheery brutalism of the experienced former Chancellor, a politician who works from instinct, not focus groups, might have worked better for the Tories than the bandwagon-jumping of William Hague. But the dominant Eurosceptics insisted that it was an ABC election – anybody but Clarke. Despite leading the first two rounds of the contest Clarke was never going to make it, not even in the grotesque alliance with John Redwood which the 'odd couple' forged in their desperation to stop Hague. It was a blatantly careerist and mercifully brief marriage of convenience which did neither of their reputations any good.

In the post-Major era, Europe has continued to have a key influence on British politics. Tony Blair came to office as a convinced pro-European at the head of the least Eurosceptic governing party we had had for a decade. There were some Labour divisions on Europe, but they were not remotely as visceral as those in the Tory party, and the sceptics had no real leadership.

'I don't feel any internal pressure on Europe. It only comes from a small group of elderly MPs,' Blair had told me in his Commons room one afternoon in 1996. He would, he said, demonstrate early on the practical advantages of being in Europe. But entry into the single European currency, he conceded, 'could be very tricky' in the early days when he and his ministers would have 'too much on their plate' to make that a priority. What he meant was that even with a big majority – and he was, of course, to have a huge one of 179 – he was not prepared to take on the might of the Eurosceptic press for a European cause, at least not until he had been re-elected for a second term.

Certainly Europe has been one of Blair's chief concerns in office. Doug Henderson told me when he was Europe minister in 1998, 'I scarcely dare even clean my shoes without checking the brushes and the colour of the polish with Tony Blair.' Blair promised to seek solutions in Europe, not confrontation, and to see the EU as an opportunity, not a threat. 'I feel when I am in Europe that I am among friends,' he told me in June 1998. He believes he has made progress in changing the psychology of Europe, teaching people to accept that in any organization of fifteen countries there will be occasional spats, but that you don't have to throw up your hands in horror about the future of the whole organization when that happens: you simply get over the rows and get on with the business.

In his attempt to take Britain to the heart of Europe, Blair has had a lot going for him. He became Prime Minister as a young, charismatic leader seeming to represent New Wave politics. Others wanted to associate with him in case a little of the glitter rubbed off. Not only that, he had behind him a whopping majority which meant that his fellow leaders had to assume he would be a two-term leader, a man they had to do business with.

His first-term opponent William Hague, by contrast, came to the Tory leadership as a gut Eurosceptic who had no interest in fighting that section of his party. Having observed John Major's experience, Hague opted for the tactic of weighing in with the anti-European instincts of the majority of his party, thus largely avoiding the sniping from Lady Thatcher which had so undermined his predecessor. But even with the Tories agreeing to rule out entry into the single currency 'for the foreseeable future' there was a problem. As one prominent Euro-enthusiast in the Conservative party put it to me, 'The foreseeable future means never for John Redwood, ten years for Michael Howard and "a week is a long time in politics" for me.' Hague found his way round that. By staging a referendum within his party on the key question of the single currency and winning 84 per cent support for his line that there should be no entry during the next parliament, he was able to sideline the pro-European 'big beasts' of the Tory jungle, Michael Heseltine and Kenneth Clarke, as an unrepresentative minority. Steady development of the Eurosceptic pitch, promising to renegotiate Britain's whole relationship with the EU, did not, however, bring any greater electoral popularity, save for one contest alone – the European Parliament elections of 1999, the first national test of opinion since 1992 which Labour had failed to win.

Euro-elections tend to be a kind of national by-election in which voters feel free, perceiving little to be at stake, to indulge in a protest vote. The New Labour government, nervous of stoking a battle over the single currency which the media might exploit, in effect left a policy and personality void. They published no specific European manifesto, offered no clear policy lines and fielded few top ministers in their campaign. The nearest they got to a slogan was the less than catchy refrain 'integrate where necessary, decentralize where possible'. They hoped the elections would be a mid-term verdict on the government's over-all performance and the Prime Minister's leadership as demonstrated in the Kosovan war. Hague took a risk. He could have suffered in a pincer movement between disgruntled pro-European Conservatives and the United Kingdom Independence Party. But in a contest with a pathetically low turnout of just 24 per cent his campaign, focused tightly on 'saving the pound' and with the effective slogan of 'in Europe but not run by Europe', paid off. The only snag was that it bought the Tories no extra popularity on domestic issues and did nothing in the long term to boost their position in the opinion polls.

The Tories' Euro-election success did have one significant effect. It made Blair, with his eyes firmly fixed on winning a second term in Westminster, even jumpier about stirring any national debate on the single currency. Sometimes you could hardly blame him. At the Cologne Euro-summit in June 1999, the first gathering of EU leaders after the European Parliament elections of that year, I interviewed him on a sunny hotel balcony overlooking the cathedral. When I asked him if, after the upset of the European elections, the single currency would be pushed further onto the back burner, he declared that the need was for a constructive attitude.

> Look, on the single currency there are three positions, two of which in my position are daft. One daft position is to say you go in straight-away, irrespective. That is not our position. I am not arguing that Britain should join the single currency today, the economic con-ditions aren't right. That is one position. Another position is that you rule it out for ten years or some arbitrary period of time or you rule it out forever. Now why that is wrong is that it may be in Britain's

interest to go in: we may need it for British jobs and British industry. The sensible position is to say the test is our national economic interest: lay down the conditions that are necessary to meet it and then make a judgement. To exclude the option, to do as the Conservatives are saying, cancel the changeover plan so that we can't join in the future even if we want to, just doesn't seem to me to make any sense at all.

It was no more than a restatement of the Prime Minister's well-known position; but it was a handy explanation in straightforward terms, and that one little four-letter word lifted it into a story. As soon as Fleet Street saw the transcripts of the interview they were off, and the next day's screaming headlines declared, as I knew they would the moment I heard him utter the word: 'Blair says it's DAFT to join the euro.' It was written up as a significant cooling within Number Ten on the single currency.

Although I reckon that Gordon Brown did indeed undergo a significant loss of enthusiasm about the euro during Labour's first term, I believe it has long been Tony Blair's determination to take Britain into the single currency. He has described himself in private as 'the man with the plan'. His aim on Europe, he once told me with a clear implication, was to 'get the politics right first'. People won't want monetary union, he says, until they feel more in control of Europe's institutions. There must be more democratic accountability, which can come either from building up the Commission and the European Parliament or from building up the role of national governments and parliaments. He favours the latter course.

Blair's plan has been to persuade the British public that there are practical benefits to be had from enthusiastic British membership of the European Union. While Hague insisted that Europe was a threat, Blair saw it as an opportunity. He has tried to break down the suspicion which a Eurosceptic media had bred in Britain that every move made by the EU was a continental conspiracy against Britain. Once people have been convinced that the rest of Europe is not hell-bent on driving towards a federal Euro-state, they can, he believes, be convinced of the benefits of a single European currency and, if the economic circumstances are right, be persuaded to back British entry into the euro in a referendum. He has insisted to me in interviews that with 60 per cent of British exports going to EU countries, 'constructive engagement' with Europe has to be the way for Britain. He won't, he says, sell out Britain's interests by 'swaggering around the place trying to say I have had to handbag everybody to get my way', thereby letting down what he perceives to be the real national interest in the process.

Blair recognized from the start that the Franco-German axis which has for so long been the driving motor for Europe was unlikely to break down (although it has since had several splutters). So, instead of trying to break it, or break into it, he has built up a series of single-issue alliances with different European partners to demonstrate Britain's eagerness to be a co-operative European, participating on the field of play rather than eternally whingeing from the touchline. Thus he has linked with the Scandinavians on enlargement, with Spain on employment and with Portugal on the 'new economy', seeking to make Europe a world power in IT and modern technology.

There have been snags. Robin Cook charged off to Paris and Bonn in his first week as Foreign Secretary and announced: 'We want to make sure that from now on there are three players in Europe, not just two.' This caused such ructions with the Italians that Tony Blair had to have a special soothing session with the Italian Prime Minister. The New Labour team put a series of continental noses out of joint by insisting that they would be 'leading in Europe'. Others rapidly pointed out that the only leading in Europe Blair would be likely to do was his effort on two wheels at the Amsterdam summit in 1997. On that occasion all the leaders were presented with bicycles. It was not supposed to be a race, but Britain's Prime Minister, who can spot a photo-opportunity blindfold at seventy paces, made sure that he was the first to pedal past the cameras at the other end. Britain had no hope of even sharing the leadership of Europe, it was pointed out, while staying out of the EU's biggest single enterprise so far, the single currency.

The lack of clout in Europe consequent on staying aloof from the euro has worried Blair. It was that, together with his genuine dismay at how ill-equipped Europe was militarily to cope with the Kosovo crisis on its own doorstep, and his frustration with the American unwillingness to commit ground troops if required to a Kosovo invasion, which led Blair to one of his biggest U-turns in office. He had come to power critical of the idea of the EU developing its own 'defence dimension', fearing that it threatened to undermine NATO. Now, however, he became an eager convert to the idea of a European Rapid Reaction Force and joined French President Jacques Chirac in pushing successfully for its adoption. It was the biggest demonstration he could contrive of his pro-European credentials; but it has, of course, led to difficulties with the Americans, who still believe that the Rapid Reaction Force represents a threat to NATO – which is hardly surprising since Jacques Chirac, who loves to tweak American tails and who benefits electorally from doing so, rarely loses an opportunity to stress how independent of NATO the new force will be.

Blair has told me several times that Britain does not have to choose between its traditional alliance with the United States and its membership of the European Union. He cherishes the notion of Britain as a bridge between the two, and used precisely that argument to sell himself to Vladimir Putin as a big player. But the dual allegiance makes his fellow European leaders feel uneasy. A German official expressed his cynicism as Blair was about to become the first European leader to visit the George W. Bush White House. 'The trouble is that all the traffic over this bridge seems to be one-way,' he sniffed.

Part of the trouble, in my view, was that continental leaders soon found a gap between Blair's rhetoric on Europe and the practice. He was determined above all to win that second term with a good working majority. He could not afford, therefore, to have the press too much against him; and with the Eurosceptic tendency so strong in Fleet Street, Blair's Europeanism has been severely restricted. Even a man with a majority of 179 has been reluctant to go into pitched battle with the papers over too many European causes, especially the single currency, although there have been moments when the Downing Street calm has snapped. In July 2000, for example, Blair and Campbell raged at Fleet Street's coverage of European issues as 'a joke', accusing the papers of 'distortion and misrepresentation'.

Blair may rail at the unfairness; it certainly affects his policies. The man who has been such an eager modernizer of the British constitution has not been prepared to see Europe's constitution modernized too far in accommodating the EU's enlargement. Other member states urged the sacrifice of the national veto on a whole range of issues so that the decision-making apparatus would not be paralysed once the EU swelled to twenty-eight or thirty countries. There must be more qualified majority voting, they said. But Blair, looking back over his shoulder at Fleet Street, argued that Britain must keep its veto on taxation, social security, defence and all treaty changes to the EU constitution. That did not leave much to change.

Blair and Gordon Brown fought a long rearguard action against the so-called 'withholding tax', a proposed levy on the savings of EU nationals held in other countries. It was a tax which they feared could wreck the bond market in the City of London, hitting thousands of jobs, and in the end they won. When the EU budget came up for reform, Blair insisted on keeping the British rebate. Again he knew that since it was Lady Thatcher who had won that concession, Fleet Street would savage him as a political pygmy if he were to give it up. As such instances stacked up, the continentals muttered that Blair might talk about European co-operation but he didn't do much about it in practice. He told me himself, with a distinct touch of Thatcherite defiance, in an interview at the Helsinki summit in December 1999: 'If we are isolated and we are right that is the correct position to be in.' At least he didn't add that he was sorry for the other fourteen.

Blair is not averse to headlines saying that he has fought and won battles for British interests in Europe, even while he is emphasizing to his fellow summit leaders how co-operative he is being. Politicians do it facing both ways. And he plays along with Fleet Street's Eurosceptics from time to time, as for example by fighting a phoney battle in 1998–9 – which he knew he would never win – to secure a reprieve for duty-free sales. He had raised not a peep about it when Britain was holding the European presidency, taking up the cause only when the tabloid papers did.

To be fair, Tony Blair has made progress in ending the idea of Britain as a permanently beleaguered minority of one in Europe.

He does try to accentuate the positive. Rows have been compartmentalized; but struggling with the Eurosceptic British media does complicate his life in Europe, and sometimes he and Alastair Campbell are plumb right about the coverage which Europe is given. At the time of that Helsinki meeting, British newspaper readers might have imagined that the whole summit was dominated by the French refusal to lift the ban on British beef. In fact, the beef question was not on the summit agenda, nobody sought to place it there and it was discussed only in the margins by the British, the French and European Commission officials. The summit business dealt with European enlargement, how to handle Turkey's inclusion on the list, European defence and savings taxes. And while thirteen EU countries were accepting British beef forty others outside the EU, including the United States, were not.

I have, however, seen Blair becoming visibly disillusioned with the European Union's way of doing things. Just as they had done with John Major, the other leaders listen gravely to Blair's arguments about the need for more flexible labour markets, and then go back and make concessions to their unions which negate the whole idea. They nod sagely as he argues that they must stop constitutional navel-gazing and do more to make their electorates feel engaged with Europe and its institutions. Then they go home and draw up another grand plan for a federalist future.

As a man with a majority of 179 used to getting his own way, Blair was obviously frustrated in his first term by Europe's way of doing things. The 'You scratch my back, I'll scratch yours' style of continental politicians used to coping with coalition governments does not come naturally to him. I used to watch his body language in the group photos. At first it was all arm-grasping jollity and friendly nudges. Soon he was to be glimpsed walking on his own, frowning worriedly. On more formal occasions Blair's pencil would be tapping on the table as Commission President Jacques Santer, a pink-cheeked man with the permanent air of having lunched well, droned on with a worthy statement. Alastair Campbell would be a few paces behind, ostentatiously looking at his watch. These days they dash to the concluding press conference with almost indecent haste and are off to the airport the first moment they can get away. After the Nice summit in December 2000 was prolonged into an all-night session as the leaders wrangled over their national voting weights in European Councils and the number of European commissioners and MEPs each country should have, Blair exploded.

'We can't go on doing things like this!' he insisted. But they will.

Nor is Blair madly enthusiastic about the meetings of the Party of European Socialists (PES), which bring together all the centre-left leaders in the EU. At one such gathering in Vienna I encountered him outside the main hall, where he asked me if I would like to do an interview. I explained that since I had done one with him the day before and a colleague had already inter-viewed him for the BBC that day, we probably had all the soundbites the BBC's programmes needed that weekend. I think he just wanted to escape a boring German speaker for as long as he could decently find an excuse.

I trace Tony Blair's disappointment with Europe back to the special Brussels summit which he had to chair while Britain held the rotating EU presidency in 1998. It was to have been a grand launching of the euro. That was awkward enough for Blair, as Britain was not joining the single currency. He was too worried about securing a second general election victory to contemplate this. Then the meeting degenerated into farce as the Germans, French and Dutch rowed over who should be the first president of the European Central Bank: Wim Duisenberg or the Frenchman Jean-Claude Trichet. Blair, representing the presidency, was supposed to broker a deal. The spat went on for eight long hours. The eventual compromise was that Duisenberg would be appointed for eight years on the understanding that he would step down after four in favour of Trichet. The official summit business of launching the euro with a great fanfare was then compressed into a few minutes around midnight while government leaders, their grandiose prepared speeches still tucked into their inside pockets, sped off to their waiting aircraft.

Rumbling tummies probably had much to do with the sharpness of the criticism directed at the British Prime Minister's chairmanship on that occasion. Imagining that he could charm things through on the day, he had failed to do enough preparatory work, essential for these occasions. It was a brutal lesson in the realities of Euro-politics for a man who, up until then, was probably hanging on to his European idealism.

Maybe he had been distracted, having attended the night before an election rally for the Dutch Prime Minister Wim Kok which served to illustrate the different styles which leaders must cope with. The meeting was held in a somewhat sleazy nightclub in Rotterdam's 'Night Town' district. Outside the hall were a sturdy group of British protesters in anoraks, holding placards demanding that Mr Blair do more to save badgers. Inside, Blair was preceded on stage by three ladies from a rhythm and blues group wearing white satin and not very much of it. The air was thick with interesting odours which had nothing to do with the marinade on the restaurant steaks, and the crowd, eager to see the latest European political phenomenon, were chanting 'Tony!

Tony! Tony!' The young man next to me enquired how he might contrive to meet Mr Blair and present him with the single red rose which he was clutching. I advised him to write to Peter Mandelson.

By the end of that long night in Brussels, Blair knew he had not distinguished himself. At the final press conference I had charged him that he had promised to launch the euro successfully despite Britain's non-participation and yet what we had seen was a chaotic mess, a classic EU fight ending in a classic EU fudge. He answered me in detail at the press conference and then, unusually, I received a telephone call from him in his car on the way to the airport in which he argued how much had been achieved. He said that he had been led to believe they had a deal sorted out before coming to Brussels, but that in fact the French and Germans had been at loggerheads. A month or so later, when I spent a day travelling with him to four European capitals, he described the Brussels summit as 'a short-term mess with a long-term solution for the better'. That, I believe, was wishful thinking.

The embarrassment of the Brussels summit, I am sure, had a part to play in Blair's cool response throughout his first parliament to the Liberal Democrats' urgings that he give them the referendum on proportional representation for Westminster which John Smith had promised them. Both Blair and Alastair Campbell (no fan of PR, or, for that matter, of deals with the Lib Dems) complained to me that slowness in dealing with problems in Europe was caused not so much by battles between the national leaders as by battles within their coalition governments: not a problem faced by a man with a majority of 179 in his legislature.

For all his enthusiastic pro-Europeanism, Europe has not been a success for Tony Blair. Despite his more positive approach, the opinion poll evidence is that the European Union has grown less rather than more popular in Britain during his time in office – a measure of the continuing strength of the Eurosceptic media. But Blair himself tends to talk a better Euro-game on the continent than he delivers at home. The Cardiff European summit which Blair hosted in June 1998, at the conclusion of Britain's six months in the European presidency, was a lacklustre affair enlivened only by the presence of South Africa's retiring President Mandela, invited to say his European farewells. Even then, they did not manage to tie up the Europe–South Africa trade agreement, which might have been more use to Mandela and his people than another round of photo-opportunities. Little was done in the six months Britain was in the EU chair to advance the cause of European enlargement, supposedly a British enthusiasm, and we had the ludicrous hyping halfway through of a list of forty-five supposed 'achievements' of the British presidency. These included a claimed improvement in the conditions of zoo animals across Europe, an increase in police drug seizures across the continent and the fact that Margaret Beckett had made a speech at the European Parliament. All the early talk of Britain 'leading in Europe' – an impossible concept for a country which was staying out of Europe's biggest single project, the single currency – evaporated, as did all the exaggerated rhetoric about the creation of a 'people's Europe'. The best ministers could claim after Cardiff was 'steady work' on enlargement, the extension of driving disqualifications from one EU country into others, and an agreement in curbing drift net fishing. That was the dolphin vote sewn up, then.

Throughout New Labour's first term in government the biggest source of tension in the Blair Cabinet was over when Britain should join the single currency. It proved to be a constant cause of sniping among several key Cabinet ministers, exacerbating the personal enmities which already enmeshed them. Robin Cook and Gordon Brown have not got on since their student days. Brown fell out with Peter Mandelson over what he saw as Mandelson's desertion to promote Tony Blair's claims for the leadership rather than his after John Smith's death. These personal animosities became mixed up in the battles over the euro as Cook, Mandelson and trade secretary Stephen Byers sought to urge the case for Britain's entry, fearing that the euro's opponents were being allowed to dominate the field in the run-up to a referendum in the next parliament, while Brown grew noticeably cooler, not wanting to have anything intervene in the 2001 election campaign to divert attention from his stewardship of the economy as Chancellor. The tensions over the euro led in October 1997 to one of the biggest rows between Blair and Brown when, with Blair concentrating on the Commonwealth Conference in Edinburgh, Brown seized the opportunity for some media manipulation to force the Prime Minister's hand.

Clare Short had been involved in some personal trouble at the Labour party conference that year and had been called into Downing Street for a fraught meeting with Tony Blair. The late Tony Bevins had written a story in the *Independent* saying that the Chancellor had been 'thwarted' by the Prime Minister over the party line on the euro, and Brown, in one of his emotional moods, rang Number Ten and insisted that the policy had to be settled there and then. Blair, preoccupied by the immediate problem with Clare Short, told him to 'sort it out with Alastair' (Campbell), whereupon Brown went to Campbell and said 'Tony agrees that I should settle the euro policy,' telling him that he would do it in an interview with my former colleague Philip

Webster of *The Times*, a man they both trusted. Phil was called off the golf course and was given a chunk of text from Brown. As one of Blair's closest colleagues put it to me: 'The Prime Minister was bounced.'

Blair was furious with Brown's interpretation as it was relayed to *The Times*, and the reason why he appeared so preoccupied during the Commonwealth Conference in Edinburgh over the next few days was that he and Gordon Brown were negotiating line by line the statement that it had been agreed Brown would make in the Commons two days later. Their battle over its wording became so furious that at one stage Blair threatened to take over and make the Commons statement himself if Brown would not accede to his changes; but eventually they hammered out a compromise formula – one which has been trotted out ever since by Labour ministers as the definitive policy line.

Most of the troubles within New Labour over the euro during the next four years derived from accusations by Cook, Byers and Mandelson that Brown was backing away from the deal agreed in October 1997. This simmering tension will undoubtedly be the biggest source of potential division in the new Cabinet appointed in June 2001.

14

THE NEW TROUBADOURS: LABOUR
AND THE SPIN DOCTORS

IF YOU ARE NOT ENTHUSED BY THE TURNING OF A NEW PAGE YOU should not be a journalist, and I was excited by Tony Blair's arrival in Downing Street in 1997. There was, of course, careful choreography involved in getting all those party workers planted there to wave their Union Jacks (made in China, I believe) as Tony and Cherie glad-handed their way to the famous door, but as I walked up the street before they arrived to the camera position opposite Number Ten it was hard not to be affected by the wave of effervescent optimism for New Labour. Party workers, a few of whom I knew, most of whom I did not, waved and shouted out, 'Give us a good report, Robin!' and I hoped there would be some genuine good news to cheer them. Even for journalists, experience does not always dull expectation: with a party returned to power after eighteen years there had to be a rich vein of stories coming our way. I was looking out not just for the interest of new policies but for a new style of politics too. It duly came, but not altogether in the way I had hoped.

Tony Blair has been in many ways the ideal party leader for a media age. He is sensitive to mood, he has a barrister's ability to pick up a brief swiftly and to strip out the essentials of an argument, and he arrived in office young and good-looking, with an attractive working wife and children who have helped him carry conviction as a politician who understands family life. Downing Street has seemed less of a stuffy outpost of the political classes. In an advertising-led world where 'new' passes as a synonym for 'better', he is an eager modernizer. He lends himself instinctively to photo-opportunities like the walk down Whitehall to the Commons for his first Queen's Speech, in carefully staged contrast to the sovereign's arrival by state coach. But while a recognition of the power of the media helped to bring New Labour to power, their obsession with image has in a way become the party's biggest handicap. It has bred caution where there should have been the boldness conferred by a big majority; and it has undermined rather than reinforced the government's real achievements.

Until he was zapped by the slow-handclapping ladies of the doughty Women's Institute and by those leaked Downing Street memos which revealed him demanding policies which would make him look good, Blair appeared to have an appealing on-camera sincerity. Of all the senior figures I have interviewed he is the only one who has mastered a particular key technique. Most top politicians know how to get away without answering a question they do not want to answer. Gordon Brown does it the most blatantly, particularly in pre-recorded interviews, reproducing his carefully crafted soundbite whether or not it is an appropriate response to the question; others, with differing degrees of deftness, use a diversionary reply. But Blair is the master of not answering a question while still appearing to do so.

The only time I really caught him and got him to say

something he seriously regretted was at the party conference in 1994, when he sprang the surprise of announcing that he was to review Clause Four of Labour's constitution, the clause which used to signal the party's opposition to private enterprise and profit by calling for nationalization of large chunks of business and industry. In an interview immediately afterwards I asked him if he was thereby conceding that those who left Labour for the SDP in the 1980s had been right, and if he was trying to entice them back.

'It's not a question of welcoming back individuals, but of course I welcome back those people who left the Labour party in the early 1980s for reasons that were understandable at that time. The Labour party went through a bad period then,' he replied.

Tactically, as he conceded later, this was a mistake. His admission that there had been good reason for people leaving the Labour party irritated most of those who hadn't left in difficult times. Blair had enough on his plate trying to persuade the Labour party to drop Clause Four without alienating those who had kept the faith and stayed in Labour's ranks by giving the impression that he was trying to create an SDP Mark II. But it was a rare scalp. Sometimes, in other, later interviews, his eyes would widen at a question and he would go into his 'Oh, come on, be reasonable,' mode. But I never really caught him out again.

For a man who talks so much about modernization and change, and who has indeed changed so much of his party's and the country's constitutions already, Blair is a surprisingly cautious politician. I remember going round for a talk with him at his Islington home as the Labour leadership contest was beginning in May 1994. John Smith had won his leadership election by a margin of 9–1. Given that there was some nervousness in the party about what a new broom Blair might be and how much he might upset Old Labour, I suggested the new would-be leader had two choices. He could blur his modernization message a little and maximize his vote, so increasing his authority; or, assuming that he was going to win anyway, he could go in with all guns blazing and setting out an uncompromising vision. That way, although he might lose a few traditionalist votes, nobody could complain afterwards that he didn't have a mandate to make the changes that he wanted.

'No question,' he assured me. 'I'll be going for the second option.'

But he never really did. The plan to scrap Clause Four, for example, emerged only after he had won the leadership. What he did spell out that May was his insistence that the party had to be 'New Labour' if it was to win the next election, and that rights had to be combined with responsibilities. He outlined a view of the state not as a universal provider but as a liberator of individual potential, and on that he has been consistent. Tony Blair had not expected to be facing the leadership contest, he told me, for another seven or eight years; but he knew that the reason for choosing him would be 'electability'.

When I went to see him for a further talk in September that year, after he had won the leadership, he was already differentiating himself from John Smith, talking of his determination to ensure that Labour was no longer seen as a tax-and-spend party.

'Middle England has suffered enough,' he said. 'We can't let them say that tax would be even worse under us.' The march to occupy the middle ground of politics had clearly begun. Ideological baggage was being jettisoned, and he was clearly more interested in solutions than in where the ideas came from. From the start there was a sense of impatience with his own party and its slowness to adapt. Labour, he argued, had to offer clarity and to define a set of core beliefs. He was also interesting on the subject of the Liberal Democrats.

'I've tried to send messages that aren't tribal,' he revealed. There were, he insisted, people among the Liberal Democrats who were 'modern Social Democrats'; and, perhaps surprisingly in view of his later close co-operation with Paddy Ashdown and his cooler relationship with his successor, it was Charles Kennedy, rather than Paddy, whom he named as an example. Blair, an instinctive believer in the Big Tent politics of co-operation so long as it did not prejudice Labour's majority, argued forcefully that there were ways the two parties could work together, and he said the Lib Dems would be 'daft' (a favourite Blair word) to manufacture differences or to seek to outflank Labour to the left.

But was he thinking co-operation or takeover?

'There are two parties in the Lib Dems and I wouldn't want the beards and sandals people,' he told me, perhaps giving an unconscious clue.

A chat with Tony Blair is always a serious affair. He does enjoy talking policy. But the burdens of office are taking their toll. The lighter side we used to see sometimes in opposition has been well-nigh invisible in the last few years, although occasionally one still catches a glimpse.

At the end of the party conference season in 1999 the four TV political editors for the BBC, Sky and Channel Four were invited to conduct the usual end of conference interviews with Labour's leader. Michael Brunson, then ITN's political editor, was about to retire, and there had been gossip column stories suggesting that he had pleased Downing Street enough to be in line for a peerage. As he got up from the interviewer's chair and I went to sit opposite the Prime Minister for my turn, I bowed and jokingly doffed an imaginary cap to Mike, saying, 'Good morning your lordship, your honour, your grace.'

'What's all that about?' asked Blair, and I explained.

'I'd like to be Lord Brunson of Abingdon Green, since I've spent so much time standing on that bit of turf in front of the Commons,' said Michael.

'Tell you what, Robin,' said Blair, turning to me with a grin. 'Ask the right questions and you can have a hereditary peerage.'

Michael had to be content in the end with an OBE, seemingly the going rate for the job, and I too remain un-ennobled. It must have been something I didn't say.

New Labour, which found such willing listeners in the press as it harried the doomed Tories over sleaze and disunity in the latter days of John Major's government, has taken media management to new levels, investing enormous effort in revamping the whole process of communication. I remember Blair aides telling me of their shock on coming into Number Ten at the lack of basic office equipment and news agency wire printouts. 'It's all so amazingly amateur,' said one.

The media, and the old-style government information service, soon found that a step-change was taking place. As early as September 1997 Alastair Campbell wrote to Whitehall press officers with a clear signal of the new government's style. 'Decide your headlines,' he commanded them. 'Sell your story, and if you disagree with what is being written, argue your case. If you need support from here, let me know.' Significantly, he went on to argue that media-handling had to be an integral part of the policy-making process. 'My sense is that in many departments policy is discussed and then developed on a completely separate track, and the media plan is then added on at a much later stage. We need to be in there at the start,' he argued.

Inevitably, after such initiatives, much attention has been

focused on the so-called 'spin doctors', most of whom we in the media used to know merely as press officers. Newspapers print nearly as much now about how some stories are sold as they do about the story itself. My long-time colleague Nicholas Jones, one of the best reporters the BBC has on its staff, has made a small industry out of books about the spin doctors' profession. In fact we have had spin doctors ever since the troubadours in medieval courts used to sing about the qualities of their monarchs. It is just that in the media-dominated world politicians now inhabit they have become much more proactive, and some of them have become more important to their parties' prospects than many members of the frontbench teams.

The Spin Doctor Supreme, of course, is Alastair himself. You have only to sit as I have done on the Blair helicopter during an election campaign and watch Campbell lean over to slash out great sections of his leader's prepared remarks for the next venue, or to watch the long-time press secretary's body language as he wanders in and out of the Prime Minister's room munching an apple and firing out sardonic asides, to sense the power that he wields. He is an essential part of the New Labour Project, and looms even larger following the exile of Peter Mandelson.

Like Bernard Ingham with Mrs Thatcher, Campbell has been close enough to the Prime Minister to lay down the Blairite line with the media even when he has had no time to check it out with Blair himself. Ingham, too, was partisan, but his Rottweiler role and 'bunkum and balderdash' tantrums with the media expressed a basically personal loyalty to his chief. Campbell is more deeply entrenched in the whole process of New Labour government. Though he disapproves of the Prime Minister's schooling arrangements and of his flirtations with the Liberal Democrats, Campbell is both a personal and political soulmate.

He attends Cabinet as he wishes and the rules have been rewritten to allow him to pursue a political role while being paid as a civil servant. His contract imposes Civil Service regulations 'except to those aspects which relate to impartiality and objectivity'. That exception has caused much fluttering of constitutional fans and inspired a fair measure of pomposity in editorial columns, but I believe it is right that such a change has been made, because it strips away pretence. In the modern political world, with the media so omnipresent, it is impossible for the press secretary to the Prime Minister not to have a political role. Sooner or later they all slide into it; and, usually, into a fairly intense personal relationship as well.

At times it seems Tony Blair resents the power his press secretary enjoys. There looked to be a touch of wounded pride and self-assertion in the way he spoke of him in Michael Cockerell's BBC documentary, *News From Number Ten*, in 2000 as the 'best hired help' available. Blair's confirmation to Cockerell that he had himself urged Campbell to step back from the twice-daily lobby briefing sessions and take on a more strategic role like the one he enjoys in the new parliament may have masked his worry that the messenger was becoming part of the message, even sometimes obscuring it with the force of his personality. Certainly Cabinet ministers have resented Campbell's power and manifestly enjoyed the occasional chance to get back at him, as when in February this year John Prescott and David Blunkett hit out openly over Campbell's reference, when discussing education policy, to 'bog standard' comprehensive schools.

But ministers tangle with Campbell at their peril. Back in January and February 1998 he sent furious fax messages to Harriet Harman and Frank Field, the squabbling ministerial colleagues in social security.

'Given the speculation on welfare changes in the Budget in recent days and the fact that the two have become inextricably linked, I think it important that you both enter a period of pre-Budget purdah,' he demanded. 'This should include all interviews that may cover Budget issues. I would also urge extreme caution in relation to lunches' (by which he meant: no cosy chats to journalists). Campbell chided the two for giving interviews without seeking permission from Number Ten and complained in a second memo about 'congenital' (or excessive and habitual) 'briefing'. Blair was to make a keynote speech on welfare reform issues in the Midlands town of Dudley that day. 'Today's exercise will only work if it is focused entirely on the Prime Minister's Dudley meeting,' Campbell added.

There have been control freaks at Downing Street before. Harold Wilson's press secretary Joe Haines confessed freely that ministers could not make statements in the Commons, broadcast or write articles without his permission, 'because my say-so was the Prime Minister's say-so'. What was significant about Campbell's missives was that they went out under Alastair's own name, not that of the Prime Minister. Harriet was apologetic, Frank muttered – and neither of them survived long in government thereafter, although she has now mabe a comeback in a legal role.

Campbell has, of course, been indispensable. A Prime Minister who is the best actor-politician in the role since Harold Macmillan needs a talented scriptwriter. Remember September 1997 and the death of Diana, Princess of Wales: 'She was the People's Princess and that is how she will stay . . .[gulp] . . . how she will remain in our hearts and memories for ever.' It was a key passage which summed up the instincts of the nation; and it came from a Campbell–Blair discussion.

A mutual friend told me that for some months Alastair

preserved on his pager the message first informing him of the fateful crash in Paris. It was certainly a moment I will never forget. My wife Carolyn was in hospital at the time after a serious spinal operation. Woken by a telephone call at 3.00 a.m., I was terrified what kind of news I might be about to hear, and in a sense I was actually relieved to find it was a summons from the office to get to Westminster and start broadcasting as soon as possible. Coming round in her hospital bed the next morning, Carolyn was surprised to find me on screen in the early hours.

In our media-dominated age, and in what is becoming an ever more presidential style of politics, the Prime Minister's chief link with the media has become the most important job in his government. Politicians now judge themselves by their impact in the media; they fight their elections through the media; and those who fail in their relations with the media rarely last. Lady Thatcher's key media operatives – Bernard Ingham, her advertising guru Sir Tim, later Lord Bell, her PR man Gordon Reece, her speech-writer Sir Ronnie Millar – lasted much longer at her side than most of her ministers.

It is a testament to how effective Campbell has proved, stonewalling when necessary, creating diversions and on occasion simply soaking up the government's punishment and coming back for more with a wolfish grin, that his professional skills were sought both by the royal family over the death of Princess Diana and by NATO over the Kosovo war. Over Diana's death, incidentally, it was not a case of Campbell stepping in to grab some glory for Downing Street; he was specifically invited by Sir Robert Fellowes, the Queen's private secretary, to join the Palace committee organizing Diana's funeral. Alastair is no monarchist, as his past columns as a journalist confirm, but I remember him arguing privately at the time that the Palace was not being given due credit for what it was trying to do. And it was Diana's family who urged that the Prime Minister, who had encouraged her in life to seek a new role, should speak at the funeral.

The techniques employed by Campbell and Co. have been pretty standard. He has come a long way from his early days in the job, when he refused to help the BBC get much needed preview shots at the conference hotel before Blair's first leader's speech. Now he thinks nothing of sending the Prime Minister out for a mysterious fifteen-minute journey away from Number Ten simply so that the television news companies can get the leaving or arrival shots they need on an otherwise quiet news day. It was Alastair who held back the car on the South Bank for a few minutes on the morning after New Labour's first election victory so that Blair arrived, symbolically, just as the new dawn broke.

Such cosmetics and choreography are part and parcel of modern media management; and the Blair team know all the classic moves. If there is a story running that they do not like, they will toss the media a bigger bone for them to worry. In the summer of 1997, for example, the *News of the World* revealed the story of Foreign Secretary Robin Cook's affair with his then secretary Gaynor Regan, now his wife. Learning the revelation was coming, Labour's spin machine went into overdrive and let loose not just one but two counter-stories. It was revealed to the *Sunday Times* that MI6 was conducting an examination to see if Chris Patten, the former Tory chairman and then Governor of Hong Kong, had broken the Official Secrets Act. (He hadn't.) And then, in a radio interview, Peter Mandelson suggested the government was thinking about reprieving the royal yacht *Britannia*. (In the end, it didn't.) The result was that not a single paper led on the Monday with Robin Cook's affair.

There was even a suggestion at the time the defence review was leaked in 1998 that that too had been orchestrated from within the government as a diversionary tactic. Ministers were under pressure at the time over the 'cash for access' affair, with New Labour lobbyists allegedly taking payments for providing access to ministers with whom they had worked in opposition. I cannot prove that the defence review was leaked deliberately from the highest quarters; but, with the notable exception of the defence secretary, Labour's top team did not seem much upset that the leak had occurred. They certainly needed a good diversion at the time of the 'cash for access' affair, because 'cronyism' was a label which stuck. The spectacle of sharp-suited former insiders cashing in on their contacts books was no more attractive than that of Conservative MPs on the take during the 'cash for questions' episode when John Major was in power.

The cronyism charges, of course, came to a head in December 1998 over the affair of Peter Mandelson's mortgage and the £373,000 advanced by Treasury minister Geoffrey Robinson when they were in opposition two years earlier. This loan had helped Mandelson, one of those politicians who like to move in fashionable circles, to buy a property in trendy Notting Hill. When Mandelson was forced out of the Cabinet a second time in 2001, over the Hinduja passports affair, it was as a result of prime ministerial panic in the face of media pressure; but his first resignation was patently his own fault. That too might have been averted were it not for the sheer extent of media coverage generated simply because he was who he was and because sections of Fleet Street saw a way of getting back at the man who had forged his career in the red rose days as Labour's reforming director of communications and who had made plenty of enemies in his days as a spinner supreme.

With the department which he then headed investigating

Geoffrey Robinson's affairs, even though Mandelson was playing no part in that investigation, Mandelson should have disclosed the house loan both to his own department's permanent secretary and to the Prime Minister. When the loan came to light – probably thanks to his enemies in the Treasury – he was in trouble. But on the first night, as he toured the TV studios insisting that he had neither flouted the code of conduct for ministers nor offended against the rules on the register of MPs' financial interests, it looked as though he could survive. There were strong indications of the Prime Minister's backing and, when I was asked on the *Six O'Clock News* if he would be forced to resign, I got it wrong. Having absorbed some fairly heavy Downing Street spin, I said that the affair had demonstrated an astonishing lack of judgement and that it would probably limit Mr Mandelson's future career, denying him the role of Foreign Secretary which he coveted; but I thought he would survive.

Immediately after the programme I took a call from Peter, who sounded, for one so disciplined in his public appearances, surprisingly emotional. I had been very hard on him, he argued. 'What have I done that was so wrong?'

Amazed that one so acute still seemed to be having trouble accepting how wrongly he had behaved, I repeated what I had said on the programme – that his failure to disclose the loan was highly culpable and put him in a position no minister should have occupied. With Downing Street still firm, I repeated in another two-way on the *Nine O'Clock News* that I thought Peter would survive, adding, however, that it was an example of how ministers who were sharp in their political judgements could go awry when it came to their own personal lives.

By the morning Peter had resigned. Late at night he had seen the Prime Minister and told him that he was minded to go. I believe that at that point he was hoping for reassurance that he need not do so. Blair told him to think about it overnight, and when they woke and saw the morning's papers both men knew that he had to step down. The sheer scale of the media barrage made it inevitable. With other questions outstanding about whether he had filled in his mortgage form correctly, it was clear that the pressure would be impossible if he were to try to stay on. The arch-manipulator of the media had been brought down by the sheer weight of the media's interest in him. And since Mandelson had gone Robinson had to go too, which he did a few hours later.

That afternoon, I went round to the trade and industry department to interview the departing minister. Mandelson's face was even paler than usual and his eyes were a little puffy, but he managed a wry smile and he held himself together with dignity through one of the toughest interviews I had had to conduct with anybody. I did not want to be seen by viewers to be kicking a man who was down, and yet I was determined to tackle the serious questions which remained.

Why, I asked, had he resigned from the government after first insisting that there was no question of his doing so?

'If you remember, we said before the election we were going to make sure we were better than better, whiter than white, squeaky clean,' Peter said. 'I feel that I have been in all that I have done in government but, through my own misjudgement, I have allowed the impression to be created of wrongdoing.'

Shouldn't he have told the Prime Minister and the permanent secretary about his loan?

Yes, he admitted. 'If I had told the Prime Minister, if I had mentioned it to my permanent secretary at the same time as standing aside I wouldn't have generated the headlines, the treatment of me that we have seen over the last two days. That was my mistake. I should have been open about it.'

Had there been any impropriety in the way he had filled in his mortgage application to the Britannia Building Society? Had he disclosed the loan to them?

'I know people are talking about the form I filled in for the Britannia. It was nearly two years ago and I cannot remember every question. I can't remember every answer . . . having tried to find a copy of the form I filled in and failed to do that, I cannot clarify that even now.'

On a personal level I felt sorry for Peter, who is an acute political strategist when his own life is not involved and a entertaining companion, even if his ascetic habit of drinking only hot water with a slice of lemon in it is a little disconcerting. But the weakness of such an answer made it plain why he had had to go. Both he and I knew that that last reply was not a convincing answer to the ticking time-bomb of the question I had put to him, especially as less prominent people might not have found their building society or other authorities quite so understanding. And we in the media could certainly not slide over such facts in the way that some of Peter's colleagues seemed prepared to do. It was amazing that Blair, who had promised a new approach and a purer than pure administration, was prepared to let him back in government so soon. Lady Thatcher, too, had had her favourites; but after the entanglements in Cecil Parkinson's private life forced him to resign, she waited for him to be re-endorsed by the voters in a general election before she put him back in her Cabinet.

Peter Mandelson's career has been a real tragedy. Let me confess: I rather like Peter. Although I have never been one of his media intimates, he has never denied me reasonable access and we have always had amiable relations. He is very talented. But a taste for conspiracy, an irresistible urge to give a swirl of his cloak and a curl of the moustache he no longer wears to draw a hiss from the audience will always let him down. He has been more 'in the know' than most people. But he can never resist the urge to pretend he knows the lot. This has led others to believe he was the author of their misfortunes, and it has left him short of friends at vital moments.

I had a minor example one day of the sort of thing which, repeated on a wider scale, so irritated some of his colleagues. Over dinner one night in Tristan Garel-Jones's Westminster home, Mandelson deliberately goaded me.

'Ah, Robin, the Prime Minister was telling me the other day that he must have done well at Question Time because even you had said so.' The implication was that the Prime Minister regarded me as prejudiced against him. Stupidly, I rose to the bait and defended myself as someone who always treated Blair, or anyone else, fairly, receiving in return the famously quizzical raised Mandelson eyebrow.

A few days later I was chatting to Alastair Campbell. 'What's all this about Tony thinking I'm hard on him?' I asked, and repeated the Mandelson conversation.

'That's balls!' Alastair said. 'I can tell you exactly what happened. Tony came out of Question Time feeling he hadn't done well. Tim Allan [Alastair's number two at that time], who had been watching you on *Westminster Live*, said, "But Robin Oakley has just described it as one of your best performances." At which point Tony said, "Oh, well in that case it must have been better than I thought."'

Peter Mandelson had merely been winding me up. One of his ministerial colleagues told me – in a comment which says as much about Blair as about Mandelson – 'The thing about Peter is that he is a natural courtier whose social life has blossomed on the strength of his closeness to Tony. He didn't prosper under John Smith because there was no court.'

Shortly after Mandelson's departure in December 1998 Tony Blair went off on holiday to the Seychelles, without having commented publicly on the affair. From there, a chartered British Airways jumbo with the media team already on board picked him up to head onwards to South Africa, where he wanted to develop his relationship with the new President, Thabo Mbeki. As soon as Blair joined us on board we started pressing him for his reactions on the Mandelson affair. From our questioning on the plane, the Prime Minister and Campbell rapidly realized that the issue was likely to dominate the British coverage of the South African trip if they did not defuse the situation. So the first thing that happened when we arrived in South Africa was that all the broadcasters were offered sit-down interviews with the Prime Minister in which we quizzed him about Mandelson and his relationship with his Chancellor Gordon Brown, whose entourage had been blamed for the disclosures which had brought down Peter Mandelson. It was a classic example of the power of the media to dictate the agenda, and a classic piece of damage limitation. You can holiday, I reflected, but you can't hide.

I asked the Prime Minister how he and Brown could live, long-term, with Brown's obvious resentment that he hadn't got Blair's job.

'That's rubbish!' Blair replied. 'Our relations are probably closer than any Chancellor and Prime Minister have been and we are able to have a relationship in which we construct the economic policy together.' But he looked truly uncomfortable.

There was a spate of other 'personality' stories around at the time, most of them pretty irrelevant to political performance. An old tale about trade secretary Stephen Byers having had a 'love child' when he was seventeen had been recycled, along with revelations about Robin Cook's alleged drinking and womanizing habits from the former wife whom he had dumped in a Heathrow departure lounge when under pressure from Alastair Campbell to regularize his domestic affairs. John Prescott, too, was manoeuvring none too delicately to ensure that the departure of Peter Mandelson would mean less cosying up to the Liberal Democrats. Seeing some story potential there, I goaded an irritated Blair into saying that the relationship with the Lib Dems would intensify rather than decline – a comment which brought little joy, I heard, back at Prescott's Department of the Environment, Transport and the Regions.

On the plane back from South Africa, via a visit to British forces in Kuwait, a clearly bruised Tony Blair told us that there would be a good deal less foreign travel in the year ahead and much more concentration on the 'core political agenda' of health, education and fighting crime. He also produced the interesting theory that the government was being handicapped by the failure of the Tories under William Hague to attack them effectively enough. Blair's complaint was that since the media were interested in reporting only clashes, not policy announcements, and the Tories were making so little impact, nobody was reporting what the government was actually doing. They were focusing entirely on personality stories. It was a convenient theory, with a grain of truth in it; but there was also the question of under-performance and over-selling from a government which always overdid the sales talk.

It was around that time that the Blair team's disillusion with the media set in. Spin doctors always tend to become more active in the second half of a parliament as the gloss begins to flake off a government. Most administrations come to office suffering from the sad delusion that the media are on their side. In most cases, and the Blair government is a particularly good example, they have arrived in office because journalists have given much space and attention to their criticisms of the predecessor regime and because their performance in opposition has been contrasted favourably with the efforts of the previous government. When they first set up shop themselves, they are given a fair wind and allowed an error or too without too much fuss. For one thing, the media know the public expect them to be given a chance; and for another, new faces in the jobs and new ways of doing things are story enough for a while. But as the business of government goes on and they make their own mistakes, the new ministers are puzzled and then hurt to find that the correspondents whom they had fondly imagined to be their friends are becoming increasingly critical of them. They find they are devoting less of their energies to the fine new policies they had in mind and more to the sheer arts of survival and keeping out of trouble. Stung by an ungrateful electorate and what they see as an impatient media, Prime Ministers come back to the media quarters on their planes for a friendly chat less frequently. Spokesmen in Downing Street go surly and retreat, threatening from time to time to call off the whole briefing process. Indeed, under Harold Wilson, Joe Haines did precisely that for a time, restricting access to a small group who became known in those less politically correct times as the 'White Commonwealth'.

Tony Blair's Downing Street team reacted to growing criticism a little petulantly by seeking to bypass a Fleet Street which they regarded as obsessed with personality. But while I believe that their criticism was justified to some extent, I disagree fervently with their definition of stories about the cost of ministerial flights and hotel rooms as 'trivia'. Governments and their ministers become self-important and start to believe that the way they are doing things is the definition of how they should be done. We need a vigilant media to help protect the public purse.

Alastair Campbell argued that the national dailies with their falling circulations were out of touch with true public concerns and were incapable of reporting serious issues. The information machine therefore decided to put the emphasis on Commons statements and other outlets through which ministers had the chance to speak directly to the people. They began doing more radio and television interviews, especially on live programmes, and making more contact with the regional media. For an initiative on youth employment, for example, fifteen regional editors were briefed in detail by the Prime Minister and employment secretary David Blunkett, complete with slide show. The national papers were ignored. There was extensive coverage in the regionals, none in the nationals, and ministers insisted they did not care.

At the same time Downing Street branched out. In the press office and in the Strategic Communications Unit they installed two people to work full-time on targeting women's publications. Two more were set to work on European media outlets, and others were taken on to deal exclusively with ethnic publications and with the internet. Campbell and Co. launched an assault designed to separate the broadcasters from Fleet Street. Any example they could find of the broadcasters picking up and running with the tabloid agenda was seized upon and ridiculed. I received regular phone calls in which Alastair would insist that this was an era of opportunity for the BBC to assert its independence and make its own decisions on story worth. So long as this meant independence from the government machine too, I was happy with the theory. But it underestimated the cannibalistic nature of the media world. It cannot be compartmentalized so easily. Nor does public cynicism about politics and politicians derive solely from tabloid excess. The government's own reputation for excessive spin-doctoring and media manipulation, with selective leaking of its own documents and decisions, plays a big role too.

Just how badly wrong the government could get it on occasion was shown by Home Secretary Jack Straw's attempt, eventually abandoned, to seek a legal injunction early in 1999 against publication of leaks from the inquiry into the police handling of the death of Stephen Lawrence. Straw said he had sought the injunction in the interests of the family and the Metropolitan Police, and to ensure that Parliament learned the details first. This was rubbish. The Lawrence family were not bothered what extracts were printed; it made little difference to the Metropolitan Police, who had faced months of criticism already; and there has rarely been a government so ready to bypass Parliament by making announcements of what it was doing in the media before the Commons were told. The normally sure-footed Straw was suffering from a rare dose of ministerial pique, and his intervention switched the emphasis – unfortunately – away from race relations and reform of the Metropolitan Police to the government's handling of the media.

In general, Jack was one of the New Labour government's first-term success stories. In the Home Office, a department where the unexpected always happens, he managed to build a reputation for steadiness and good preparation. There are snags for both sides, though, in the full-time security operation which he and his family have to accommodate in such a role. On a rare weekend off, Jack decided one day to take the family to the cinema. He picked on a title showing at the Ritzy, Brixton, not far from where we both live in Kennington. The family Straw and the Special Branch officer on duty for their protection duly went off to the cinema, where the film proved to be a dreary Scandinavian epic, with sub-titles, about the life of two drop-outs on the dole. While the younger Straws fidgeted in their seats, the Home Secretary and his wife did their best to follow what plot there was. As the numbed audience filed out at the end, Straw enquired of his Special Branch man how he had enjoyed the film.

'Enjoy it, sir? I was so depressed I nearly went down to Brixton nick and handed in my sidearm for fear I might turn it on myself.'

What was curious about the Labour media operation, which had been so astonishingly successful in opposition, was how in government they failed to learn from their mistakes. In November 1997 Labour was forced to hand back £1 million which it had received from the motor-racing tycoon Bernie Ecclestone, who had earlier been invited into Downing Street to lobby (successfully) for his sport to be exempted on job-creation grounds from the government's policy of banning cigarette advertising from sporting events. It was a double blow because the party had been hoping to gain further funding from the same source. Facts were dragged out slowly from a reluctant and therefore shifty-sounding Downing Street, ensuring that the story ran for longer than it otherwise would have and demonstrating the clear lesson that when the sticky stuff hits the fan it is better to bring all the facts into the open swiftly rather than turn the episode into an involuntary and extended striptease.

The lesson, though, was not digested, because we saw the same pattern all over again in March 1998 over a story involving Blair acting as an intermediary between the newspaper magnate Rupert Murdoch and Romano Prodi, then the Italian Prime Minister and later to be the successful Blair-backed candidate to become President of the European Commission. It began when the Italian newspaper *La Stampa* claimed that Blair had phoned Prodi to lobby him over Rupert Murdoch's interest in buying the Italian media conglomerate Mediaset, owned by the politician Silvio Berlusconi. That was only partially true. It was Prodi who had called Blair on other matters, and the Murdoch deal was not the main point of the conversation. But Alastair Campbell and his team of Downing Street spokesmen knew that many in the Labour party were sensitive to any evidence of Blair seeming to suck up to a media magnate whom they loathed; so, using those minor inaccuracies, they sought to browbeat journalists and to obfuscate the main point of the story in the hope of killing it off.

At first they used the old formula that they had 'no knowledge' of the story, a spin doctor's way of suggesting there is nothing in it without actually denying something has happened. Then they refused to say whether or not the Mediaset deal had been discussed in the Prodi–Blair conversation, insisting that they did not brief on private conversations. Mostly they don't, it is true. But reporters are often given titbits from such conversations when it suits the government's purpose – as, for example, when President Bill Clinton praised John Prescott's role at the Kyoto environment summit.

We enquired further. Could Downing Street assure us that there had not been any discussion of Mr Murdoch and his deal in the conversation? They could not. Pressed further through a series of briefings, they became angry and insisted that it was 'balls' that Mr Blair had 'intervened' in some deal. The next tactic was abuse. Reporters who persisted were accused of 'talking crap' and lacking principle. The *Financial Times* was targeted, becoming the focus of Campbell complaints about 'a diary story lifted to the front of a once-serious newspaper'. Next, the government spokesmen complained that they were being used as fodder for a Fleet Street war – and, in fairness, the involvement of Rupert Murdoch did give journalists on rival newspapers an added zest in pursuing the story, which by now was being described by Downing Street as 'a complete joke'. At one stage Campbell challenged the assembled lobby to follow the Tories and claim that he had lied. None did, because he had not lied, although he had sought to lay smokescreens. The Number Ten official who had monitored the Prodi conversation was said to be out of the country in the Middle East and unavailable for checking details. Was he at a hotel with no phone? Poor chap. It is scandalous how badly we treat our public servants.

Downing Street had got as far as making the hardly surprising concession that any British Prime Minister would do his best to help the interests of British firms when one of Mr Murdoch's own newspapers, *The Times*, provided a new development. It reported that Murdoch had used information supplied by the Prime Minister in deciding not to bid higher for Mediaset. Murdoch told his own paper he had made a perfectly innocent request for information from the Prime Minister who had telephoned him, after speaking to Prodi, to say that the Italian government would prefer to see an Italian bid but would not block the Murdoch bid if no other were forthcoming.

It was not surprising that Murdoch should have sought help and information from the Prime Minister over such a deal or that Mr Blair should have acceded to any such request. What was extraordinary was the prickliness of Number Ten about the whole affair. It did not accord with all Labour's promises of 'open government' when in opposition. But of course, the revelations came at a time when Labour MPs were beginning to complain about the Prime Minister being starstruck by business leaders and to become suspicious that he had a 'special relation-ship' with Murdoch so as to keep the *Sun* newspaper on his side.

Some Labour MPs did not like the degree of power wielded by unelected figures such as Alastair Campbell, and it was at this time that Campbell's earlier memos telling Harriet Harman and Frank Field to take themselves into purdah were leaked. The same weekend there had been leaks of a document from a Labour fund-raiser, Amanda Dellew, reminding the Prime Minister that big donors to Labour would expect invitations to Number Ten. 'Just an early draft never seen by ministers,' said the spin doctors. But from a party which had coasted to office criticizing Tory sleaze it did not look reassuring.

Governments always have had spin doctors and always will have them. What has been striking about New Labour is the sheer scale of the operation. Labour had taken a long time in opposition to learn the discipline which helped to bring it back to power after eighteen years, and the new regime were deter-mined that it would not be relaxed once they came to office. They resent the label of control freaks, but that is what they were and are. We saw it over devolution, when the Prime Minister blessed the creation of a Scottish Parliament and Welsh Assembly to decide affairs in their localities, but still could not kick the habit of wanting to control what kind of Labour representatives led or were elected to the new bodies.

No other administration in my time worked so hard at keep-ing its foot-soldiers singing from the same hymn sheet or at seeking to manipulate the media; but it is my firm belief that Labour in its first term actually suffered more from its spinning than it gained. I do not altogether blame them. They had learned from bitter experience how much indiscipline and mixed messages can harm a party. Today's media, given an inch, will take a mile, and with the advent of twenty-four-hour news there is much more exposure. If politicians don't seek to run the media, the media will run them.

15

LABOUR AND THE MEDIA; OR, THE STRANGE CASE OF HUMPHREY THE CAT

THE 1997–2001 LABOUR GOVERNMENT WAS ONE OF STRIKING initiative and considerable strength of purpose. It gave us Scottish and Welsh devolution, an independent Bank of England in charge of interest rates, a national minimum wage and the working families tax credit. It repaid chunks of national debt, began the much-needed reform of the welfare system and began to turn round Britain's serious underspend in public services. It conducted a war in Kosovo with credit and fought successful battles in the European Union over the British budget rebate and the withholding tax. Tony Blair and his government deserved the credit electors gave them for their first-term achievements. But because it proved as evasive as the Tories before it when scandals surfaced, it failed to renew public faith in politicians as a breed; and because it was so obsessed with its own image, it bred a public cynicism about the whole process of government.

'We need two or three eye-catching initiatives ... I should be personally associated with as much of this as possible,' read one of the leaked missives Blair sent to his Downing Street team. Of course, this was manna for Rory Bremner and Co.

Public cynicism was redoubled by the way in which the general election of 2001 was postponed from May to June. Blair's decision to do so when the focus groups told him he would look arrogant if he went ahead on 3 May, in view of the gravity of the foot-and-mouth crisis, raised one particular problem. New Labour has set great store by keeping the *Sun* newspaper on side. Blair went to a News Corporation shindig in Australia to win over Rupert Murdoch and his key tabloid; Gordon Brown went to another in America to help keep them sweet. As part of sugaring the *Sun* before the election, the paper had been given an exclusive tip-off when Blair first decided the date would be 3 May, which it ran alongside its declaration that it would be backing New Labour in the election. Delaying the poll to 7 June was going to leave a potentially angry *Sun* with egg on its front page. So the solution was simple: give the *Sun* another exclusive that it was now to be 7 June. Margaret Thatcher, like Harold Wilson, sought to keep Fleet Street happy with judiciously distributed knighthoods and peerages; Tony Blair does it with scoops. But the need for haste in employing the new stratagem meant that the *Sun* was informed about the new date before many of Tony Blair's ministers were, and while some of those ministers were still rehearsing the arguments as to why the government should not budge from 3 May.

Nowhere was the Blair team's attempt to manipulate the media more blatant. As an *Independent* leader tartly observed: 'The *Sun* now seems to occupy the role once allotted to the monarch in our constitution – "the right to be consulted, the right to encourage, the right to warn".' The cumulative result of this bit of clever news management can only have been to irritate most of Blair's fellow ministers and MPs, the rest of Fleet Street and a fair proportion of the general public to boot.

*

As part of its attempt to dominate the headlines and dictate the quality of its coverage, New Labour initiated a ruthless purge of senior civil service press officers across Whitehall. Within a single year after the 1997 election, twenty-five heads of information or their deputies had quit or been sacked. Some, it is true, were past their sell-by date; but some highly competent officials appeared to be excluded simply because, as Thatcher would have put it, they were not 'one of us'. Under New Labour the government information service was professionalized, but it was also politicized. The simultaneous building up of a huge panoply of rapid rebuttal units, strategic communications units, research departments and electronic knowledge networks fed an image of media obsession.

Then there was the vast influx of ministerial 'special advisers'. No minister feels happy these days, it seems, without two or three such walking comfort blankets. There were around thirty of them in Whitehall when the Major government left office. By the time the Neill Committee on Standards in Public Life reported on them in January 2000 there were nearly eighty, with Downing Street's own quota up from eight to twenty-eight; and the bill for such appointments had risen from £1.8 million to £3.9 million. These advisers have brought their own problems, for not only did they strike many as an indulgence and an unnecessary expense, they actually helped to undermine the new government. New Labour's troubles have never been over policy disputes; their difficulties have been personality clashes involving the big beasts like Gordon Brown, Robin Cook, Peter Mandelson, John Prescott, Jack Straw and David Blunkett. The corps of special advisers, each of whom owes a personal loyalty to his or her minister rather than a general loyalty to government or party, have been behind most of the stories which have embarrassed the government. Although the principals rarely rubbish each other in front of journalists, their apparatchiks are seldom reluctant to do so. If they had no regularly available 'friends', why, even Gordon Brown and Robin Cook might be on friendly terms by now.

The Neill Committee's report of January 2000 called for a cap on the number of special advisers, some of whom are genuine policy experts, some of whom are links with the Labour party or extra press officers, and some of whom are merely cronies. It also urged a Civil Service Act laying down a code of conduct for them. So far, nothing much has happened.

Labour's advisers and spinners, and some ministers too, have also been too sharp for their own good in the use of statistics. If they feel they have not been given due credit for what they have spent and done in the fields of health and education, it is because they have bred cynicism with their constant repackaging of the same initiative and the double and triple counting of their sums. Jack Straw's 'blitz on burglary blackspots' and 'crime reduction programme' seemed to pop up once every two or three months at one stage. So did the £100 million for schools to be hooked up on the internet to the National Grid for Learning. Ministers constantly talked of Gordon Brown's '£40 billion boost for health and education' once he agreed to open the Treasury purse strings; but they did so for the best part of a year before the money actually came on stream, and then wondered why their constituents were so irritated that their own local hospital or school appeared to have been totally unaffected by the government's largesse.

The most irritating trick was double counting. If the government was spending £8 billion a year on something and then announced it was to spend an extra £2 billion in each of the next three years this would be presented as an increase of £12 billion, on the reasoning that it had increased spending by £2 billion in the first year, £4 billion in the second year and £6 billion in the third year. Any business organization which presented that as more than an increase of £6 billion would be accused of false accounting.

Then there has been the question of tone. Alastair Campbell in most respects has been probably the best press secretary I have known. I sometimes find it hard to see why there has been such a fuss about what he has done. It was his job to generate coverage for the achievements to which the government wished to draw attention and to put the best interpretation on what they did. I was never worried by his occasional assaults nor, I suspect, did he expect me to be. There was an element of ritual about attacks like his condemnation of the BBC as a 'downmarket, over-staffed, over-bureaucratic, ridiculous organization', and I felt some of my lobby colleagues were far too sensitive about his rough tongue. As journalists we dish it out and we should be able to take it. He also has a sense of humour; but he could have been more effective still if he had curbed his aggression and heeded the words of Bernard Ingham: 'The function of a press secretary is to manage relations with the media, not to make war with them, whatever the provocations.' In the Michael Cockerell film about Downing Street's media operation in 2000, Campbell confessed that he was not managing relations. 'I have got myself into a situation where combat was the only language that was really being spoken,' he conceded.

Like most press secretaries, Alastair and other New Labour operators have had their trusties in the media, to whom they would drop a story or two. I was rarely a chosen conduit for breaking a story because such favours usually come with a string or two attached, and the BBC could not and should not be in that game. But I have no complaints. Campbell worked all hours, a steer was normally available on request, and I could always count on getting the flavour of a developing story.

Campbell's case is that it is the journalists who are now the spin doctors. The twenty-four-hour news programmes, he says, make anything seem old hat by the evening. The event has been analysed to death by then; so the next day's newspapers want a new angle. Their journalists will indulge in interpretation and speculation, and will try to sell their line to broadcasters so that they are invited on the electronic media to pontificate and to publicize their papers. Their motto, says Campbell, is: 'Better be first with the speculation, however inaccurate, than right at the same time as the others.' The speculation can always be written up as a 'government change of tack' if it proves wrong.

Alastair's case is not without substance, but what he does not mention is the strength which such a situation gives to the spin doctor. If the papers, beaten constantly to the punch on hard news by the electronic media, have to rely on forward projection, they are ever more dependent on the spin doctors to move on a story which hasn't happened. Jill Rutter, one-time civil servant head of the Treasury press office, summed up the process acutely. 'Once the news is out – in a speech or an official release – it is a free good,' she argued. 'But unreleased information is a valuable commodity. The genius of the government's news managers is to recognize and exploit the fact and use it to create a long-term dependence.'

The lesson for governments is that journalists are excited by information which people seek to withhold, and they will persist in their efforts to get hold of it. If you want to persuade them not to write about something, well, Dr David Clark, the former

Cabinet Office minister, has told us how that is done. When the government was wrestling with the problems of the millennium bug, he wrote to all ministers for their plans, then called in journalists for a briefing.

'They were suspicious, as always. In effect, they said, "Well, you are just telling us this and that." I said, "I will give you the whole lot." I gave them twelve hundred pages each on which were set out our plans – and they wrote nothing about the millennium bug.'

Certainly Tony Blair and his team have a sharp eye for presentation and for the kind of subjects they like to be associated with. Following a chat with the then sports minister Tony Banks during which I discovered how much effort was going into Britain's bid for the 2006 World Cup, I arranged to do a report on the subject for the *Nine O'Clock News*. I set up an interview with Banks and collected some suitable archive footage of the 1966 World Cup. At one stage I mentioned to Alastair Campbell that I was doing this piece, to see if I could excite the Prime Minister's interest and grab a quote. Within twenty-four hours I got a phone call from a startled Banks.

'What the hell have you been doing?' he asked. 'I've been called round to Downing Street to give the Prime Minister a special briefing.' Surprise, surprise, I and my camera crew then received an invitation to film Banks and Blair chatting with the Football Association's Graham Kelly on the Downing Street terrace. The only things they hadn't laid on were a referee, two linesmen and canned crowd noise. I don't think I would have got quite the same priority if I had requested an interview in Number Ten on the single currency.

If Downing Street showed their speed on the draw and lack of stuffiness over that piece, I am afraid the BBC did not. I thought it would be fun to go on to the sacred Wembley turf for my 'piece to camera' to end the report on the World Cup bid. My producer, Audrey Green, had the bright idea of throwing a ball for me to head during the concluding sequence and, determined to show my football enthusiast son Alex that I had headed into the Wembley goal, I went for it. Amazingly I managed the perfect header, twice out of the three versions we shot. But, just for safety's sake, knowing the BBC's ways, we filmed a straight version as well, with no header. We sent the piece to the *Nine O'Clock News* with both versions of the piece to camera, with the header and without. Executives huddled, and the verdict was given. They would use the version without me heading the ball. The action sequence 'wasn't quite appropriate for the BBC's political editor'.

I did have my small revenge over this piece of stuffiness. The sequence, including my header, appeared on TV not long after, in Terry Wogan's show *Auntie's Bloomers*. 'I wonder how they got their hands on that?' tutted one BBC Millbank manager afterwards. I closed my bottom drawer rapidly, just in case my return envelope was showing.

Tony Blair's New Labour government has made so much use of the photo-opportunity that it has become a TV cliché. No education announcement is made without a classroom full of fresh-faced children on hand. No step forward in the NHS is marked without ministers mingling with pretty blonde nurses in crisp, clean uniforms. At times, this makes the relationship between politicians and broadcasters much too cosy. We justify the collusion, with both sides of the political spectrum, on the grounds that there is a genuine story to be told and that it is better to make it visually attractive. But there were, I have to say, some pretty dubious cases when an item made it on air less because of the story content than because 'the pictures are so good'. On those days my old newspaper instincts twitched and I did not feel the complete TV animal. Certainly some items moved higher up the bulletin on sheer picture quality, rather than by virtue of their political importance.

We should not, however, think that it was New Labour who invented the photo-opportunity. Remember Margaret Thatcher cradling that calf? At one stage she was doing so many hospital visits to demonstrate her concern for the health service that *Private Eye* offered to supply tokens to readers which they could enclose with their kidney donor cards, specifying: 'If I am taken into hospital for emergency treatment I expressly DO NOT wish to be visited by the Prime Minister.'

The relationship between politicians and television has never been an easy one. In some ways, the fairer we try to be on television, the more we succeed in turning politics into a shouting match. During the 1997 election, following a public complaint from Alastair Campbell, one newspaper ran a headline which said 'Government accuses BBC of being too fair'. I kept it taped to my desk computer; and the story was not quite as bizarre as it sounds. Campbell's complaint was that the BBC's style of reporting involved a soundbite from Labour attacking the Tories, a soundbite from the Tories attacking Labour, and a soundbite from the Liberal Democrats saying what a nasty argumentative pair the two major parties were. That, he said, was in itself producing the kind of tit-for-tat politics of which the nation despaired. The Campbell complaint followed a furious public row I had had with Peter Mandelson in Labour's Millbank headquarters, when he accused broadcasters in general and the BBC in particular of 'ruining the election' because of our style of reporting.

I could see their point, repeated in post-election seminars as parties, pollsters and pundits debated the lessons of the campaign, but I could not agree with Campbell's solution. He wanted us virtually to take out the intermediary/reporter altogether and let the politicians speak directly to the people. In my view this is but a small step away from the 'waving sheaves of corn' style of broadcasting so beloved of communist governments in days gone by. While I agree that there need not be an excess of interpretation by the unelected, we need to supply the context. That is why broadcasters should resist the pressure for ever shorter items.

In the extended *Nine O'Clock News* run during the 1997 election I was given four to five minutes for packages confined at normal times to two or three minutes. The result was that we were sometimes able to run the journalists' questions as well as the politicians' answers. In the 'normal time' bulletins there was room only for the soundbite reply, which often sounded impressive on its own; but in election-length packages the inclusion of the question often showed what an inadequate response the politician's reply had been. The longer the package, the greater the chance you have of actually explaining what the policy argument is all about.

What I used to suggest to the parties who complained about the style of 'tit-for-tat' coverage was that they should drop the insistence on every one of them being represented in every report. The parties should be given a clear run when they had something new and interesting to say, so long as we balanced the time they all got over a period. This would let each of them play to its strengths. Senior figures in all parties nodded to the theory, but were never willing to make that leap of faith in practice. And all of them from time to time try it on, seeking to influence the prominence given to particular stories.

The most celebrated argument of that kind I remember was when Tony Blair's leader's speech at a Labour party conference coincided with the verdict in the O. J. Simpson trial. When the *Six O'Clock News* ran with the Simpson story as its top item, Alastair Campbell fired off faxes to demand that the *Nine O'Clock News* should not do the same. When the *Nine O'Clock News* ran the Blair speech as top item, we were accused of following the Downing Street agenda, but this was not the case. Some of us had been arguing all day that we should lead with the Blair speech on the grounds that what Blair had to say was far more likely than an American trial to affect the lives of ordinary people in Britain. For the *Six O'Clock News* there had been a different argument because the Simpson story was actually due to break as they went on air. The only point at which our argument was in serious danger of losing was when Campbell's fax arrived: he very nearly lost the top slot for Blair simply because we did not want to look as though we were being shoved around. The one thing TV programme editors will always fight is attempted political browbeating or censorship.

I had a few spats with all the parties from time to time, but no grudges were ever held for long, I believe, in any quarter. One of the most bitter rows I ever had was with Paddy Ashdown, a man for whom I have the greatest regard and with whom I have always had the friendliest of relations. On the day Roy Jenkins published his report on electoral reform, a subject of immense importance to the Liberal Democrats, I went to do the main BBC interview with Paddy, for use across a wide range of programmes, in his room in the Commons. Among a series of nine or ten questions I asked him if the report and its reception by the government would be sufficient to end any speculation about his leadership of the party. Since there were some Liberal Democrats grumbling about his closeness to Labour and whether the Lib Dems had gained sufficient benefit from it, it seemed to me a legitimate area of questioning.

Amid our exchanges, he answered the question perfectly well; but after the interview had concluded he went ballistic, saying that I had no right to ask such a question when he had scored such a success, that any question about his leadership was 'history' and that I was pursuing an agenda set by a Labour minister. If the BBC ran that question and answer, he said, our good personal relations would be sundered. I explained that it was not for me to select which clips from the interview were taken into different reports on different programmes, at which he and a rather inexperienced press officer expressed derision.

I was interested that so senior a politician, after all his time in the job, could still have so little knowledge of how the BBC worked. I told him that I had spoken to no minister on the subject and that I would not have been doing my job if I had failed to ask the question. What I did not say, but what should have been obvious to him and his media team, was that if I started ringing round a dozen programmes saying, 'Please don't use this question because Paddy is chucking half-bricks,' nothing would more effectively whet their appetite to use it. We parted on bad terms. The first programme on air afterwards, the *PM* programme, used the exchange which had so irritated Ashdown without a word of steering from me, although I am sure Paddy never believed that. We had, fortunately, mended our fences before, less than a year later, Ashdown announced he was stepping down from the leadership and leaving Parliament. Paddy, Jane, Carolyn and I happily enjoy a good bottle together still.

Of various spats with the Tories, I remember one over coverage of the pre-Budget report in November 1999, when party chairman Michael Ancram wrote to Sir Christopher Bland, the BBC chairman, with a long series of complaints about the day's coverage, starting with the fact that the special programme had been presented by David Dimbleby, 'who is associated strongly in the public mind with matters of national importance'! Specifically, there was a complaint that in my *Nine O'Clock News* report the shadow Chancellor Francis Maude's remarks were 'clipped and not in any way contextualized'. What they did not know was that I had very nearly left out Maude altogether, having listened to his entire performance twice through searching desperately for a usable clip. If there is one task resting on the shoulders of an opposition spokesman in such circumstances, it is to form one memorable soundbite encapsulating his case in a viewer-friendly way which can be used across the airways; and Maude, for all his abilities, had that day fallen down on the job.

Like most governments, the Labour administration of 1997–2001 soon came to believe that the BBC was determined to cause it trouble. But the Tory party has a deep and abiding belief that the BBC is permanently biased in Labour's favour. This is equally wrong. It is almost certainly true that there are more people who vote Labour working for the BBC than there are Conservative supporters, but that is as much to do with the kind of people who are attracted to media work as anything else. It would probably be equally true of the staff of newspapers thought of as Conservative. But in my eight years with the BBC, nobody ever urged me to alter the balance of a report to make it more favourable to Labour or less favourable to any other party. All the programme editors with whom I worked were scrupulous in their efforts to eliminate bias. Programme editors and news executives are entirely robust, too, in beating off pressures from all the parties when they try to dictate the relative importance of stories and to affect programme running orders.

Not all of those who try to sway the opinions of political journalists are in the government or opposition parties, however. Single-issue pressure groups, commercial organizations and others all try in their different ways. One of the most intriguing efforts I encountered was from the security services when the government decided in 1993 to bring in legislation to put them on a statutory basis. They wanted to influence the shape of that legislation and so were keen to talk to a few political editors. It gave me the chance in return to learn something of their hidden world.

The three senior spooks who gave me a decent lunch and presented me afterwards with calling cards which were rather short on detail insisted that the Secret Intelligence Service (or SIS) does not set its own agenda but does what it is tasked to do by government departments. They claimed already to be subject to tight budgets and close networks of supervision within Whitehall. Pressed, they admitted to a 'two-way suggestion process' on the work they did, but said that it was not worth their while to bend the rules and carry out actions which had not been sanctioned. They were, they insisted, more a 'brolly and pen' operation than one involving much military bravado. They did not kill and they did not use blackmail – although MI6, they agreed, did break the law, while MI5 was there to uphold it. They hoped that bringing in a degree of parliamentary scrutiny of their activities would make them new friends, as oversight by Congress had done for their counterparts in the United States. They were anxious, however, that the Table Office, the body which decides which parliamentary questions are allowable and which are not, should not allow too much latitude in their case. The debate in Parliament at that time was over whether they should be supervised by an ordinary Commons select committee or by a committee of privy councillors (senior ex-ministers and the like), and there was no doubt which they preferred.

From the spooks I learned, too, that MI6 would use economic means to turn Middle East and other terrorist organizations against each other; that they would deliberately screw up technology to hinder arms proliferation; and that they would give help to British firms keen to ascertain which of their competitors abroad were giving bribes. Leakage of technology was one of their main areas of activity, and economic casework was growing all the time. Their relations with some Third World leaders, whose security chiefs tended to be big wheels in government, were often better than those with the Foreign Office. Their role in countering the narcotics trade was growing. They were not keen to 'demythologize' their service too far, and they wanted govern-ments to be able to disown their actions if they went wrong. They admitted to having a 'recruitment officer' in every major university and to making much use of 'loners'.

Later, in November, I attended a select Foreign Office briefing on the new bill, an occasion which saw the first appearance before the media of Sir Colin MacColl, the then head of MI6. We in the media are all small boys really, except those of us who are little girls, and Sir Colin confirmed in response to some typically journalistic prompting that he was still referred to within his team as 'C' in respect for the founding figure Admiral Cumming. Green ink, he admitted, was still in use. No pictures of him were allowed, as a reassurance, said Sir Colin, to operatives in the field that they were 'not about to be publicly undressed'.

'Secrecy is our absolute stock in trade,' he added encouragingly.

Douglas Hurd, presiding as Foreign Secretary, ruled some questions out of order and said that the supervisory committee of MPs which was to be set up would be 'within the ring of secrecy'.

'The people who traffick in darkness,' said Hurd, 'tunnel underground. And we need counter-tunnels.' I felt for half a day as if I were living in a John Buchan novel.

I never had any complaint from C, or anybody else in the counter-tunnels, about our coverage of the bill. But I would have listened if I had, as I did to all complaints which came my way. Most alleged political bias, and I dismissed these so long as they were stacking up on both sides of the political spectrum. But there are some complaints from parties and from the public which broadcasters would do well not to brush aside as vigorously as they do attempts by politicians to determine journalistic priorities.

One besetting sin of modern TV journalism, I believe, is that of moving on too fast, a tendency that has been exaggerated by the arrival of the round-the-clock news services. We as journalists have been watching the stuff all day and are desperate to 'take the story on'. We want to give it a fresh face to demonstrate our originality. But we are not broadcasting for an audience of other journalists. We are broadcasting to people who have been out earning their daily bread and who have probably had no time to watch or listen to the news all day. Then in the evening they are presented with analysis and commentary on the likely next moves in a story whose basics they have yet to grasp.

A former presenter of *Panorama* was once rebuked by a senior BBC figure: 'No, don't tell them what happened. Tell them what it *means*.' I understand what he was getting at, of course, but there must be a happy medium. We want to move fast into analysis and deconstruction, but people need to be told the basics first. What is wrong, I sometimes ask, with the occasional 'New readers and listeners begin here' recap?

We should not be frightened on TV of going back to basics. When I first joined the BBC and started doing live two-ways I was quite nervous – actually, I was pretty scared – and I was therefore grateful for the common practice of programme editors or presenters telephoning in advance to discuss the questions to be asked. To my surprise, I soon found that I much preferred it when there was no time for such run-throughs and I had no advance notice of the questions. If you pre-discuss, you start forming a reply to the question in your own mind. When it comes to the real thing on air, the questions may be asked in a different form or in a different order, and then, instead of answering spontaneously, you struggle to get back to that pre-formed structure in your mind. You should not be there answering questions at all if you do not know enough about the subject to answer spontaneously.

John Sergeant and I agreed that pre-discussion was not for our benefit but for the benefit of the presenters. They wanted to avoid asking questions which might have us saying, 'Well, it's not quite like that, Fred.' Not unreasonably, they were keen to ask complicated questions which demonstrated how much they were on top of the subject. But too much presenter knowledge is not always a good thing. Often viewers and listeners would like an answer to some very basic questions, like 'What the hell is going on here?' CNN presenters, I have found, are much readier to ask those questions than most British TV presenters, and I believe the audiences benefit. We do viewers and listeners no service by assuming too much knowledge, and sometimes in the process we play into the hands of politicians who see our insatiable appetite for the new as the opportunity for the news management at which they have become so adept.

It is time, too, for some grown-up journalism about 'splits' and 'rows'. As journalists, we complain about the cloning of modern politicians and the 'on message' caution of the pager generation. The tendency was best summed up in the Westminster joke which did the rounds in 1998 about the new-intake Labour MP who went into the Commons barber. The barber asked him to take off the headphones he was wearing while he cut his hair.

'Oh no, I can't do that,' said the worried-looking MP, so the barber did the best he could until he noticed his client had fallen asleep. He removed the MP's headphones to finish the job, whereupon the parliamentarian turned blue in the face and collapsed. Picking up the headphones after he had called for an ambulance, the barber wondered what the MP had been listening to. He put them to his ear (the joke goes), and heard Peter Mandelson's voice saying, 'Breathe in . . . breathe out . . . breathe in . . .'

It is not quite that bad in reality, but there are genuine problems, and they persist. Early in the life of the Labour government I lunched one day with Harriet Harman, then social security secretary, and she became truly passionate about some aspect of social security policy.

'You've convinced me completely,' I said. 'But why don't you sound like that in the Commons, where it matters?'

She found it hard to do that any more, she told me. 'I got so used to being cautious in the run-up to the polls, not daring to utter a phrase that might contribute to losing us an election that we had to win. I just can't let go any more.'

We may deride this generation of 'safety-first' politicians – but what did we expect? Given the kinds of stories which find space on air and in print these days, journalists examine the sub-clauses of every article, the stresses of every speech for something which can be presented as a gaffe, a split or a party division, especially if there is a personality angle attached. Because the media are obsessed with splits, the spin doctors have become paranoid and work harder still to close down debate and argument in all parties.

For a senior minister to go against collective Cabinet responsibility once the policy has been agreed is, of course, a story. But when policies are being formulated, should every nuance of difference be splashed across six columns as a split on a par with the divisions over the Corn Laws? Should we not be encouraging healthy debate, not stultifying it? How is there to be any advance without debate within the parties as well as between them? Once again, the obsession with personality and 'splits' at the expense of policy gets in the way of informative journalism; and politics is the poorer for it.

Sometimes, though, there is a lighter side even to the media battle with the Downing Street machine. In November 1997 lobby correspondents became aware of a sinister development. Humphrey the Cat, who had been in Downing Street long before the Blairs, was no longer to be seen. Suspicions grew, and the question arose: never mind entrusting the economy to New Labour, could the Blairs be trusted with the well-being of the nation's best-known cat? There ensued a bizarre episode involving secret journeys to an undisclosed destination for the supposed victim to be photographed apparently well and stalking round a goldfish bowl. This is an abbreviated version of how I wrote it up at the time for the parliamentary journal *The House Magazine*:

The suspicion was stirring that without public debate Humphrey had become an ex-cat. Cherie Blair, once photographed cuddling

Humphrey with all the enthusiasm of somebody invited to take a bath with a piranha, was known to be less than enamoured of the hairy beast. There were fears that the announcement he had been retired to a less stressful situation was a cover-up and that he had disappeared from Downing Street paws upwards, in a box. An edging down in the opinion polls could have become a serious slide.

Never mind that he was a mangy old mog prone to leaving the wrong kind of presents on the Downing Street carpets and that the previous occupant, one John Major, had had to defend him against charges that he was a serial killer of baby birds. Humphrey had caught the public's, or at least the media's, imagination. And it was a thin day.

Fleet Street's finest, aided and abetted by a broadcaster or two, were not to be pacified by assurances from Prime Ministerial sources that Humphrey had gone to a quiet place in suburbia. That could have been a cemetery, or six feet under a new motorway, the hacks protested. They wanted photographic evidence. 'Don't let's have this one leaking out in dribs and drabs,' cried the media (even if that was what Humphrey had been doing). For an hour or two Downing Street vacillated. But the lessons of the Ecclestone affair had been learned.

By the afternoon a Press Association cameraman had been despatched to Humphrey's secret new suburban abode, travelling, no doubt, blindfolded in a shuttered van. Pictures were taken of a surprisingly frisky-looking Humphrey set, Middle East hostage style, against copies of that day's papers.

It was officially announced that the Blairs did like cats, that any suggestions Cherie had wanted Humphrey done away with were a vile slur and that the Blair family were all sorry that Humphrey's failing health had required him to move away from the hectic pace of life in Number Ten just when they were getting to know him.

Fearing a furry flood, Downing Street appealed to the nation not to send in cats or even pictures of cats. Already a substitute was being groomed, we were told, for the role of new First Cat.

But now the questions would really begin. Was it the real Humphrey who had been shown to the PA cameras or just some long-haired agency lookalike hired by the hour? Were paw-prints taken? What about a DNA test?

How much credence could be given to the story that Humphrey had needed a quieter life – after all, Downing Street is a cul-de-sac with no through traffic. If Humphrey really was as sick as Downing Street had first claimed when his 'retirement' was announced how come his regular vet said he was in comparatively good health? How come he was leaping around that goldfish bowl in such sprightly fashion?

Had he been positively vetted by Peter Mandelson and found wanting?

This, Alastair Campbell was warned, was only the start of it.

16

SOME OF MY BEST FRIENDS
ARE POLITICIANS

'DO YOU BECOME FRIENDS WITH POLITICIANS?' PEOPLE OFTEN ASK
me. And, 'If you do, doesn't that make it difficult to report on
them properly?'

The truth is that in general there is a particular kind of
relationship between many journalists and politicians. It is more
than acquaintanceship and less than close friendship: perhaps we
might be called 'good acquaintances'. Some of the more clearly
partisan journalists develop deeper friendships, but those who
have taken my route of trying to report from the uncommitted
centre generally seek to put a curb on them. Nevertheless, there
are politicians in all parties whom I hope to see more often when
I do finally hang up the microphone. As for reporting on them,
well, when a surgeon rolls up his sleeves and makes the first in-
cision on a friend he is just another body; and it has to be the
same with politics. If my reporting fractures a budding relationship that is just too bad, but, if you are fair, few politicians resent
the fact that you have said critical things about them – and the
ones who do are probably not worth bothering with anyway.

A common involvement with Westminster means that politicians and political journalists share both interests and lifestyles. Indeed, to the outside world it probably looks all too cosy from time to time. One BBC research study found that the BBC's practice of standing the political team against the Palace of Westminster for reports and interviews made political journalists and MPs pretty well indistinguishable: 'They're all men in suits,' was the repeated comment.

Shedding my suit in company with a political figure, however, did once lead to a certain amount of hassle. The diary columns got themselves in quite a spin in October 1994 when they discovered that in the summer of that year Carolyn and I had joined a group of other guests aboard a yacht which had been loaned to Jeffrey Archer and his wife for a cruise down the coast of Turkey. Jeffrey, as it happens, is an old, though not particularly intimate, friend, who had been associated with my old Oxford college, Brasenose, and with whom I shared a strong interest in athletics and in the theatre. I have known him for around thirty years and have found him an entertaining companion, a useful source of stories and a generous host of parties where you met a string of interesting people, always useful to a journalist. My journal records a lunch one day in 1997 at Archer's Thames-side penthouse, for example, at which the guests included actors Michael Caine and Alec McCowen, heart surgeon Magdi Yacoub, sports journalist Ian Wooldridge, Tory frontbencher Peter Lilley, and former Olympic athlete Alan Pascoe.

When Jeffrey almost went bankrupt and was forced to leave the Commons Carolyn and I felt sorry for him, knowing his passion for politics, and we continued to entertain him occasionally as he forged a new life for himself. Over lunch one day he read me the early chapters of his first novel, *Not a Penny More*, and I made a few minor suggestions, as I did with drafts of some of the more political books which followed. Along with other friends who had thus stuck by him I found my name used as a character in his novels, at least until Jeffrey judged me well enough known to be disqualified, and he was kind enough to dedicate his first volume of short stories, *A Quiverful of Arrows*, to Carolyn and me.

I was pleased to see him succeed with his alternative career, and have sometimes wished since that he could have been content with his success as a popular novelist. But he was consumed by the political life and always preferred talking politics to anything else, particularly politics of the 'who's up, who's down' kind. What is endearing about him is his Tiggerish enthusiasm, his ability always to bounce back and the fact that he rarely criticizes anybody else. He is always happy to celebrate someone else's success, even if he likes to imply that that success was somehow due to him and his contacts. His judgement, alas, is another thing, and most of his friends have become aware over the years of what his wife Mary tactfully describes as Jeffrey's 'gift for inaccurate précis'. I see him only two or three times a year, but I would feel it deceitful now to desert a man whose hospitality I have gladly accepted over the years – as have hundreds of fellow journalists, politicians, actors and personalities from various fields – simply because he has made some serious mistakes and paid for them.

What is sometimes forgotten – deliberately by most of the Conservative party hierarchy – is the degree of access to the top Tories which Jeffrey enjoyed for so long, even allowing for a certain amount of Archer embroidery. He was at times a favoured court jester, permitted into private rooms denied to more formal figures. He may have used the party to some extent as a self-promotional vehicle; but the party used him too, some-times pretty ruthlessly. Neither Major nor Thatcher entirely trusted his political judgement, but both found it useful to employ his considerable energy in rushing around the country speaking to Tory groups, raising funds for the party and report-ing back to them on the flavour of what he had been told at the grass roots. He touched a populist chord and people opened up to him with a freedom which they would not have felt in conversation with party grandees. Various senior figures used Archer, a big draw on the after-dinner circuit, to coach them on their speaking techniques for big occasions.

Sometimes when Margaret Thatcher had wearied of the latest draft of her party conference speech she would dismiss the official speech-writing team and call Jeffrey in for a run-through which was really an exercise in reassurance. What she did not know was that the familiars like Ronnie Millar and Stephen Sherbourne would have grabbed Archer beforehand and told him which sections to praise.

With John Major, a surprisingly lonely figure at times, in Downing Street, the millionaire novelist would sometimes drop into Number Ten on a Sunday night for a cheery chat, taking it as a signal that his presence was not wanted if the Prime Minister turned instead to his official papers. It was useful to me, and to Jeffrey's other occasional lunch companions like the *Sun*'s Trevor Kavanagh, to feed off the information Jeffrey tapped into at either end of the scale.

When Jeffrey invited me and Carolyn that summer to join him on the luxurious *Taipan* for a cruise around the Turkish coast, the list of fellow guests was one no journalist would have turned down the chance to join. It included a senior former Cabinet minister, an important figure on the American political scene and a distinguished judge (all of whom did come), and a very senior Whitehall mandarin (who in the end did not). Jeffrey at the time held no political office with the Tories and I saw no harm in joining them – but, just to be certain, I cleared it with my BBC bosses before I accepted.

It was, I have to say, a very enjoyable holiday with excellent food and very good company, even if each of us did have to give an after-dinner lecture on a subject unconnected with the day job. I did not, however, distinguish myself when I swam from the boat to some rocks beneath a Turkish military base, thus precipitating an alarming visit to the *Taipan* by a heavily armed military patrol who dripped oil from their sub-machine guns on the carpets. Nor did my host thank me for taking him clambering up a rather craggy mini-mountain. When we had to jump across a few fissures and he panicked about our prospects of ever getting down, I opted for a shortcut which involved us, in shorts, sliding through a few hundred yards of spiky thorn bushes, which was not comfortable. I have been watching for the scene in Archer novels since.

When news of the trip suddenly came out during the party conference season later that year, a cluster of diary columnists descended on me. Somewhat surprised that I was entirely happy to confirm I had been on the holiday, they did little but record the facts. Just one paper, the *Daily Star*, decided that the story was worth more than a diary item. They ran an inside-page lead headed 'Oh dear, Oakley', declaring that 'In taking a holiday with Archer, some believe the BBC's political editor has taken leave of his senses.' None of the 'some', of course, were quoted.

I could see absolutely no harm in our having holidayed with the Archer group; no more, indeed, than I see in accompanying my Liberal Democrat chums Menzies Campbell and Richard

Holme to rugby internationals, or in having Labour friends like the Prime Minister's adviser Roger Liddle (whose former house we bought) to dinner. I regularly swop tips on the racecourse with Robin Cook and the Labour peers Lord Lipsey and Lord Donoughue. Politicians who have become friends include Chris Patten, Lord Baker of Dorking (better known as ex-Home Secretary Kenneth Baker) and my Kennington neighbour (Lord) Paddy Ashdown. In journalism you simply have to compartmentalize your life. And ironically, one of the first stories I reported on after the yacht holiday was Jeffrey's difficulties over the allegations of insider dealings in Anglia TV shares. Neither he nor I would have expected anything else.

There have been days when I have walked back across St James's Park to the House of Commons after an amiable lunch with one of John Major's or Tony Blair's Cabinet team and worried that I was being drawn into the establishment. But for a journalist it only takes one phone call, one hint in a Members' Lobby conversation, to get you up and running. It is also worth remembering that while we co-exist quite happily, journalist and politician belong to different tribes with differing instincts. Of course you enjoy being with some politicians more than you do with others, and you do sometimes develop a different relationship with a good contact, even if there is some calculation on both sides. But for a journalist the story always comes first, and the politicians know that.

I saw a lot of David Mellor, for instance, in his days at the always newsworthy Home Office. Underneath the braggadocio which irritates some he is, like many of us, a typical middle-class boy with a slight sense of wonder at having got where he has. When the BBC disposed of me and other prominent figures

349

suddenly did not want to know me (until they caught up with my new role at CNN), David was the first to offer wine and sympathy. He has helped to introduce me to the enjoyable world of the after-dinner speaking circuit. But our good relationship could not and did not affect the way I reported his downfall.

In September 1992, with the Tory party in crisis over the ERM, Mellor's career was hanging in the balance after revelations of an extra-marital affair and of hospitality he had accepted from foreigners. I noted in my journal on 18 September: 'Things look blacker for David Mellor. The Tory Party always needs a sacrifice, a public hanging, when things get bad and John Major has made it clear they are not going to get the Chancellor's head on the railings. It may turn against D. Mellor instead.' Six days later comes the note:

When I phoned for David Mellor this morning and spoke to Judith [his then wife] I knew it was all over. I was going to tell him that his support had evaporated; it had slipped on the back benches and he would have to go. She had already spoken to the Prime Minister and David was seeing him this morning. If the whips felt it couldn't be held he would go before the 1922 Committee [the assembly of Tory backbenchers] demanded it, that way keeping open the possibility of a later return.

I felt a heel, particularly when talking to Judith, but the job still had to be done. I have seen a good few politicians whom I know well fall off the high wire. Some explain away their tangles and misdeeds as a consequence of the parliamentary hours and lifestyle. I think it is more complicated than that: some of them are habitual risk-takers who feel their lives empty without some element of danger.

The political world is a sociable one, and at one stage we used to give quite a few political dinner parties. After a while it was the reputation of Carolyn's cooking rather than my political drawing power which continued to fill our table in Epsom. But Carolyn does not share my anorakish interest in every little detail of the political scene, and she employed one basic rule. Any politician would be invited for the first time on my recommendation, but they did not get invited a second time if they proved capable of talking about nothing but themselves or politics. One who fell foul of that rule was David Owen in his SDP days. Another was one of my favourites, Tristan Garel-Jones, the long-time Tory whip and Europe minister. Tristan, a good raconteur, told us the story of how he had encountered Alan Clark when the Tory maverick was in the final stages of his first volume of famously indiscreet diaries.

How had the elegant Euro-sceptic treated him? Tristan enquired.

'Don't worry, dear boy,' cried Clark. 'You emerge as a hero.'

He had not taken too much comfort from this, said Tristan, since the only two others he knew to have been accorded that status by Clark were Adolf Hitler and General Stroessner.

I think perhaps it was the fact that he arrived an hour and a half late for dinner that put paid to Tristan's chances of a recall *chez* Oakley.

I spoke to Tristan the day he announced he was going to resign as Europe minister once the Maastricht Bill had completed its progress through Parliament. It was a curious thing to do. A minister known to be on the way out loses clout immediately, with civil servants, opponents and colleagues alike. Who was going to accept any assurances of government intent from him after that? But, in a rare glimpse of the human side of politics, he told me that he had promised his wife Catali and the family that he would cease being a minister after the 1992 election but had been persuaded to stay on. Then he had postponed it to Christmas; then to the end of the mammoth bill. He made the announcement in advance of the action as an irrevocable public pledge to his family that he would succumb to no more arm-twisting, and because he could bear keeping the secret no longer. The final straw, he said, had been when a much-postponed meeting with his son's in-laws-to-be had been put off yet again for a ministerial dash to Strasbourg.

I felt genuine sympathy for Tristan's difficulties, as I too have tried and frequently failed to combine politics with a civilized life.

'Look, Robin,' he told me. 'I love pictures and I haven't set foot inside an art gallery for five years.'

I knew the feeling. Ever since my student days, I had been a keen theatre-goer; but for eight years while I was at the BBC Carolyn did culture for the Oakleys, and the social life went too. We had intended to continue having the more interesting politicians to dinner, but once I joined the BBC those gatherings steadily fell away. By the time New Labour were in power we had virtually given up entertaining. With senior politicians you have to fix dates well in advance, and *Nine O'Clock News* duties meant that Mondays to Thursdays were out and most weekends were pretty iffy: pre-planning was almost impossible.

Political journalists have more to do with those in power than those in opposition, for that is where the stories are mostly to be found. But while column inches and broadcast soundbites have, I hope, been fairly divided, the Tories did better at the Oakley dinner table than New Labour. The Blair team arrived in power too late in my career to get a fair crack at Mrs Oakley's chicken pudding or halibut with herby crust.

There is the occasional day out of school at Westminster. Colleagues who can play golf without digging up half the turf in Surrey and threatening innocent bystanders' lives, as I do when let loose on the course, regularly play golf with parliamentarians. There are football and cricket matches, too; but even in their sporting activities, it seems, politicians retain certain modes of behaviour. I used to lunch regularly with the Labour front-bencher Graham Allen, a talented cricketer who turns out regularly for the Lords and Commons XI. Another good cricketer is the lanky Tory Eurosceptic Bill Cash. At one meeting of the Lords and Commons cricketing fraternity a few years back, sixty Tories who were not normally seen at such occasions turned up. Two minutes before the meeting began, the Tory Lord Orr-Ewing took Cash, the existing club secretary, to one side. Cash came back and announced that, after eight years, it was time for him to step aside and that he was delighted to hear that the members wanted him to be an honorary vice-president. Were there any nominations, Orr-Ewing asked, for secretary? A huge posse of Tories immediately insisted that Graham Allen, who had not been consulted in advance and who knew nothing of what was going on, was duly voted in as club secretary. He was deeply impressed by the whole performance.

'Lady Thatcher,' he told me soon afterwards, 'clearly had no chance.'

Poor old Bill. He has paid a price for voluble devotion to his Eurosceptic cause. But such is his obsession that, as one Tory minister put it cruelly: 'When Cash addressed an anti-Maastricht rally in Trafalgar Square even the pigeons left.'

Apart from a few squash games over the years with Alan Haselhurst (later the Deputy Speaker) and Labour luminaries Jack Cunningham and Barry Jones, my sporting life with politicians has largely been confined to the Turf. Nobody could keep a horse in training on an MP's salary, but since there are fifty-nine racecourses in Britain a fair few MPs have a constituency interest in the subject. I certainly won't forget going racing one day with Spencer Le Marchant, a large, generous and expansive soul who was a Tory whip and a renowned party-giver. Cecil Parkinson, once a fellow whip, told me of a morning with Spencer which involved two double Bloody Marys before 11.00 a.m. Spencer suggested another drink and Cecil demurred: 'I don't think I can go on downing them like that,' he protested.

'Quite right,' said Spencer, summoning the waitress and ordering 'Two more, without the tomato juice.'

Spencer, having extra-parliamentary means, owned a horse which on this occasion was running at Windsor in a race which, he was convinced, it would win. He rounded up a small group of parliamentary racing enthusiasts and took us down from the Commons in a large limousine copiously stocked with champagne (although for me it simply does not taste the same unchilled and out of paper cups). Carolyn, tempted by the dinner at the Waterside Inn at Bray which Spencer had promised us all on the proceeds of his expected victory, drove over from Epsom to meet us at the course. Alas, the Le Marchant horse ran a stinker and failed to make the first three. Spencer, a somewhat mercurial character, had a row in the unsaddling enclosure with Willie Carson, who had ridden it. And he was in such a bad mood afterwards that instead of dining at the Waterside Inn we finished up eating takeaway pizza out of a car boot in a Holiday Inn car park. It took me some time to entice Carolyn to come racing again.

As a journalist who has found his holiday arrangements, his jogging habits and even his in-flight entertainment appearing in the papers, I have over the years reflected on the rights of politicians to a private life. If actors should be chary of appearing with animals or children, then politicians should be pretty careful about highlighting family values. Aware of how John Major's Back to Basics campaign, embellished with moral overtones by Tory spin doctors, became a kind of *laissez-passer* for Fleet Street to probe the private lives of Tory MPs, Tony Blair was more careful in 1998.

'I challenge the media: don't use it as an excuse to dredge through the private lives of every public figure,' he said as he announced a boost for 'family values'; but it takes more than brandishing the stake and the garlic to frighten off a media weaned on the Major years. Affairs outside marriage and strings of mistresses are no longer quite such a big deal with Fleet Street, it seems. The robust Steve Norris has seen to that. But in the New Labour years we had a different emphasis for a while with Ron Davies's wanderings on Clapham Common, Matthew Parris's 'outing' of the gay Peter Mandelson on *Newsnight* and the *News of the World*'s pursuit of Nick Brown, the agriculture minister, who emerged alongside Mr Mandelson and Chris Smith as the third gay minister in the Blair Cabinet.

Brown was forced merely by the threat of newspaper revelations to confirm his sexual orientation. 'I had hoped that I could have a private life, like other people do, that was private,' he lamented. But Fleet Street had decreed otherwise. I believe Nick was entitled to the hope, but the odds are against anybody who goes into public life keeping their private one private. The code of conduct to which most British newspapers subscribe declares that everyone is entitled to respect for his or her private and family life, home and correspondence unless that right is overridden by the public interest, but it rarely works out like that in practice.

If no crime is committed or suspected, if there is no evidence of a lapse of judgement that could affect a minister's performance and if there is no evidence of hypocrisy, it is hard to see the justification for forcing men or women to reveal that they are gay. Ron Davies's admittedly bizarre behaviour and resignation made media probing inevitable, but there was no public interest defence for prurient interest in Mr Brown's sex life. As Peter Tatchell of Outrage put it: 'There is no justification for outing MPs unless they are behaving in ways that are hypocritical or homophobic. Mr Brown has supported the gay community and voted in favour of gay equality. His public pronouncements are consistent with his private behaviour.'

But life moves on, as the former racehorse trainer Gay Kindersley once observed, pointing out in an after-dinner speech that he had been christened in an age 'when gay meant happy, clap meant applause and only generals had aides'. Nick Brown's forced outing as a homosexual did not produce howls of rage from the tabloids as some might have hoped. By no means all the Monday papers made it a front-page story, and even in those that did, the tone was moderate and mostly sympathetic. As the Prime Minister's press secretary remarked, there seemed to be a greater understanding than before of the difference between public roles and private lives.

The *Sun*, the *News of the World*'s stablemate, made the case for those who believe there is a legitimate public interest in the sexual orientation of MPs who do, after all, come to vote on issues like the age of consent for gay sex, sexual education and homosexuality in the armed forces. But opinion polls at the time of the Brown affair showed a majority seeing no harm in openly gay ministers holding Cabinet posts, and with 56 per cent accepting homosexuality as 'morally acceptable' it looked as though the country had become more tolerant than many tabloid editors believed.

We are, thank heaven, slowly becoming a more tolerant society. At the 1997 election, openly declared gays like Ben Bradshaw suffered no visible penalty with the voters. To my mind quite rightly, a greater penalty was paid at the ballot box by sticky-fingered MPs who had been improperly involved with brown envelopes than by those whose sexual peccadilloes had been raked over in the public prints. The comparative calm with which the media coped with Michael Portillo's admission of homosexual experiences in his youth, and his subsequent selection and election for Kensington and Chelsea, marked another stage in the development of public and media perspective about the gap between public and private lives. Slowly, steadily, a politician's sexual conduct in private life is becoming less crucially linked with his or her political fortunes, and that is all to the good. In my book, behaviour that impinges on a minister's performance of his duties is fair game for reporters, and so is conduct blatantly at odds with the publicly professed beliefs which may have contributed to getting an MP elected. But those categories apart, politicians are entitled to private lives. We are on the way: the only thing you can't confess in a Blair Cabinet if you want to keep your job is that you are an old-fashioned socialist.

17

TRIUMPH WITH A SHRUG

THERE ARE SWINGS AND ROUNDABOUTS FOR JOURNALISTS AS WELL as politicians. When the BBC disposed of me a year early, my biggest disappointment was the thought that I might miss reporting the 2001 general election. Instead, thanks to the American giant CNN, which has made me its European political editor, I reported it for an international audience that broadcasts to 239 countries. Of course, I and many others had confidently predicted that Tony Blair would return to Number Ten with another landslide behind him; but, sitting in CNN's election-night studio overlooking Parliament, interpreting the flood of results with Christiane Amanpour, I was still impressed by the sheer scale of the victory achieved by the party which Tony Blair has refashioned as 'New Labour'. No party has ever won more than 400 seats at two consecutive elections; no Labour government has ever before had a majority sufficient to ensure two full terms in office; but Mr Blair has returned to power with a margin suggesting that this one will not only serve a second term but gain a third term too, unless it meets with absolute disaster.

Of the ten elections I have now covered, this campaign was certainly the least exciting; John Prescott's punch, adding the Straight Left tendency to Labour's Hard Left and Soft Left factions, was the only election event to become a genuine talking point in the public bar. Quick off the mark with their tax-cutting agenda, the Tories began well. Labour, fixated as ever with their media planning and wedded to their pre-determined grid, were initially leaden-footed, not wanting to unveil their own renewed pledge not to raise the standard or higher rates of income tax through this next parliament before their planned announcement at the following week's manifesto launch. But they were soon forced to respond to bad headlines by leaking their tax intentions, so getting the worst of both worlds.

From then on, however, it was all downhill for the Tories. For me, the symbolic moment of the campaign came when their economic spokesman Oliver Letwin briefed the *Financial Times* that a Conservative government would not be content with the £8 billion of tax cuts they had already promised, but would be aiming for reductions of as much as £20 billion. Labour leaped in to say that that would mean severe cutbacks in public services, and the Conservatives rapidly went into anguished denial. This exchange marked a truly significant change in the terms of trade in British politics. At every previous election I had reported, the 'spending' party had been on the back foot, having to justify how it would pay for its pledges without taxing the nation to the hilt. Now, suddenly, here was the tax-cutting party forced onto the defensive while Labour ploughed on day after day with its big-spending pledges, promising to renew the health, education and transport services.

Never have I known a party keep so relentlessly to a single issue as Labour did through the 2001 campaign. Whatever the

question, a frequently shirt-sleeved Tony Blair and a fiercely concentrating, brow-knitted Gordon Brown endlessly repeated the
message that they had ended the years of boom and bust and
stabilized the economy so that in their second term they could
boost Britain's crumbled public services by pumping money into
health, education and transport. The polls told them, us and an
unheeding Tory party that better public services were exactly
what the public wanted to hear about; and day after day Prime
Minister and Chancellor emphatically repeated their promises to
provide 10,000 extra doctors and teachers and 20,000 nurses,
together with a £180 billion plan for transport improvements over
the next decade.

In truth, the election was won less during the predictable
campaign itself than through the four years which preceded it.
With that second-term target constantly in mind, Blair and
Brown proceeded with caution. They knew that they had to avoid
both the troubles with trades unions which had helped to bring
down the previous Labour government in 1979 and any
semblance of an economic crisis, and they ensured that they did,
despite a wobble over fuel prices when protesters took to the
streets in September 2000.

Thanks to a good economic legacy from the Major government
and Brown's tight-fistedness over public spending in the first two
years after May 1997, they had, at least for a while, ended 'boom
and bust' and they had the dividends to hand out. By giving
control of interest rates to the independent Bank of England and
keeping their pledge not to raise either the standard or the higher
rate of income tax, Brown and Blair won the confidence of the
business community, even if it chafed at some of their regulation
and what the Conservatives called their forty-five 'stealth taxes'.
By instituting a national minimum wage and the working families

tax credit for low-income earners, by pressing on with devolutionary parliaments and assemblies for Scotland and Wales, and by successfully prosecuting a war in Kosovo, they proved their strength of purpose as a government.

There were blots on their record, of course. They had alienated some in country areas with apparent insensitivity to rural needs, mishandling of the hunting issue and early blunders over the attempt to contain the foot-and-mouth epidemic. But with employment at a record high and interest and mortgage rates low, election victory was assured. The media and the chattering classes might mock their obsession with image and their control freakery, but there was no reason for people to hate the New Labour government as the Tories had been hated, for example, over the poll tax.

For Blair, and for his campaign supremo Brown, the depressing aspect of the election of 2001 was the appallingly low turnout, with four in ten voters staying at home: the lowest level of participation since 1918. The voters may have given Tony Blair a second landslide, but with only 59.3 per cent voting, they did so with a shrug. Less than a quarter of those eligible to do so cast a positive vote for the new government. A string of factors, I believe, contributed to the low turnout. In the first place, at times of high employment and low interest rates, fewer people bother with politics. Second, opinion polls which had shown a settled pattern over four years, bar the September 2000 fuel protests, encouraged most to believe the result was a foregone conclusion, whatever they did with their own vote. And third, we have been in a period of declining participation: the vote was artificially inflated, I believe, in 1997 because so many people wanted to give the Tories a kick after eighteen years. Voters are always readier to vote against something than for something.

All of which brings me to the Tory party and their problem of leadership credibility. William Hague relied on playing two cards in the election: tax cuts and the euro. Yet, despite an effective poster campaign before their campaign opened, enquiring: 'You've paid the taxes, now where are the operations/policemen/teachers?' the Conservatives never settled to a consistent pattern of attack on the ground where Labour was weakest: its delivery so far on the public services, which had become the main focus of the election. The Conservatives tried to make headway on violent crime, on political asylum (dubbing the Labour government 'a soft touch') and on tax scares, such as the suggestion that a re-elected Labour government would abolish the ceiling on national insurance contributions, in effect introducing a 50 per cent tax rate. But they were sunk by the Letwin gaffe, and their constant chopping and changing of targets robbed most of their attacks of conviction. Polls showed the public happier by far at the thought of Labour continuing to run the economy.

Hague, who had scored a success by employing similar tactics in the European parliamentary elections of 1999, insisted that the election was 'the last chance to save the pound'. Blair insisted that, with a referendum promised if Labour did decide to recommend entry into the euro in the new parliament, it was not; and the people believed Blair. In an ICM poll listing eleven issues which people saw as influencing how they would vote, joining the euro came eleventh. It was the prime example of the Tories talking to their own core activists and not to the general public, who did not share their obsession with Europe, an obsession dating from the dumping of Margaret Thatcher. The Tory pro-Europeans were careful not to speak out of turn through the election. They wanted Hague to go down with all guns blazing on Europe, so as to demonstrate to the party that Euroscepticism was not the way back to the heart of the British people. And he was only too happy to oblige, in an election in which his own credibility and personality, perhaps somewhat unfairly, had become an issue.

William Hague's resignation as Tory leader was almost inevitable given his complete failure to dent Labour's huge majority. In four years he had led his party to the second most humiliating defeat in its recent history, gaining just one extra MP. In his dignified and compellingly honest resignation speech outside Conservative Central Office on the morning after the election, he admitted: 'We have not been able to persuade a majority, or anything approaching a majority, that we are yet the alternative government that they need. Nor have I been able to persuade sufficient numbers that I am their alternative Prime Minister.' He added: 'It's also vital for leaders to listen and parties to change. I believe it is vital the party be given the chance to choose a leader who can build on my work, but also take new initiatives and hopefully command a larger personal following in the country.'

The election debacle and Hague's decision to go has forced the Conservatives to do some hard thinking, not just about their leadership but about their policies. They appear to have lost touch with the mass support required to win an election. Before the campaign began, Hague was criticized for jumping on too many short-term bandwagons in his efforts to please the media and land a blow on Labour; similarly, once it was under way, there was little consistency in the targets chosen day by day. Those they did choose to emphasize – Europe and tax cuts – turned out to be the wrong choices, a blunder for which the leader had to take the blame. The Tories sang the old tunes on tax, but the public refused to join in the chorus.

The failure to make significant inroads into Labour's majority at the 2001 election means the Tories now face two more parliaments in opposition. They cannot hope to overturn a majority of 167 at one go. It makes leadership of the party a less than enthralling prospect, involving sustained exposure to media battery through a minimum of eight years in opposition. You cannot blame William Hague for quitting swiftly. But a rushed resolution of the leadership question did not profit the Tories in 1997, when John Major precipitated an immediate contest, and this time around many Conservatives wanted a chance to stop and think as the pattern of the new parliament was established – especially because of the complicating factor of the referendum on the euro that looms if, as many expect, Tony Blair decides two years into the parliament that he will recommend British entry and Chancellor Gordon Brown decides the economic conditions have been met. Most Tories, apart from the Europhiles like former Chancellor Kenneth Clarke, are pledged to fight to Save the Pound. But, by insisting that the election was the last chance to reprieve sterling and that a Labour government would 'rig' the referendum, Hague has weakened the anti-euro cause. The new Labour government is unlikely to stage the referendum unless it believes it will win it. So, Hague having departed, the Tories face the risk of choosing a new leader who, having gone down to defeat in the referendum contest, is thus instantly devalued.

William Hague ought to know the dangers of swift decisions made on the rapid departure of a party leader. He probably made his worst career decision when John Major stepped down and he pulled out of a deal to run as the older Michael Howard's running mate and went for the leadership himself. If he had stepped back and let somebody else don the leadership mantle in 1997, Hague, who as a parliamentary performer is a class above any of the contenders to succeed him, would probably have emerged as a hero of his party over the past four years, and would have been the post-election shoo-in for the leadership of a devastated party much readier to change its views than the one he inherited at the end of a Conservative civil war in 1997; as it is, he is the first Tory leader since Austen Chamberlain in 1922 not to become Prime Minister.

While William Hague is a gut Eurosceptic, happy to weigh in with the party activists on that issue, I have always found him in private discussion entirely open-minded and of no great fixed conviction on other subjects. Had he been the new man taking over in 2001 rather than in 1997, he might have led his party in a very different direction. Early on in his leadership he went through a period when he made speeches suggesting that the Conservatives could become the party of the public services; but then Peter Lilley tactlessly chose the twentieth anniversary of Lady Thatcher's becoming Prime Minister to develop the theme that the market was not the answer to everything. Activists leapt to defend her legacy against what they regarded as a sell-out, Mr Lilley lost his job, and William Hague took fright and retreated into the familiar Thatcherite territory of tax-cutting and Euro-bashing. The rest is now history.

As the Tories face up to eight years in opposition they have to resolve some fundamental debates, such as that between the 'inclusivists' like Michael Portillo, who want a softer, gentler Conservatism, and the social authoritarians like Ann Widdecombe and Iain Duncan Smith. Harder-line right-wingers will insist that, with a Blairized Labour party now occupying the 'enterprise society' ground they used to call their own, the Conservatives need greater clarity – a clarity, they will no doubt have been arguing by the time you read this, which can be obtained only by moving to the right. Kenneth Clarke is probably the one politician the Tories have who possesses both the personal clout and the public recognition to make a difference to his party's standing in the opinion polls; but, as it demonstrated in 1997, the current Tory party is likely to prove too embedded in its Euro-scepticism ever to put that to the test. Modernizers want the party to be more inclusive, to broaden its appeal to gays, single parents and ethnic minorities, and to talk the language of twenty-first-century urban Britain. They may also be inclined to revive the arguments for turning the Tories into the party of effective public service delivery; for, since Tony Blair has scored another scorching success by appealing to the country to turn its back on Thatcherism, some Tories may now decide they have their cue to do the same. As Michael Heseltine puts it, 'The Conservative Party must alienate some traditional supporters to stay alive.'

In a candid passage in a speech towards the end of the election campaign Tony Blair put his finger on the Conservatives' problem. He declared: 'When they lost power in 1997 they did not believe that they deserved to lose at all. What they believed was, "It is a time for a breather. Labour will come in to screw up the economy and then we will go back in again." The Conservatives did not learn anything from that defeat at all. In fact they are a more extreme version of what this country rejected in 1997.' The Tory party, he insisted, was incapable of moving on from Thatcherism. It was a theme which Labour had illustrated with the most amusing poster of the campaign, which super-imposed Margaret Thatcher's hairdo on the close-cropped pate of William Hague. Never mind that *The Economist* responded play-fully by superimposing the Thatcher blue rinse on Tony Blair's thinning locks, and that *The Times* declared its first ever backing for a Labour leader by suggesting that Tony Blair was the safest pair of hands around to be entrusted with bearing the Thatcher torch. The high visibility of the lady herself in the campaign underlined Mr Blair's point. Whether she was 'helping' William Hague by developing his 'keep the pound for this parliament' line with her insistence that she would never support the introduction of the single European currency to Britain, or warning unheeding voters of the dangers of a Labour landslide, she was a constant reminder of Christmas past. When she joked about the poster she had seen on the way to one rally advertising the film *The Mummy Returns*, she summed up unconsciously the problem which her reappearances pose for her party. Tory activists love her as a symbol of the great days when she was for so long the dominating figure in British politics and their party looked impregnable in power. But to middle ground voters in 2001 she is a visible reminder of the party they rejected in 1997, an electric-blue-suited symbol of eighteen years of Tory rule. As long as the Conservatives prove incapable of letting go of Mummy's hand, one must ask whether they will ever conduct the proper self-examination and updating which are required to put them back in touch with the mass of British voters.

One other worry which now looms for the Tories is the further emergence of the Liberal Democrats, a much weightier force than they used to be with their strength in local government behind them and the courage to tell the truth about taxation (a luxury, perhaps, in which it is easier to indulge when you do not have the immediate prospect of election to government). Shrewdly, Charles Kennedy, a leader who found himself during the election campaign and who clearly began to enjoy his role as never before, began to present them as an alternative opposition force who would keep Labour up to the mark while the Tories spent the next few years in introspection. Before the campaign their opponents were sure that the Lib Dems, who had doubled their number of seats in 1997, would slip back. Instead, they forged on past the psychological barrier of fifty seats. They are, I believe, here to stay in British politics as a serious third option.

Tony Blair and the Labour government seemed to take curiously little joy in their election victory. The message had clearly gone out on the pagers: 'Not a scintilla of triumphalism.' Party workers even blacked out the windows of the Millbank Tower headquarters so no-one could be seen celebrating. In a way this was appropriate; they had deliberately struck a note of humility in the campaign, recognizing that they had not delivered all that they had promised and asking to be given the majority to finish the job. Tony Blair set the tone, acknowledging a historic victory but saying that he would learn, too, from the mistakes. 'It is', he said, 'a mandate for reform and investment in the future; and it is very clearly an instruction to deliver.'

Labour now has an unquestioned mandate of its own, not just, as in 1997, a thumping majority handed over by a populace keen to get rid of the Tories. But perhaps the lack of celebration also marked the realization that in a second term the alibis have gone. No longer can Labour blame the Tories for a poor inheritance. Pressure to perform in the future will mean battles with the public sector unions, who do not like the tone of what they have heard about using private contractors where public services cannot deliver, and with left-wingers resistant to the welfare state reforms which Tony Blair did not dare attempt in the first term. Mr Blair's sober mien probably reflected, too, the recognition that in this term the question of entry into the European single currency, probably Britain's biggest post-war decision, has to be resolved. That, of course, is where Gordon Brown comes in.

Ever since 1997 the Labour government's problems have been

more to do with personality than with policy. Hence the demotion after this election of Robin Cook. Tony Blair will have to find some gainful occupation for Peter Mandelson if he is not to become a destabilizing factor. Few will forget his tortured assertion on election night: 'I am a fighter, not a quitter.' As for Gordon Brown, as Chancellor of the Exchequer he is, in effect, the custodian of the five economic tests by which the government will, in theory, determine whether or not to enter the euro at some point within the next two years, although in practice the choice will be a political one. But Mr Brown wants to be not just the next leader of the Labour party but also the next Prime Minister after Tony Blair. What happens over the euro and the promised referendum will be the key to Labour's future prospects and to Mr Blair's place in the history books, always a consideration with second-term prime ministers. It will add new tensions to an already complicated relationship; indeed, perhaps the key factor for Labour in this new parliament will be the state of the Blair–Brown relationship. If Labour is to take Britain into the euro then public opinion, two-thirds against the idea as Labour returned to office, has to be turned around. With Gordon Brown's active support this can probably be achieved; without it, Mr Blair's chances of doing so are probably slim. A deal has to be done.

British politics, largely because the media likes it that way, is becoming ever more presidential. But New Labour has not just been about Tony Blair. The party may owe its modernizing leader a great debt for the Clause Four revolution and for reforging its image to make it electable again. But it owes a huge debt too to Mr Brown, the most intellectually dominating figure in the government. Through the years of opposition he was the one who worked ceaselessly to destroy the crippling concept of Labour as a 'tax and spend' party whose arrival in office would inevitably lead to higher taxes. Week after week as shadow Chancellor he would stage a press conference on Labour's latest economic initiative. Grumbling, with justification, that it would prove only to be the recycling of sub-paragraph 17(b) in some previously published policy document, we would all troop along just in case. And week after week Gordon would go through his routine, driving home his insistence that the Tories were no longer the party of economic competence and that Labour was no longer the party of tax and spend. This relentless emphasis had, I believe, a crucial drip-feed effect on the media and on public perception of the two parties in the run-up to the 1997 election.

Labour's success in winning a second term with a working majority again owes much to Brown and his effective stewardship of the economy. As Blair said to a few of us aboard the prime ministerial plane returning from the Commonwealth conference in South Africa in 1999, 'At the last election the one remaining question in people's mind was, "Can this lot be trusted to run the economy?" That question has now been answered.' It has indeed, and it was Brown who provided the answer. He reassured the City and weathered the first potential mini-recession by sticking to tough spending plans outlined in advance by the Tories (plans, Ken Clarke confesses, to which they would never have kept themselves). He had the confidence to hand over the control of interest rates to an independent Bank of England, so terminating the ability of future Chancellors to meddle with this key economic tool for political reasons. And, through the public service agreements with Whitehall departments, which have to agree their programmes for three years ahead in detail with the Treasury, he has had more influence on more aspects of policy than any Chancellor I have ever observed.

Such control has not made him popular with his colleagues. His intense concentration on the job in hand has at times made him a remote figure. We see less of the buccaneering speech-maker who used to please the party conference with cracks like the one about the Tories and the rail network: 'The only network they want to preserve is the old boy network and the only train running that will always run on schedule is the gravy train.' It is as if he feels these days that ordinary politicking is a bit below a Chancellor's dignity. But he is a figure of real stature, and it will be a travesty of justice if he does not succeed Tony Blair as Labour's leader.

What, though, is the relationship between him and Blair? I believe that it is one of the most extraordinary partnerships in politics. Over a period, it is something I have attempted to discuss with both of them and with their closest advisers. Blair has great respect for Brown and great confidence in him. Brown has considerable intellectual self-confidence but knows instinctively that Blair has a surer touch in the front-of-house stuff required in modern politics. Each knows that many in their respective entourages would like for their own reasons to drive a wedge between them, and they do sometimes exchange strong words. But that is not just because of Brown's resentment that his friend is in the top job. It is because they are, as Blair puts it, 'ideologically *simpatico*' and therefore do not need to talk about things in a roundabout way. They test things out on each other in a dialogue, a dialectic even, which can sometimes be quite fierce, and yet they remain friends politically and personally. When young Euan Blair was found drunk in Leicester Square, with his mother abroad, Brown was the first person Blair turned to for counsel and comfort.

Brown may be readier to use Old Labour language than Blair,

and happier with social justice themes, but each is fully committed to the 'project' of modernizing both party and country. Both have 'New Labour' stamped through them like the legend in Blackpool rock. It is only when Blair is charged that he is playing company president to Brown's company chairman that he bridles somewhat, insisting that he follows things in detail too. One man who knows them both well said to me: 'Tony remains eternally vigilant for fear of Gordon trying to dismantle the structures on which his power is based.' Brown remains broodily concerned about the power balances between their favourites and followers in every reshuffle, and a tension will always be there until Brown one day comes into his inheritance.

In the weeks following the election there was much agitation among leader writers, politicians and academics about voter apathy. I believe that this apathy is evidence of a deeper distrust of the political process which has much to do with the way we pay for our politics. Voting levels will stay depressed, especially among young people, until this issue is addressed. Partly because of the dominance of the media, parties these days need slick packaging, expensively mounted conferences and eye-catching advertisements to sell their wares. They have developed the habit of testing opinions with pricey opinion polls. They canvass by direct mail, phone and e-mail – and it all comes expensive. Tony Blair told David Frost this year that it costs £25 million annually to run the Labour party. But in an age of low voting turnouts and cynicism about the political process, fewer people join parties and pay subscriptions. Young people are often more attracted by membership of single-issue pressure groups involved with causes like the environment. Politicians, who know there is no such thing as a free lunch, have turned more and more to rich benefactors to fill the holes in their party budgets. Labour used to deride the Tories for their dependence on such people. But now Labour too has faced unwelcome publicity, eventually and reluctantly admitting, two years after the Ecclestone affair, to having received donations of £2 million each from Paul Hamlyn, Lord Sainsbury and Christopher Ondaatje. For the Tories there was a £5 million cheque from Stuart Wheeler, the spread betting millionaire. Sometimes I can't help feeling that if it goes on like this, we will have a British Prime Minister answering in the same terms as President Kennedy did when asked why he had only narrowly beaten Richard Nixon. 'My father', he said, 'could not afford to buy me a landslide.'

The more the parties turn to expensive professional techniques, the more they surrender control of their message to the professionals and to those who are prepared to fund their efforts, and the more they alienate the idealistic young people who should be drawn into the political process. We have seen, too, the steady enmeshing of the business and political communities, with Labour appointing some 2,000 businessmen to around 300 task forces, inquiries and study panels. Some of this is healthy cross-fertilization; some of it is likely to end up in grubby deals. Businessmen like to get close to the source of power and legislation, and parties need the money to which those businessmen have access.

All the recent benefactors to British parties insisted there were no strings attached to their money, and the parties promised that they would have no input on policy. But in no time at all Mr Wheeler was saying that he would not continue to support the Tory party if a Euro-enthusiast like Kenneth Clarke were to become the next leader, and very soon the Tory party was backing changes in the law which would benefit spread betting firms. Sheer coincidence, of course; but what are the impressionable young to believe?

There is, has been, and probably will continue to be a direct trade-off, too, between contributions to party funds and preferment to the House of Lords or other honours. Harold Wilson's former press secretary Joe Haines has confirmed that honours were traded for contributions when he was in Downing Street, and while there may be more subtlety about the process these days, few politicians would pretend that you cannot still buy yourself ennoblement. We have seen the introduction of new laws banning foreign donations, limiting the amount which parties can spend on future general election campaigns and forcing them to identify donors of more than £5,000. But these stipulations do not go far enough, and if the experience of the latest US election is anything to go by, they will soon be evaded by a huge plethora of political action committees. Personally, I would like to see the limit on personal or company contributions to political parties set at, say, £5,000; a sum for which no Prime Minister would be tempted to sell an honour. Such a restriction would also force the parties to go out and rebuild themselves mass memberships, and consequently to listen to a wider public, not just to their own activists. Party funds could be topped up with a measure of state aid, but only as matching funds for properly certificated individual donations.

The situation was bad enough when politics was financed by major companies and trades unions; but now I believe it is becoming steadily poisoned by money. The more money that is raised from rich benefactors, the more cynical the public become and the less inclined they are to join in the political process. This in turn feeds into the media's interest in political parties and in their desire to raise money by any means, as they relentlessly pursue stories like the Hindujas' passports or the business affairs of politicians like Keith Vaz, alienating still more people from what they perceive to be an embedded part of the political process. Nothing could be more calculated to induce public cynicism under the old doorstep slogan of 'they're all the same', and it is time our politicians woke up to it.

Was there anything which could have been done to boost interest and lift turnout at the last election? There was; but, sadly, Tony Blair chose to sacrifice it on the altar of party interest. I believe it was an insult to the British public that there was no national TV debate among the party leaders before the election on 7 June. Yes, I know that such debates are a key feature of American presidential elections and that elsewhere I have argued that there is too much Americanization of our politics. Yes, I know the arguments against: ours is not a presidential system; such a debate would represent a further 'dumbing down' of politics. Was not the 1960 US presidential election decided by Richard Nixon's sweaty face and heavy six o'clock shadow? Didn't George Bush senior lose hundreds of thousands of votes in 1992 merely because he glanced nervously at his watch? But I would have more respect for the 'dumbing down' arguments if they did not tend to come from the people who would in 1988 have preferred to keep the House of Commons as an exclusive London club, refusing to allow TV cameras into the nation's debating chamber. It is not only the US electors who get the chance to see their would-be leaders in extended debate. There are debates too in Canada and Australia, in the Netherlands and Sweden. Does anybody suggest that their politics have been dumbed down in consequence?

We have to accept the reality that, thanks to a powerful

media's concentration on personality, a British general election is anyway becoming an ever more presidential contest. And I believe that, far from dumbing down the election, a Blair–Hague–Kennedy debate would have resulted in far more attention being given to the parties' policies. The debates between George Bush and Al Gore did not just offer the opportunity to see the two men in competition and under stress; they covered a wide range of sometimes complex issues. I cannot think of anything that could have been done to contribute more to electoral education.

In Britain we usually have an extended tease along the lines of Will It Be A White Christmas This Year? In the run-up to each election little groups of BBC and ITV executives huddle over their laptops contriving programme formats for a leaders' debate and lunch well for weeks on the negotiations. The Brothers Dimbleby have a word with their colour consultants and search through their wardrobes for suitable ties. And then brutal reality sets in. The favourite in the polls – in 1997 Blair as opposition leader, in 2001 Blair as Prime Minister – finds a reason not to have the contest for fear of sacrificing an advantage.

In refusing this time I believe that the Prime Minister did British democracy a disservice. The excitement of a new element in the election campaign would have seen a huge response to the broadcast debates. In the United States, presidential debates have drawn audiences of up to 80 million, compared with 4 million for top talk shows. And the leaders would scarcely have been able to put the focus on personality for a whole hour, or however long the programme was given. A new, extended audience would have been given prolonged exposure to the issues. And election turnout, I am sure, would have been boosted. We had seen low turnouts virtually every time a section of the electorate had been invited to enter the polling booths since 1997. Blair knew that a low turnout in the 2001 general election was a risk. But he ducked the one chance of injecting a new interest and significantly boosting electoral participation.

The politicians can tinker with the fancy ideas of voting in supermarkets and post offices; they can insult our intelligence with all the irrelevant pop stars and sports stars they choose in their party political broadcasts. But there is no substitute for getting people engaged with the issues, and leaders' debates are the best hope of achieving that. If we don't see our leaders in debate on television next time, I predict that turnout will be even lower.

18

NEW HORIZONS – AND A FEW REFLECTIONS

WORKING AS I HAVE BEEN THROUGHOUT THIS YEAR WITH THE zesty young CNN team, I have rarely been busier during an election, with the intriguing difference that, as this one got into its stride, I was commentating not just on the British poll, but on Silvio Berlusconi's victory in the Italian general election and on Basque elections in northern Spain as well. I was also finishing scripting a CNN documentary on illegal immigration across Europe, a project which had involved filming in Turkey, where we were harassed by policemen who were highly protective of the immigrant smugglers on their patch, and in Bosnia, where we were shadowed by local Mafia heavies. Never in my BBC days did I expect to find myself in a Bosnian brothel at 3.00 a.m. as I witnessed police and UN experts on a raid near Tuzla designed to rescue some of the women who are the most pitiful victims of the people-smuggling rackets. Within a week of the election I was in Gothenburg for the EU summit attended by President Bush, where I was free to search for the story as it developed, not handicapped as I would have been at the BBC by programmes' unspoken, perhaps even unconscious, but nevertheless potent pre-occupation with 'How did our boy do?'

Carolyn, who felt the trauma of my departure from the BBC as keenly as I did, keeps saying to me, 'I can't believe you're so happy.' But truly, variety is the spice of life. I am enjoying television work more than I have ever done, and because I am no longer tied to the BBC schedules, I have a freedom which was denied to me before. I am able to fit in more work alongside Millennium Dome rescuer David James and trainer Simon Dow for the Epsom Training and Development Fund, a charity enterprise which is seeking to improve life for Epsom stable staff and to restore Epsom's former glory as a training centre. I have also been appointed to the Epsom Race Committee, a source of real pride after the glorious success of this year's Derby Day, even if it has made little improvement as yet in my ability to back winners. I am able to indulge my enthusiasms for the worlds of both politics and racing on the after-dinner speaking circuit, and to get my own back on a few long-winded politicians by chairing conferences. Carolyn and I have a new happiness in the shape of our beautiful little grand-daughter Isabel. We relish too the burgeoning legal careers of our daughter Annabel and her husband Ben and the success in the film world of our son Alex and his partner Sara. One day soon I hope we will even find time for the holiday together we have not managed for the past two years.

I hope to continue, too – at least until certain BBC executives discover how much I enjoy it – as one of the presenters of my old radio favourite *The Week in Westminster* on Saturday mornings. I retain my relish for the British political scene. I would never wish to quit it entirely; but if I am now able to spend less time than I did in the Palace of Westminster itself, I am not entirely heartbroken about that. I know just what John Major meant when he said, 'I will miss it as it was, but not as it is becoming.' The veteran Canadian Prime Minister John Diefenbaker once advised an aspiring MP, 'You'll spend your first six months wondering how you got into Parliament and the rest of your life wondering how the others got there.' Many of those who entered the British Parliament in 1997 must now in their heart of hearts be asking themselves another question: 'Why did I bother?'

Certainly in my thirty years and more of political reporting I cannot remember a time when proceedings were so limp or when parliamentary performance mattered so little to public reputation as during the 1997–2001 parliament. I wrote a 'Week in Westminster' article for *The House Magazine* in 1999 saying so. It was quoted, selectively, at Prime Minister's Questions by William Hague and in the House of Lords, and many MPs came up to me to say how much they agreed with my conclusions. It seemed appropriately symbolic when I observed that there were more parliamentarians at the 1999 Brit pop awards with Robbie Williams and the Manic Street Preachers than there were on the Commons benches for a debate on reforming the House of Lords.

It has become increasingly obvious that Parliament has lost power to the executive, to Europe, to the courts, and especially to the media. A Scottish Parliament and a Welsh Assembly now do chunks of the work the Commons used to do, although the number of Westminster MPs has not been reduced. MPs themselves have done little to arrest the decline of the Commons and the media has positively assisted the process. Although there was a slight revival of parliamentary reporting in the year 2000 with the approach of an election, most newspaper reports have been confined in recent years to the entertaining, waspish efforts of a talented band of parliamentary sketch-writers who see the

Commons largely as a kind of vaudeville theatre, a mere back-cloth to a string of witticisms. Even the BBC, which still reports the daily proceedings so well on *Today in Parliament* and *Yesterday in Parliament*, the beloved '*TIP* and *YIP*' as they are known at Number Four Millbank, has made it harder for listeners to gain access to those reports by shifting their slots.

MPs confess freely that they would rather do a stint in front of the cameras on College Green than stand up and speak in the chamber. In the age of the soundbite and the two-way between TV presenter and correspondent, oratory appears to count for little. If you are looking for clearer evidence that the Commons is now an irrelevance, then look at the poll ratings which so dogged William Hague. Even his critics admit that within the Commons chamber he is a first-rate performer; yet this talent did nothing to make him acceptable to the nation. Debates themselves have become formalized, ritual exchanges with no trace of spontaneity, a development encouraged by the 'Speaker's List'. Nowadays MPs have only an outside chance of being called for a spontaneous contribution in response to an argument just heard. This is because any Privy Councillor (the Rt Hons, as they are called, most of whom are retired ministers with time on their hands) has to be given precedence. Chairmen of appropriate select committees and specialist backbench groups come next in the pecking order. Finally, the Speaker will be expected to look to regional balance and to make sure that minority parties have had their look-in before he can take the less formalized contributions. Knowing all this, fewer and fewer MPs bother to come into the chamber. It was wrong that until recently some MPs had no offices and had to dictate to their secretaries in Commons corridors. But now they all have comfortable offices with TV screens, there is the temptation to stay there to cope with the hefty in-trays and crammed e-mailboxes resulting from the generally increased constituency workload. And because throughout the last parliament the government's majority was so large and the result of every vote a foregone conclusion, the Commons chamber has been virtually devoid of any element of drama. MPs knew that a Prime Minister who bothered to vote only 14 times in 325 divisions in his first year was not making a priority of being around the Commons, and ministers took their lead from him.

Without consulting the other parties, the new Labour government switched Prime Minister's Questions from two quarter-hour sessions on Tuesdays and Thursdays to a single half-hour session on Wednesdays. This no doubt made life more comfortable in Number Ten, but it has further diminished interest in the Commons chamber. Somehow, too, it produces fewer stories as both sides slug themselves to the point of verbal exhaustion on a key topic over a concentrated half-hour. The modernizing process has done away with most late-night sessions and introduced morning sittings on Thursdays. This enables business to be completed by 7.00 p.m. so members can travel to their constituencies that night. It has also ensured that many leave even earlier. Not only is the Commons sitting on fewer Fridays, but few MPs hurry back on Mondays either. Add to this the new half-term holidays and 'constituency weeks' for some members, and woe betide you as a journalist if you are counting on finding any particular MP at Westminster other than twenty-four hours either side of Prime Minister's Questions. Like a moribund factory with weeds in the car park, the Commons is now effectively working a three-day week. Most of the time the Members' Lobby has all the buzz and excitement of an undertaker's waiting room.

The executive is almost totally dominant. It cares little for

Parliament because it does not have to. Even if there is the occasional flurry of protest over invalidity benefit restrictions or asylum and immigration laws, the votes are assured. Ministers do not need Parliament to get their message across: they can do that more directly through interviews on radio and television, and in the 'exclusive' articles which now appear in every kind of publication under the Prime Minister's name.

I'm not even sure that people these days look to Parliament for the righting of their wrongs. When Stephen Lawrence was killed in Eltham in 1993 the then MP for the area, Peter Bottomley, demanded action, met the Metropolitan Police Commissioner and repeatedly raised the case in Commons questions. But it was not until the 1997 inquest and its verdict of 'unlawful killing' were followed by a huge *Daily Mail* campaign naming five suspects that the case began to attract public, media and political attention on a large scale. Bottomley, himself an ex-minister, now argues that a newspaper article is much more likely than a parliamentary question to engage a minister's attention. Having spent so many of my working years in Parliament's precincts I winced to hear the expression, but Labour MP Austin Mitchell was right when he said last year that, with the executive so strong, Parliament's role has been reduced to 'heckling a steam-roller'. More and more the wronged, the disadvantaged and the single-issue pressure groups feel they have to rely not on parliamentary representation but on legal or direct action. Publicity is their best weapon; and these days it is more easily obtained outside Westminster.

Direct action, aided by modern technology, now works for the people at street level, as we saw during the fuel protests in September 2000. Why go through the long-winded process of writing to your MP and seeking to stir him to action when you can jump on a tractor, summon a few tanker-driving friends via your mobile phone or your home laptop and block the M1 within hours in front of a battery of cameras churning for twenty-four-hour television and accompanied by the assembled might of the country's top columnists?

Nor is it enough for MPs simply to ally themselves with a particular protest. William Hague's bandwagon-jumping promise of a 3p a litre reduction in petrol prices did not make him the hero of the fuel protesters. Labour had regained its massive opinion poll lead within three months. Politicians appear to me to have reacted to the loss of the tribal loyalties on which they used to count by behaving more and more like advertising men. They research what product the public wants with their focus groups and promise it to them. But the product is never as good as they say, and few trust their promises. No wonder that in his seventies Tony Benn, one of the best debaters and truest parliamentarians whose contributions I have watched over the years, announced that he was standing down from Parliament 'in order to go into politics'.

The trouble is that there seems so little will within Parliament to do anything about the decline of the Commons. Select committees are among the few institutions which MPs have under their control that can show independence, rattle ministerial cages and stand up to the government. But MPs continue to go tamely along with a system which allows the whips, the 'don't rock the boat' business managers, to control who sits on those committees. And the biggest disgrace of all occurred in October 2000 when a new Speaker had to be chosen. Michael Martin, who emerged from the process as victor, is a decent, amiable man, but in seeking the job he offered no thoughts on whether he shared his predecessor Betty Boothroyd's views on the excess of spin perpetrated by a government neglectful of the Commons. Nor did he describe in any detail how he might build up the rights of the legislature against the executive. As a result only 370 MPs – just eleven of them Tories – bothered to vote for him on a dangerously low turnout. And the Commons themselves allowed the twelve candidates for the Speaker's job to be whittled down to one in a convoluted parliamentary version of pub skittles, using a process designed for a field of two, not of twelve.

There should be a proper contest for the role of backbenchers' champion, with open manifestos and a secret ballot. Thanks to Tony Benn, backed by independent-minded Tories like Andrew Tyrie and David Davis, later to enter the field for the Tory leadership, MPs had the chance of participating in such a transparent contest with all the entrants competing on equal terms. To their shame, they decided it wasn't worth the fuss. They let the Father of the House, Sir Edward Heath, who presided over the process, get away with refusing to allow a vote to change the procedure on the grounds that 'such a motion requires notice', and the day was won by the 'we've always done it this way so we'd better do it this way again' school. It made a laughing stock of the Commons, it was unfair to the candidates who failed, and it was unfair to the new Speaker, who emerged from such a tarnished process with questionable authority. When MPs prove so incapable of fresh thinking, so careless of public opinion and so unwilling to battle for what a large proportion of them believed to be right on a subject so central to their own lives, the rest of us are left feeling that their rights are hardly worth fighting for.

It was symptomatic of our times, I thought, that Robin Cook's move from Foreign Secretary to Leader of the Commons in the post-election reshuffle was described in the media as a humiliation. It should not be seen as such, and I hope that Robin, as good a Commons debater as I have heard in my time and a man who enjoys exercising power, will use his new position to reassert the role of the House of Commons and of Parliament in general. I hope, too, that this time Tony Blair will make his contribution to the reputation of Parliament by living up to his promise in 1997 that Labour in government would be purer than pure. Allowing MPs in safe seats to barter early retirement for positions in the House of Lords or other perks, and perverting the system to parachute an ex-Tory millionaire into St Helens South as a reward for defection from the other side is not exactly an encouraging start.

But it is easy for us journalists to criticize the politicians. I hope that some of my colleagues in the media will recognize that we too must bear our responsibility for the pathetic turnout in the 2001 general election. If politics is not coming alive for the voters, it is to some extent our fault. Politicians cannot any longer practise their trade solely by personal contact. As Alastair Campbell puts it, 'The political party that does not understand the needs of the media is doomed.' We are in it together, and if democracy is to mean anything at all then sometimes we in the media, while recognizing the importance of our part in the process, have to be content to be facilitators. If we want to be players instead, we should go out and submit ourselves for election. As journalists, we should be there explaining what is happening, how it is happening and sometimes why it is happening. We should be prepared to unravel the intricacies of policy as well as to poke fun at the personalities. We should help people to participate in the dramas and to enjoy the spectacle, though we should not shrink from challenging anybody as we seek to get as close to the truth as we can.

I have never been shy of putting the bluntest of questions to our leaders on behalf of my readers, viewers or listeners. But I have, I hope, done so without aggression or partisanship, and in my reports I have tried not to over-editorialize, because I do not think reporters should be telling audiences what they should believe. We should give them the facts and the flavour and let them decide what they want to do, or whether those involved in a situation are right or wrong. Too many people in the business today, I believe, see journalism as an offensive weapon. They are more interested in putting the boot in than in passing on information. But journalism is about reaching the commuter in the suburban bus queue as well as about being the hot topic in the bar of the Groucho Club.

Personally, I now relish wearing my European hat for CNN, a broadcaster with all the BBC's concern for accuracy and being fair to all parties, but also with a more internationalist dimension which frees up the reporter. My career has been a progression from the Wirral to Westminster and now – where next? With every national leader pitching into the debate about the shape of Europe's institutions, with the fifteen-nation European Union preparing to absorb as many as twelve new members in the near future, and with Britain about to take the momentous decision whether or not to adopt the euro, the five years ahead look like being a lot of fun. But then, they always have.

INDEX